Recovering *the*
Unity *of the* Bible

Other Books by Walter C. Kaiser Jr.

*An Introduction to Biblical Hermeneutics:
The Search for Meaning (coauthor)*

*The Promise-Plan of God:
A Biblical Theology of the Old and New Testaments*

The Messiah in the Old Testament

The Expositor's Bible Commentary, Revised Edition: Exodus

Proverbs: Wisdom for Everyday Life

Psalms: Heart to Heart with God

Recovering *the* Unity *of the* Bible

One Continuous Story,
Plan, and Purpose

Walter C. Kaiser Jr.

ZONDERVAN

ZONDERVAN

Recovering the Unity of the Bible
Copyright © 2009 by Walter C. Kaiser Jr.

This title is also available as a Zondervan ebook.
Visit www.zondervan.com/ebooks.

Requests for information should be addressed to:
Zondervan, 3900 *Sparks Dr. SE Grand Rapids, Michigan 49546*

This edition: ISBN 978-0-310-52993-4 (softcover)

Library of Congress Cataloging-in-Publication Data

Recovering the unity of the Bible : one continuous story, plan, and purpose /
Walter C. Kaiser, Jr.

   p.   cm.

Includes bibliographical references and indexes.
ISBN 978-0-310-32024-1 (hardcover)
1. Bible — Criticism, interpretation, etc. 2. Bible — Theology. I. Title.
BS511.3.K34 2009

220.1 — dc22   2009020884

Interior design: Melissa Elenbaas

Printed in the United States of America

*T*o Bill and Judy Pollard—
dear friends, mentors, and leaders
of the Wheaton College Board

Contents

Preface. 9

1. The Unity of the Bible: Introduction 11

2. The Unity of the Bible: Diversity as an Accompanying Reality . . .25

3. The Harmonization of the Diversity 35

4. The Unity of the Hebrew Bible 47

5. The Unity of the New Testament 59

6. The Unity of the Bible in Its Messianic Promises. 69

7. The Unity of the Bible between the Two Testaments:
   The God of the Old Testament and the New. 85

8. The Unity of the Bible: Two Testaments:
   The Morally Offensive Character and Acts of Old Testament
   Men and Women. 99

9. The Unity of the Bible and the People of God. 111

10. The Unity of the Bible and Its Program: The Kingdom of God . .127

11. The Unity of the Bible and the Promise-Plan of God. 141

12. The Unity of the Bible and the Law of God. 157

13. The Unity of the Bible and the Doctrine of Salvation in
    Both Testaments 169

14. The Unity of the Mission in the Old Testament 183

15. The Unity of the Bible and Hermeneutics 195

16. The Unity of the Bible and Expository
    Preaching and Teaching 209

    Epilogue 221

    Bibliography 226
    Scripture Index 235
    Author Index. 244
    Subject Index. 247

Preface

Inever would have thought of tackling such an awesome topic as the unity of the Bible had it not been for an invitation that came from Ranald Macaulay, principal of Christian Heritage learning center in Cambridge, United Kingdom, several years ago. He invited me to deliver sixteen lectures at the Cambridge Summer School of Theology (UK), July 14 to 20, 2008. These lectures originally were to be held at the Round Church Vestry on Bridge Street in Cambridge, but were later moved down the street to Sidney Sussex College, Cambridge.

As I began this research some two years or more before these lectures, I found that most scholars wanted to celebrate the diversity of the Scriptures, but few were willing to stretch their necks out to lay any claims for the Scripture's coherency. The trail for unity by and large seemed to drop off just after the biblical theology movement crested in the 1950s and '60s. Only in recent days has there been such activity matching what was carried out about a half century ago (see the bibliography for confirmation of this point). Yet, without this component in its treatment of the Scriptures, the work of biblical theology remains piecemeal, without a set direction or an ability to locate itself in the theological curricula.

Nevertheless, I have been convinced that despite the dropping of the search for any center for a biblical theology during these same years, or a search for its unity, there is a strong case to be made for just such a unity. I have been delighted over and over again in my study for these lectures to see how strong, yet neglected, that case for the Bible's unity is. May you, too, the readers of these lectures, have the same joy I have had.

It only remains for me to thank so many who have had a hand in this project. First of all, my appreciation goes to Ranald Macaulay for his invitation to this lectureship. I am also grateful for the correspondence from Dominic Vincent and Martin Lown, student program facilitators at Christian Heritage.

Once again it was a privilege to work with Katya Covrett, Senior Acquisitions Editor of Zondervan. She has, as usual, been most helpful. My long relationship with Stan Gundry, Executive Vice President, Publishing and Editorial Operations, has continued to be a wonderful association and one of great encouragement to me. It has also been a pleasure to work with Jim Ruark, Senior Editor-at-Large, as well as with Jesse C. Hillman, Associate Marketing Director, Academic and Reference. Thanks to each one of you and to all others who had a part in making this project a tribute to the glory of our Lord.

The Unity *of the* Bible:
Introduction

In 1955 G. Ernest Wright of Harvard began his article on the unity of the Bible with this unusual assessment: "The question of the unity of the Bible's message is one that will *never be satisfactorily solved*, though it is one which every generation of Christians must seek to solve. We are continually impelled to search for the answer because the unity of the Church's message to the world is at stake."[2] That is hardly a cheerful note on which to begin this series of studies on the unity of the Bible, but at least we may be encouraged that G. Ernest Wright did acknowledge that it is important enough to the Christian church that we must still attempt to press on for the best statement of the Scripture's unity possible in every generation. Wright, however, had been even more melancholic in an earlier article. He opined:

> The problem of the unity of the Bible confronts us in all of our attempts to teach and preach biblical faith in a modern setting. No sooner do we present

---

1. H. Freiherr Campenhausen, *Die Entstehung der christlichen Bibel*, Beiträge zur historischen Theologie 39 (Tubingen: Mohr Siebeck, 1968), cited by Gerhard Maier, *Biblical Hermeneutics*, trans. Robert W. Yarbrough (Wheaton: Crossway, 1994), 188.
2. G. Ernest Wright, "The Unity of the Bible," *Scottish Journal of Theology* 8, no. 4 (1955): 337 (emphasis added).

one selection of biblical passages or books than we may be confronted with other passages which *seem to say the opposite.* When we attempt to present in some systematic way the theology of the Bible, which should be the chief agent for the presentation of its unity, we are confronted with the seemingly insuperable obstacle that the Bible was never written with any attention whatever to systematic presentation of theological propositions. For that reason biblical scholars cannot make up their minds as to what biblical theology is or can be. Is it a history of biblical ideas? But how can one make a systematic presentation of ideas undergoing historical change and exhibiting considerable fluidity through a historical process? Is it a systematic cross-section of those ideas at some one period ... ? If so, how can one call it a *biblical* theology, when it is a theology of only one period?[3]

In recent memory, most of this latest concern for the unity of the Bible took place toward the middle of the twentieth century. However, now in the twenty-first century, the emphasis has once again fallen on the diversity of the Bible, for the concept of diversity has risen to its highest point as the words of Scripture were granulated into as small bits as possible, mainly, but not exclusively, under the writings of some forms of source, form, and historical literary criticism.

Theological leaders, mainly those in the school of neoorthodox interpretation, especially during the days of the biblical theology movement of the 1950s and 1960s, were eager to discover and to set forth afresh some sense of the unity of the Bible that superseded or matched any historical, sociological, or literary findings that were emanating from the schools of negative literary and historical critical studies of the Bible.

Nevertheless, it has been the custom in many circles of biblical scholarship in the last half century to revert to emphasizing once more the Bible's diversity and discontinuity, rather than to seek for any possible strands of harmony and unity. In fact, one tends to be more readily accepted in scholarly circles if the focus of one's research avoids the topic of unity in the Bible, or a search for a center or a *Mitte* (German for "middle" or "center") that Scripture might possess. Presumably the fear is that if one gets started with the presupposition that the text might exhibit a harmony or unity, it is probably motivated by a prior commitment to a dogmatic or a systematic theology interest that understands the Bible in a more harmonistic way or one that has a single purposive mind behind it all.

---

3. G. Ernest Wright, "Wherein Lies the Unity of the Bible?" *Journal of Bible and Religion* 20, no. 3 (1952): 194 (emphasis added).

Oliver M. T. O'Donovan correctly countered such a fear and blanket accusation by asserting: "In fact, the search for diversity is as much the result of a prior methodological decision as is the search for harmony, and cannot be defended on purely empirical grounds. Empirical investigation reveals [both] points of diversity and points of harmony."[4]

To gain some insight and a possible vantage point from which to evaluate the emphases and tendencies of our own era, let us briefly look at what has happened in the history of the Christian church.

The Concept of the Unity of the Bible in Church History

In the first Christian century, Josephus (c. AD 37–38—c. 99) could claim in his *Contra Apion* (1.8) that the Jews "have not an innumerable multitude of books among [them], disagreeing from and contradicting one another [as the Greeks have], but only twenty-two books [i.e., equal to our present thirty-nine Old Testament books], which contain the records of all the past times; which are justly believed to be divine; and of them five belong to Moses, which contain his laws and the traditions of the origin of mankind till his death."[5]

Similarly Justin Martyr argued for the "seamless unity and freedom from contradictions of the divinely inspired Holy Scriptures."[6] In his *Dialog with Trypho*, Justin Martyr concluded, "I am entirely convinced that no Scripture can contradict another,… [for] I would admit rather that I do not understand what it says [should a contradiction be presented]."[7] Likewise, Augustine's *De consensus euangelistarum*, though a relatively neglected work, argued against the pagan critic Porphyry in book 1 and against the Manicheans in the remaining three books of his defense of the harmony of the four gospels. In his first book, using the Pauline analogy of the head and the body, Augustine worked to overcome the objections of the pagans by writing in this manner:

> Whoever apprehends this correspondence of unity and this concordant service
> of the members, all in harmony in the discharge of diverse offices under the
> head, will receive the account which he gets in the gospel through the narratives

4. Oliver M. T. O'Donovan, "The Possibility of a Biblical Ethic," *Theological Students Fellowship Bulletin* 67 (1973): 19.
5. Josephus, *Contra Apion* 1.8.
6. Campenhausen, *Die Entstehung der christlichen Bibel*, 20, cited by Robert M. Grant, *A Short History of Interpretation of the Bible* (New York: Macmillan, 1963), 68.
7. Justin Martyr, *Dialog with Trypho*, cited by Maier, *Biblical Hermeneutics*, 188.

constructed by the disciples, in the same kind of spirit in which he might look upon the actual hand of the Lord himself, which he bore in that body, which was made his own, were he to see it engaged in the act of writing.[8]

Many other similar citations could be gleaned from Irenaeus, Tertullian, Origen, and others.

Unfortunately, the terms "unity of Scripture" and "unity of the Bible" as such were not usually part of the vocabulary of the early church, the era that immediately followed these early church leaders, or even of the Reformers, so far as we can tell. There were, however, other terms that approximated the concept of the "unity of the Bible" during these time periods, such as *regula fidei, analogia pisteos, analogia fidei,* and *kanon pisteos,* but these were terms with related, albeit often different meanings (some pointing, for example, to texts such as 2 Tim. 1:13 or Rom. 12:7), where these terms probably were not consistently used for the concept of "unity" itself.[9] Even though the actual meaning of all these phrases was not always clear and did not always point to a uniform concept, it can be shown fairly easily that the *assumption* in these early periods of church history was that an organic unity ran through the entirety of the Scriptures; otherwise, appeal to the wide selection of texts made little sense if the fathers expected to have a cohesive statement emerge from them. It was the interconnectedness of Scripture that brought the sixty-six books of the canon into a wholeness that put the reader or interpreter at ease, regardless of where he or she was in that extensive corpus.

But there is another way of evaluating this same type of evidence from these same sources. Some have thoughtfully observed that the reason there is a scarcity of evidence in the earlier periods for the unity of Scripture is because the church faced few challenges to its unity *prior* to the time of the Enlightenment. Only then did numerous alleged contradictions to Scripture begin to appear.

While Gnosticism had led the earlier attacks against any concept of wholeness in the biblical corpus in the second to third Christian centuries, these were as short lived as those made by Porphyry or the attacks of the Manicheans, which did not make an enduring offensive against the widely held consensus that there was some type of cohesiveness within the biblical text — simply because Scripture represented nothing less than the mind and purpose of God. Campenhausen declared, "The indestructible unity and

8. Augustine, *De consensu evangelistarum* 1.35.54: CSEL XLIII, 60–61, cited by Carol Harrison, " 'Not Words but Things': Harmonious Diversity in the Four Gospels," in *Augustine: Biblical Exegete,* ed. Frederick Van Fleteren and Joseph C. Schnaubelt (New York: Peter Lang, 2001), 158–59.
9. This is the conclusion of Robert D. Preus, "The Unity of Scripture," *Concordia Theological Quarterly* 54 (1990): 1.

coherence of the Scriptures of the Old and New Testaments is the foundational biblical doctrine for Tertullian as for all the church fathers since Irenaeus in the battle against the Gnostics."[10]

Nowhere can the cohesive quality of the interconnectedness of Scripture be seen more dramatically and graphically than in its comparison with the sacred writings of other religions. James Orr, for example, made this famous contrast:

> The Koran, for instance, is a miscellany of disjointed pieces, out of which it is impossible to extract any order, progress, or arrangement.
>
> The 114 Suras or chapters of which it is composed are arranged chiefly according to their length—the longer in general preceding the shorter. It is not otherwise with Zoroastrian and Buddhist Scriptures. These are equally destitute of beginning, middle or end. They are, for the most part, collections of heterogeneous materials, loosely placed together. How different everyone must acknowledge it to be with the Bible! From Genesis to Revelation we feel that this book is in a real sense a unity. It is not a collection of fragments, but has, as we say, an organic character. It has one connected story to tell from beginning to end; we see something growing before our eyes: there is plan, purpose, progress; the end folds back on the beginning, and, when the whole is finished, we feel that here again, as in the primal creation, God has finished all his works, and behold, they are very good![11]

Nevertheless, despite these several lines of argumentation from the early church and history itself, still in our day the case for the diversity within the Scriptures continues to be so pervasive that many biblical scholars would judge that any other goal for a biblical theology than an acknowledgment of its diversity would be out of keeping with the current lines of thinking for this discipline, and it would therefore be unable to handle the wide spectrum of materials, genres, and topics in the Bible. Gerhard Maier was not convinced, for he noted that the general consensus in scholarship was against unity.

In modern times the notion is widely prevalent that biblical revelation exhibits *no* unity. Old and New Testament are said to be "everything but unified";[12] indeed, they "abound in contradictions."[13] This leads, on the

Nowhere can the cohesive quality of the interconnectedness of Scripture be seen more dramatically and graphically than in its comparison with the sacred writings of other religions.

10. Campenhausen, *Die Entstehung der christlichen Bibel*, 335, cited by Maier, *Biblical Hermeneutics*, 188.
11. James Orr, *The Problem of the Old Testament* (New York: Scribner, 1907), 31–32.
12. F. Hesse, *Das Alte Testament als Buch der Kirche* (Gütersloh: Gerd Mohn, 1966), 35; W. Wrede, *Uber Aufgabe und Methode der sogenannten Neutestamentlichen Theologie* (Göttingen: n.p., 1897), 79–80; R. W. Jenson, "On the Problem(s) of Scriptural Authority," *Interpretation* 31 (1977): 243; H. Gunkel, *Zum religionsgeschichtlichen Verstandnis des Neuen Testaments* (Göttingen: n.p., 1903), 35; and E. Fuchs. *Zum hermeneutischen Problem in der Theologie*, 2nd ed. (Tubingen: n.p., 1927), 22.
13. E. B. Redlich, *The Early Traditions of Genesis* (London: Duckworth, 1956), 11.

one hand, to the rejection of "attempts at harmonization" and to disparagement of the "unfruitfulness" of such attempts.[14]

Maier went on to decry the fact that this rejection of the Scripture's unity has likewise made deep inroads into "positive" as well as "biblicistic" circles. He was alluding to the fact that even conservative scholars had generally given up on the search for any unifying factors and had concluded that diversity and discontinuity were the more scientific ways of approaching biblical studies.

In the twentieth century there was a tendency to pose the question as to whether there was a center or *Mitte* to Scripture, rather than whether Scripture had any kind of unity. Once again, it was Gerhard Maier who surveyed the scholarly landscape that was involved in this situation. He concluded: "It is difficult to speak of a 'center' of Scripture today, because the rubric 'center of Scripture' is often separated from the 'unity of Scripture.' While the two were closely identified at the time of the Reformation, the Enlightenment disengaged them. Indeed, the 'center of Scripture' practically replaced the lost [subject of the] 'unity of Scripture.' "[15]

The concept of the center or *Mitte*,[16] or a *Mittelpunkt*,[17] or even a *Zentralbegriff*[18] of the Bible, or of either testament, tended to replace any discussion of the unity of the Bible. However, Rudolf Smend surveyed approximately 150 years of Old Testament theology up to 1970, and he concluded that "the confidence with which one has postulated the existence of a center (*Mitte*) of the Old Testament, has steadily become less and less."[19] Accordingly, what once was a reluctance to adopt or suggest a "central concept," a "focal point," or an "underlying idea" that embraced the whole of biblical theology has almost become a total abandonment of this quest.

However, if this were to be the real state of affairs also for biblical theology, why call the discipline by a name that implies some unifying promise—that is, *a* biblical theology. Why not call our textbooks in this area biblical theolog*ies* of the Old or New Testament? But in that case, how can a discipline, which historically by name and definition searches for a pattern, plan, person, and meaning from the biblical record, settle for a purely

14. M. Debelius, *Geschichtliche und ubergeschichtliche Religion im Christentum* (Göttingen: n.p., 1925), 93; cf. K. Girgensohn, *Grundriss der Dogmatik* (Leipzig/Erlangen: n.p., 1924), 63.
15. Maier, *Biblical Hermeneutics*, 202.
16. Rudolf Smend, "Die Mitte des Alten Testaments," *Theologische Studien* 101 (1970): 7.
17. Georg Fohrer, "Der Mittelpunkt einer Theologie des AT," *Theologische Zeitschrift* 24 (1968): 161–72.
18. Gunter Klein, " 'Reich Gottes' as biblischer Zentralbegriff," *Evangelische Theologie* 30 (1970): 642–70.
19. Smend, "Die Mitte," 7.

descriptive classification of the facts and information from the texts? And if the categories are coming *ab extra* from philosophy, that is, from an imposed subject arrangement, or the topics are taken from the systematic theology outline or some other external pattern of organization, would this not be an alien imposition over the texts that almost presupposes certain conclusions before we start?

Gerhard Hasel joined in the chorus of denials for any kind of center in the biblical materials. He warned that the biblical theologian "cannot and must not use a concept, fundamental idea, or formula as a principle for the systematic ordering and arranging of the OT kerygmatic message as a key that determines from the start how he will present the content of the OT testimony." Nevertheless, he surprisingly went on to advise that "the final aim of OT theology is to demonstrate whether or not there is an inner unity that binds together the various theologies and longitudinal themes, concepts, and motifs."[20]

Of course, such a center must come internally from the text itself and not be one imposed from the outside or determined in advance (as Hasel warned and as I of course agree). But, if so, is that center all that opaque? Were the writers oblivious and ignorant of any ongoing master plan in their participation in this divine revelation? One would think, from their claims, that they were aware of some type of continuity even if it were only in terms of the continuing narrative story of the Bible. Page H. Kelley came to the same conclusion as he affirmed that "the search for a unifying theme should be regarded as a valid one, else the Old Testament would be reduced to a collection of unrelated literary fragments."[21]

We will leave for another time the discussion of how, in the 1970s, *history* became the chief medium of divine revelation in the Old Testament. Let it be said in the meantime, however, that a subjective and often fallible estimate of history, as offered in the literary historical-critical theories of the day, did little to describe the heart and object of Israel's faith. As Roland de Vaux challenged, "Either the interpretation of history offered in the Bible was true and originated from God or it was not worthy of Israel's faith or ours."[22]

---

20. Gerhard Hasel, *Old Testament Theology: Basic Issues in the Current Debate* (Grand Rapids: Eerdmans, 1972), 62, 93. Also see his study "The Problem of the Center in the Old Testament Theology Debate," *Zeitschrift fur die Alttestamentliche Wissenschaft* 86 (1974): 65–82.
21. Page H. Kelley, "Israel's Tabernacling God," *Review and Expositor* 69 (1970): 486.
22. Roland de Vaux, *The Bible and the Ancient Near East*, trans. Damian McHugh (London: Darton, Longman and Todd, 1971), 57. He went on to say such a critical view attacked the foundation of all faith: "the truthfulness of God."

Types of Unity in the Bible

W. Graham Scroggie observed, "There are two kinds of unity: the one is that [used in the metaphor] of a building, which we call a mechanic [view]; the other [metaphor] is that of a body, or a plant, which, of course, is organic."[23] He asked which kind of unity characterized Scripture and proposed the test Margoliouth had suggested for the unity of the authorship of Isaiah, which could just as well serve as the proper test for the unity of the whole Bible. Margoliouth had said:

> Aristotle tells us that a work of art should be so constructed that the removal of any part should cause the whole to fall to pieces. We can, therefore, easily tell whether such a work is a unity by seeing what will happen if we take any part away. If the experiment results in leaving two unities where we fancied there was one, there will have been no original unity of plan. But if the result of the experiment leads to endless dissection, then it will have been shown that the work was originally an organized whole.[24]

If one book or part of a book of the Bible were lost, the truth of the Scripture would ... be maimed.

The second metaphor for unity was the organic one. Scroggie suggested that the laws of organic unity, summarized by the comparative anatomist of old, no one less than Georges Cuvier, could be helpfully compared to the unity of the Scripture as well.[25] Just as there is an organic unity in the human body, so that if an eye, a limb, or even the smallest joint of a finger is lost, not only has its unity been violated, but the body is forever maimed. In like manner, if one book or part of a book of the Bible were lost, the truth of the Scripture would similarly be maimed.

Cuvier's first law was: *Each and every part is essential to the whole.* When this law was applied to salvation, the various parts of the Bible yielded these types of patterns:

Genesis to Malachi: Salvation was promised and typified.

The Gospels: Salvation was provided in the death and resurrection of Jesus of Nazareth.

Acts to Revelation: Salvation was proclaimed, applied, and consummated.

---

23. W. Graham Scroggie, *Ruling Lines of Progressive Revelation: Studies in the Unity and Harmony of the Scriptures* (London: Marshall, Morgan & Scott, 1918), xvi.
24. Ibid., xvi–xvii. He gives no source for Margoliouth.
25. Ibid., xviii–xxiv. The same argumentation is found in Arthur T. Pierson, *The Inspired Word: A Series of Papers and Addresses Delivered at the Bible-Inspiration Conference, Philadelphia, 1887* (New York: Anson D. F. Randolph, 1888), 352–59.

If any one part were removed from the canon—for example, the Gospels—the link between the promise and the provision would be broken. If the Old Testament were removed, the Gospels would announce fulfillments for which there were no predictions. And if Acts to Revelation were cut off from the Bible, the salvation promised and provided would be useless, for the question would be: to whom was it to be applied and for what was it to be used? All three main parts complement each other, and each is essential to the whole.

Cuvier's second law was: *Each part is related to, and corresponds with, all the other parts—that is, all the parts are necessary to complement each other.* Scripture has a structure to it so that the combination of its parts yields a complete picture. Accordingly, Scroggie noted how the first and the last books of the Bible form a nice inclusion and a complete chiasm:

> a First Heaven and Earth (Gen. 1)
>> b Husband and Wife (Gen. 2)
>>> c Judgment Pronounced on Satan (Gen. 3)
>>> c' Judgment Executed on Satan (Rev. 20)
>> b' Husband and Wife (Rev. 21)
> a' Last Heaven and Earth (Rev. 22)

Thus the opening and closing of history are part and parcel of each other.

In like manner the four gospels are important to each other and to the message of the whole Bible, for each presents Jesus from a different teaching point of view. Matthew is written for the Jews and presents Jesus as the King of the Jews. Mark is addressed to the Romans and presents Jesus as the powerful worker of miracles. Luke focuses in on the Greek mind and shows Jesus as the Great Teacher and the wisdom of God. John is a supplement to the other three Gospels and presents Jesus as the true Son of God. Instead of there being four gospels, their combined story results in one gospel of the Lord Jesus Christ, with the first three stressing Jesus' earthly side for the most part, while John emphasizes his inward and heavenly aspect.

No less do the Epistles complement each other. All five writers of these letters emphasize a parallel part of the same organically related truth. Paul's great topic is faith and its relation to justification, sanctification, service, joy, and glorification. James, on the other hand, wants to make sure *works* are properly seen as the legitimate outcome of faith; thus he complements the apostle Paul. Peter is the apostle of hope who urges God's people forward despite trials and temptations. John is the teacher of love and the relation love has to light and eternal life in Christ. Finally, Jude warns against apostasy, which can wreck faith, hope, and love toward God.

The principle of a designed structure can be seen everywhere in Scripture and is a marked indicator of the Bible's organic nature.

Cuvier's third and final law is: *All the parts of organism are pervaded by one life principle.* The biblical text claims for itself that the word of God is "living" and "enduring" and "stands forever" (Heb. 4:12; 1 Peter 1:23, 25). Just as a seed, or a living organism, has life and vitality, so the Scripture shares that same vitalizing force that comes from God. The fact that God's Word is alive can be seen in the life it produces in all who take it up and act on its instructions.

The Nature of the Unity of the Bible

The Bible's cohesiveness can be examined under six general categories of unity: (1) structural, (2) historical, (3) prophetical, (4) doctrinal, (5) spiritual, and (6) kerygmatic. The particulars for each of these categories can be stated rather forthrightly.

The structural unity of the Bible. When a full document like the Bible is drawn from so many individual books written over such a long period of time, and the writers did not know each other and rarely were contemporaries of each other or even from the same continents, it is hard to image that any kind of coherence and ongoing strategy could be possible. But the Bible, extending over two testaments and some sixteen hundred years, and written by about forty writers in three languages, representing three continents, exhibits some strong general schemes that suggest a common archetypal plan and purpose in the story of redemption.

For example, each of the two testaments seems to be built around a similar structure that contains three parts—a historic section, a didactic part, and a prophetic section—that tend to look to the past, present, and future. This symmetry of history, teaching, and proclamation, or even past, present, and future, can be displayed even more fully: the five books of Moses were followed by twelve other historical books of the past, which in turn were succeeded by five didactic poetical books and five major prophets and twelve minor prophets. Likewise, in the New Testament there are five historical books relating the past work of Jesus and the apostles, twenty-one didactic epistles, and one apocalyptic prophetic text. Note again that the pattern is past, present, and future. There is not one isolated or orphaned book in the whole collection of both testaments, for even those that seem the remotest in thought have threads of contact with the whole canon.

One writer marveled:

> Imagine another book, compiled by as many authors, scattered over as many centuries! Herodotus in the fifth century before Christ, contributes an historic fragment on the origin of all things; a century later, Aristotle adds a book on moral philosophy; two centuries pass, and Cicero adds a work on law and government; still another hundred years, and Virgil furnishes a grand poem on ethics. In the next century, Plutarch supplies some biographical sketches; nearly two hundred years after, Origen adds essays on religious creeds and conduct; a century and a half later, Augustine writes a treatise on theology, and Chrysostom a book of sermons; then seven centuries pass, and Abelard completes the compilation by a magnificent series of essays on rhetoric and scholastic philosophy. And, between these extremes, which, like the Bible, span fifteen centuries, all along from Herodotus to Abelard, are thirty other contributors, whose works enter into the final result—men of different nations, periods, habits, languages and education. Under the best conditions, how much real unity could be expected, even if each successive contributor had read all that preceded his own fragment? Yet here [in the Bible] all are entirely at agreement.[26]

As is said in America: *e pluribus unum*. Surely there is a diversity in Scripture as there is in America, a diversity found in unity and a unity found in diversity. Accounting for all of this unity in the midst of obvious diversity spread over these centuries with some sixty-six contributions of some forty different writers in three languages on three continents is mind-boggling. There can be no real answer unless we also receive the claim of the writers that there was a supernatural aspect and a guiding mind at work in their writings as well. If God was behind the production of all these contributions, then the unity is the result of a driving plan and the harmony reflects what he has willed and purposed.

The historic unity of the Bible. The Bible tells a single story gathered around the people of Israel. Scripture's history begins with the calling of one man, Abraham, who is eventually made into the nation of Israel, and its progress continues until the people's apostasy lands them in captivity. But it doesn't end there, for the Jewish Messiah is the Christ of all the nations, and God's

E pluribus unum. Surely there is a diversity in Scripture as there is in America, a diversity found in unity and a unity found in diversity.

---

26. Pierson, *Inspired Word*, 340–41.

covenantal promises made with Israel are never relinquished; God will end history just as he began it—with the Abrahamic, Davidic, new covenant promise-plan of God.

The prophetic unity of the Bible. If holy men of God spoke as they were moved by the Holy Spirit (2 Peter 1:21), then nowhere may we expect to find a greater case for the unity of the Bible than in the prophecies of the Bible. Peter explicitly declares that "no prophecy of Scripture came about by the prophet's own interpretation" (v. 20). Yet here is the startling result: prophets separated by great distances and times formed an unbroken agreement on what they had to say about the future. Theirs was a common ministry as they spoke with one voice over the centuries. Old Testament prophets and writers in the Christian church alike, all cried out with one voice, "Prepare the way for the Lord; make straight ... a highway for our God" (Isa. 40:3). The kingdom of God would soon emerge in all its fullness.

The two comings of the Messiah, the one who would indeed come out of the loins of David, constituted the two focal centers of all prophecy. His first coming would provide salvation for mortals; his second coming would set up a rule and reign that would have no end or competitor. Overall, however, J. Barton Payne identified a total of 1,817 prophecies in the Bible, or a total of 8,352 verses, for a total of 27 percent of the Bible's 31,124 verses.[27] Payne also found 127 personal messianic predictions involving 3,348 verses in the Old Testament, while Alfred Edersheim reported that Jewish sources identified some 456 passages as being in general messianic.[28]

The doctrinal unity of the Bible. Rather than finding didactic, doctrinal, and ethical teachings conflicting with one another, we discover a oneness that fits both with what has gone before and what has followed after. True, there is a progressive development to the revelation described here, but even when the books are not arranged in chronological order, as in our present canon, the steady development of the whole is not impaired.

So in harmony are the parts with the whole canon that oftentimes some of the parts are not fully understood until the whole has been completed. Each constituent part is like a scaffolding of a building that for the moment conceals part of the beauty of the building until the final capstone is put into place and the grand cathedral of the whole Bible is completed.

27. J. Barton Payne, *Encyclopedia of Biblical Prophecy: The Complete Guide to Scriptural Predictions and Their Fulfillment* (New York: Harper and Row, 1973), table on pp. 674–75.
28. Alfred Edersheim, *The Life and Times of Jesus the Messiah*, 2 vols. (London: Longans, 1915), 2: app. 9. These numbers reflect midrashic exegesis in some cases and thus are somewhat inflated.

The spiritual unity of the Bible. There is more to the biblical text than the mere cognitive or scientific study of its parts and the whole can reveal. This book has the power to grip a person and bring changes in his or her life if followed. This claim can be made for few other books in the world. In this book, God, the subject, addresses each of us mortals as objects of his creation and love. The one who bridges the gap for us is no one less than Christ, the Messiah, who gives us the Holy Spirit as a guide and counselor.

God's word claims, "Thus says the Lord," rather than providing a series of footnotes by eminent, or not so eminent, scholars. And the unified word that comes to us from Scripture is God's everlasting promise-plan that stretches from the record of creation to the book of Revelation.

The kerygmatic unity of the Bible. The presence of a unifying kerygmatic core is what pulls together the manifold diversity found in the New Testament. Eugene E. Lemcio made this assertion, building on the famous effort to a similar effect from the research of C. H. Dodd.[29] Dodd argued for a seven-point outline of the preaching of the early church based on fragments of tradition collected from Pauline literature.[30] Even though Dodd acknowledged the presence of variety and development in the preaching of the apostle Paul, he thought he detected a great harmony in the early sermons in the book of Acts. Anglo-American scholars at first responded favorably to Dodd's proposal but then decided it was based on too much artificial harmonization of Pauline material and not enough on the speeches of Acts.

Dodd's thesis would reappear in a new form a quarter of a century later as scholars began to speak of the *kerygmata* of the New Testament. Especially prominent was the name of Rudolf Bultmann in his use of redaction criticism to get at the unique message of each gospel. But Lemcio believed that J. D. G. Dunn, in his *Unity and Diversity in the New Testament*, brought this legacy to its fullest form, even though Dunn put more emphasis on diversity than unity, despite the title of his work.

Lemcio went beyond Dunn's emphasis on diversity and abstraction of the core kerygma to argue for a kerygma in the New Testament that was concrete, and not abstract or reductionistic, and was represented broadly enough to be regarded as a core running though the whole New Testament. He identified this common denominator of the kerygmatic core as having

Each constituent part [of the canon] is like a scaffolding of a building that for the moment conceals part of the beauty of the building until the final capstone is put into place and the grand cathedral of the whole Bible is completed.

29. Eugene E. Lemcio, "The Unifying Kerygma of the New Testament," *Journal for the Study of New Testament* 33 (1988): 3–17.
30. C. H. Dodd, *The Apostolic Preaching and Its Developments* (London: Hodder and Stoughton, 1936), 9–28; 47–51; 77–129.

six constant elements, which usually, though not always, introduced what followed as the kerygma, the gospel or the word about:

1. God who
2. sent (Gospels) or raised
3. Jesus [which required]
4. a response (receiving, repentance, faith)
5. toward God [and]
6. brought benefits (variously described).[31]

Lemcio summarized his contention for a unifying core this way:

> In this spar[s]e statement (hardly more than a dozen words in many instances) lies the skeleton of every Christian conviction.... So far as content is concerned, the most fixed elements refer to God as the initiator of the redemptive act in Christ ("sending" before Easter, "raising" afterwards). And one's response is always to God. The variations within this stability occur in the descriptions of response ("believing" being the most frequent) and of the benefits promised or achieved.[32]

Conclusion

The case for the unity of the Bible, then, rests on two main theses: (1) the self-claims of the Bible and (2) the message of Scripture. Yes, God has spoken to our forefathers through the prophets in many different ways and at many different times (Heb 1:1), but the message has formed a whole cohesive unity while employing a wide variety of supporting details.

---

31. Lemcio, "Unifying Kergyma," 6. The bracketed information is mine.
32. Ibid., 12–13.

The Unity *of the* Bible

Diversity as an Accompanying Reality

[There are] three approaches to the question. One … different viewpoints are appropriate to different contexts, another that they reflect different levels of insight, and a third that they are all expressions of one underlying theology.

—John Goldingay[1]

The case for diversity in the Bible seems more apparent to most readers in our day than the case for the unity of the Scriptures. However, since these sixty-six books function as the Holy Scriptures for Christians, several ways have been suggested for upholding the case for diversity while still acknowledging the presence of some type of unity. Moreover, different approaches have been taken to the claims of an overriding presence of diversity.

For example, we begin by seeing diversity either as a *problem*, which possibly could be answered by a number of explanations, or as a *virtue*, wherein the various books of the Bible are regarded as a complex but interrelated set of documents, instead of a rather simple and uncomplicated text, with a decided emphasis on an internal unity.[2] But any religion worth its salt could not remain indifferent or oblivious to what could be viewed as

---

1. John Goldingay, *Theological Diversity and the Authority of the Old Testament* (Grand Rapids: Eerdmans, 1987), vii.
2. This contrast was suggested in John Barton, "Unity and Diversity in the Biblical Canon," in *Die Einheit der Schrift und die Vielfalt des Kanons*, ed. John Barton and Michael Wolter (Berlin: De Gruyter, 2003), 11.

outright internal inconsistencies and contradictions in the books described as being "scriptural" or having a normative status if it makes a claim to their truth, consistency, and authority. Therefore, the problem is worth investigating in a more detailed manner.

The Numerous Types of Diversity

If the Bible did not evidence a common theme and continuing thread throughout its extended library, its diverse features would not be worth noticing, for that would be what we would expect given the plurality of writers, times, and cultures. Diversity is only worthwhile noting where it is somehow expected to exhibit an ongoing coherence, consistency, or unified plan.

Nevertheless, at least seven rather elementary types of diversity can be seen immediately upon getting a general overview of the Bible and its contents. They are: (1) a diversity in language, (2) a diversity in human authorship, (3) a diversity of the writers' qualifications and backgrounds, (4) a diversity of place, of both where the written material emanated from and where the events originally took place, (5) a diversity of literary form, (6) a diversity of matter or substance, and (7) a diversity of times the material covers and in which it was written. Each of these types of diversity needs to be discussed in more detail.

1. Diversity of language. Three main languages were used in bringing to us the divine revelation of God. The Old Testament was written mainly in Hebrew, the language of Canaan, while the New Testament was composed in Koine Greek, the language of the common people. Another portion of the Old Testament was composed in Aramaic, the trade language of the day. Those texts include Daniel 2:4–7:28 and Ezra 4:8–6:18; 7:12–26. Genesis also has a sprinkling of Aramaic expressions.

2. Diversity of authorship. At least forty men were employed in the writing of the Bible, thirty-one in the Old Testament and about eight or nine in the New. To have so many over such a long stretch of time putting their hands to a work, now bound into one volume, yet arriving at a continuity of theme and goal, is nothing short of astonishing unless some guiding hand was at work.

3. Diversity of qualifications. The fact that the forty-some authors of Scripture were not from a single school of thought or similar education or cultural

> Diversity is only worthwhile noting where it is somehow expected to exhibit an ongoing coherence, consistency, or unified plan.

upbringing only increases our amazement at what they were able to accomplish. The occupations they represented are truly wide-ranging—kings, poets, fishermen, statesmen, priests, tax collectors, shepherds, physicians, and philosophers. Some were highly educated, others had little or no education at all. Some were well schooled in the wisdom of Egypt, others in schools of Babylon, and still others by the rabbis in Jerusalem or Antioch. There was no set standard in academic, physical, or religious training nor in social status that automatically qualified them for the task of writing the books of the Bible.

4. A diversity of place. The authors of Scripture wrote in the desert of Sinai, in the cave of Adullam, from a prison in Rome, in exile on the island of Patmos, on the banks of the Chebar canal in Babylon, and in the palace in Jerusalem. So disparate are the places from which the message comes that it is almost unbelievable that a chaotic mess did not emerge instead of divine revelation.

5. A diversity of forms. Scripture contains a variety of genres—narrative throughout both testaments, the law from Moses, poetry in the Psalms from David and others, laments in the Psalms and in Lamentations, prophecy, epistles from the Pauline corpus, and apocalypses in Daniel, Zechariah, and Revelation. How could so many books, with such diversity of forms and genres, have made any sense when melded together unless their authors were supernaturally directed to the same goal in writing?

6. A diversity in subject matter. The books of the Bible cover a wide scope of material—the creation account; stories about a flood and a tower; reports of the patriarchs' lives; an intriguing account of the exodus; narratives of the emergence of a nation, a conquest of a land, a collection of ruthless judges, a Davidic kingship, a Samarian exile in Assyria, and a Jerusalemite exile in Babylon; philosophical writings on suffering and on the transitory nature of life; proverbs; gospels; a history of the early church; letters written to the new church plants in Asia Minor and to the young pastors of those churches; and a depiction of the end of the age. Could any unorganized group of men, without contacting one another, have written such a combined outlook on life such as we have in the Bible on their own without any contact between them?

7. A diversity of the times covered and the times they were written in. These sixty-six books were written over a period of almost sixteen hundred years. Surely that would have provided ample time for major confusion and severe contradictions, not to mention a major change in direction and attitudes from that exhibited in the earlier writings of this collection.

Nevertheless, all forty-some writers appear to have kept on-message and contributed to one grand history that began with creation and stretched up to AD 90 with one magnificent purpose at the heart of all they said. W. Graham Scroggie summarized it this way: "But wonderful as is this diversity, perhaps the unity of the Bible is even more wonderful."[3]

Where Does the Problem of Diversity Show Up Religiously?

These rather simple statements of certain types of diversities are interesting, but this is not the list that is generally worrisome to modern advocates of discontinuity and diversity. Instead, the modern list focuses on alleged inconsistencies and contradictions in the text. The more troubling contradictions are said to appear in three main areas: (1) in historical facts of those reporting on the same events or persons, (2) in the moral teachings of the text, and (3) in the theological understandings of one writer when set alongside another. However, the degree or level of diversity recognized or easily tolerated by various theological groups also differs, depending on whether one is talking about the Jewish, Roman Catholic, liberal Protestant, or evangelical Protestant approach to this problem. For example, John Barton noted:

> ... for Jews the Bible needed to be read as presenting a coherent picture on how Jewish life was to be led, so that inconsistency was a problem where matters of *halakhah* [basically found in the mishnah, codified by Rabbi Judah the Prince, born in A.D. 135, with its 63 tractates organized under six major headings, to which the *Tosephta* was later added] were concerned.... It is not possible to tolerate diversity [there], because clear rulings are needed on matters of conduct if one is to lead an observant Jewish life.... There are no rabbinic debates about how to reconcile [the data of] Kings and Chronicles, for example, probably because in that case no issues of *halakhah* arise: consistency in telling the history of the kingdoms of Israel and Judah is not an essential part of Judaism. What is essential is that Scripture shall speak with a single voice on those matters that are essential to the actual operation of the religious system.[4]

3. W. Graham Scroggie, *Ruling Lines of Progressive Revelation: Studies in the Unity and Harmony of the Scriptures* (London: Marshall, Morgan & Scott, 1918).
4. Ibid., 11–12.

Likewise, even though Roman Catholic thought also commits itself to the infallibility of the Scriptures, it has the magisterium of the church to fall back on even if the text of Scripture is not always consistent. Therefore, while looking to Scripture for its direction in life, there is always an alternative route for getting rulings on conduct and doctrine if the text of Scripture seems to fail as a guide to doctrine or living.

In the case of liberal Protestantism, it too could afford to be very relaxed over a good deal of diversity, contradiction, or inconsistencies in the biblical record, for *reason* took a prior seat over the text of the Bible, especially as assisted by historical criticism.

But where the real tension in the strong claims for diversity came was with evangelical Protestants, whose ultimate and final court of appeals remained the Scriptures. If all authority rested in the biblical text, there was no other place one could turn to gain guidance for life or teaching for doctrine and ethics.

Theological Diversity as a Special Problem

In the precritical era of Bible study (usually over two centuries or more ago), most read their Bibles in a static way wherein they just assumed that the same truths were taught in both testaments with Christian meanings read from either testament with equal ease. But since the twentieth century, many now regard the Old Testament as possessing a "multiplex nature" with "completely divergent theologies" and "struggling contradictions."[5]

John Goldingay accepts the statement that the Old Testament has an assortment of viewpoints on meanings or concepts, themes, and institutions. For example, the concept of God is itself an ambivalent one, for Yahweh may be encountered anywhere or at a particular place. He is said never to sleep, yet he must be awakened at times (Pss. 44:23; 121:4). Thus this is an ambiguous way to present the concept of God, it is claimed.

In the same way, themes may become slippery as well. Thus the people of God may be a pastoral clan, then a theocracy, then ruled by a king or governed by God. In like manner, Goldingay sees institutions like the monarchy totally rejected and accepted wholeheartedly. Or take the covenant as

---

5. As suggested by Goldingay, *Theological Diversity*, 1, where the order of the quotes noted here come from James Barr, *Old and New in Interpretation* (New York: Harper & Row, 1966), 15; Gerhard von Rad, *Old Testament Theology*, 2 vols. (New York: Harper & Row, 1962, 1965), 2:412; and Walther Eichrodt, *Theology of the Old Testament*. 2 vols. (Philadelphia: Westminster, 1961, 1967), 1:490.

another example; it can be seen as one without qualifications and permanent or as one that has numerous qualifications.

Goldingay likes the basic distinction made by Gerhard von Rad in which he saw a break between the approach to theology in Israel's earlier narratives and the prophetic traditions as the prophets turned their backs on those earlier Yahwistic ideas. This is not the only break, in his view, but it illustrates that the same theological statements function in different ways in different parts of the Old Testament.

What could be the reason for this absence of unity of perspective, theme, conceptuality, aim, and theology? Goldingay says there are several reasons for all this diversity:[6] (1) the Bible is a *biblia*, the Scriptures (both words are plural), thus it is more of a *symposium* than it is the collected works of one person. (2) The messages of the prophets relate to different circumstances and attitudes in their listeners; therefore, since theology is a historical affair, *faith must change* with a changing world. (3) There is an *unpredictability* about how, when, or what God will choose to act or speak.

Of course, notes Goldingay, there are degrees of diversity and differences in what some would call contradictions.[7] To claim that the Bible is full of contradictions usually means that the word *contradictions* is being used very loosely. Often matters that enjoy a plurality of perspectives are suddenly frozen and one is pitted over against the other in order to force a contrasting view on what has just been said. More attention will be given to these and similar matters later on in this work.

Goldingay's Four Types of Contradiction

In this discussion, Goldingay purposely sets aside alleged contradictions where there are simple differences, but these are without inconsistencies. He illustrates this by showing that one and the same person was called both Messiah and the second Adam.[8] Such can hardly count against harmony and unity. However, Goldingay mentions four other types of contradictions, which we will examine here.

Formal contradiction. This type of disharmony exhibits a difference at the level of words, but it does not reveal a difference in substance. Illustrative of this type of difference is that it seems both to state and then deny that God

---

6. Goldingay, *Theological Diversity*, 12–15.
7. Ibid., 15–25.
8. Ibid., 16.

changes his mind (1 Sam 15:11, 29, 35). Both statements make use of the same Hebrew word *nacham*, "to repent, to change." However, since both assertions occur in the same context, we are called upon to relate them as well as to contrast them. To speak of God changing his actions is to present him as retaining his own consistent nature, for when persons change, God is free to change in his response to them. God changes in his actions to mortals so as not to change in his own being and nature.

Formal contradictions, then, are no stumbling stone for the case for unity. They are more a case of the use of words, often the same words being used in two different ways, as indicated within the context in which the dual usage is exhibited.

Contextual contradiction. Oftentimes the existence of a variety of circumstances can take very similar words and use them in two different ways. Thus the prophet Isaiah will call Judah to trust God's strong affirmation of the royal line of David and Jerusalem, while the prophet Jeremiah, for different reasons, will deny that Judah can trust God to rescue the Davidic king Zedekiah or the city of Jerusalem from the hand of the Babylonian Nebuchadnezzar. The people of Jeremiah's day were using God's promise to the Davidic line and to Jerusalem as a good luck charm, a way of avoiding facing their own need for repentance. They reasoned that no matter how poorly they failed to obey or to believe God, God would never destroy his city or his king. After all, he had promised his word on an oath to Abraham and David, so the guarantee was secure and so were they!

Therefore, the circumstances changed what had seemed to be a flat-out reversal of the divine message. Each generation, it will be seen, had to transmit the promise of God for the coming Davidic king and for the future city of Jerusalem to the coming generations, but there was no guarantee that that generation, or any particular generation, would also participate in the benefits of the promise of God unless they, too, sought God and obeyed his word. Thus the promise of the longevity of David's line and the threat of a false use of the promise both were true.

Substantial contradiction. It is in this area where true disagreement is said to arise, differences that go beyond the mere verbal or contextual sorts of examples. The area most pointed to here is the postexilic material. But the examples offered here have a number of problems associated with them.

First, Isaiah 58–66 is made into a postexilic prophecy by Goldingay, a debatable move we will set aside at this time to get at the more important

To speak of God changing his actions is to present him as retaining his own consistent nature, for when persons change, God is free to change in his response to them.

issue. It is said that the message of the chronicler was that the people had returned and rebuilt the temple, whereas Isaiah 58–66 looks to a future day when Yahweh will fulfill this return and bring safety and security to the land of Israel once again.

Both are true. Judah's return from the Babylonian exile did not fulfill the promise about their return in the end day. That "day" still remains in the future, for in Zechariah 10:6–12, the same future promise is laid out in 518 BC, well after the 536 BC return from Babylon; therefore the promise about a future return to the land still awaits fulfillment even in our day.

The charge that says that Job and Ecclesiastes "fundamentally dispute the claim that Yahweh's fairness can be perceived [to be] at work in human life, whether in the experience of the individual (Job), or in the events of History (Ecclesiastes)"[9] is not at odds with the thinking of the chronicler, who emphasizes fairness of God's dealings with each king and generation. Neither of these assessments of Job or Ecclesiastes is exactly where those books conclude. Job bows to Yahweh's different summary of his problems at the end of his book, and the last two verses of Ecclesiastes (12:13–14) come to the conclusion that book was about "fear[ing] God and keep[ing] his commandments, for [that was] the whole [of what a man and a woman are all about]." This area then is less clear as a separate category of contradictions when the issues are examined more intensely.

Fundamental contradiction. Some place in this category those types of disagreements that really are substantive and usually involve contradictions in the ethical stances or religious outlook of the texts. The examples used by Goldingay, however, are most surprising: for instance, one involves the basic Old Testament conflict between the "Yahweh alone party" and the "syncretistic cult of [Baal and] Yahweh" (1 Kings 18). Another example was the conflict with the false prophet Hananiah and the biblical prophet Jeremiah (Jer. 28).

Well, for certain these were basic conflicts. But in no way was either the Baal party or the Hananiah prophetic perspective registered as a normative point of view in the Bible. To argue differently is to side against the narrative of Scripture itself. There are indeed fundamental differences here, but they are presented as such in the text as being just that, and in no way do they disturb the case for unity.

9. Ibid., 22–23.

The Case for Theological Coherence in the Old Testament

"This quest [for coherence, some fear,] mistakenly posits some [sort of] meta-historical entity that stand[s] … behind the various historical expressions of OT faith."[10] It also ignores, the objectors continue, the Old Testament's own reticence for forming a systematic view of things. And it does not account for the so-called primitive mind's allowance for tolerance, or earlier writers' open acceptance of representatives of divergent viewpoints, where modern westerners would see both of these as outright contradictions.

But is that not the point? The claim of the text is that there is a "meta-historical entity" called God who revealed the text. The narrative purports to be his mind and his purpose and his attitude to things. Is that not the real claim of the Scriptures themselves?

P. D. Hanson concluded that it is dishonest to try to account for such contradictions in the text when that very text itself does not point to a theological solution to the disharmony.[11] However, as Goldingay has correctly pointed out, this assumes that historical exegesis is the only valid interpretive way of understanding the texts. It is also possible to look for an understanding of these tensions on theological grounds and on the grounds of the context of the whole Bible. This argument for the wholeness of Scripture grounds itself in the claim that there is an organic structure to the canon in which it comes to its fullness of expression in the later revelation of God. It is to be unexpected, then, that the Old Testament will be theologically coherent, for the differences of views in an earlier document of the Bible may often be gathered up in the larger unity of the whole collection of the books of the Bible.

Conclusion

The theological unity of the Bible celebrates the diversity of the Bible but does so with the conviction that even though that unity can be tested historically, ethically, and otherwise, it has not detracted from the central case for the theological harmony that is found in the text. This has been the general conclusion of two millennia of Judeo-Christian exegesis.

---

10. Ibid., 25.
11. Paul D. Hanson, "The Theological Significance of Contradiction within the Book of the Covenant," in *Canon and Authority,* ed. George W. Coats and Burke O. Long (Philadelphia: Fortress, 1977), 118.

The Harmonization
of the Diversity

> When we meet an apparent error in a good author, we are to presume ourselves ignorant
> of his understanding until we are certain that we understand his ignorance.
>
> —Samuel Taylor Coleridge[1]

Much modern biblical scholarship tends to disparage most, if not all, attempts to "harmonize" biblical texts that appear to exhibit discrepancies where matters of biblical history, doctrine, or ethics are involved. Some bias against this type of exegetical activity can be attributed to differing definitions of the term *harmonization*, but a good part of the opposition rests in the unwarranted assumption that when factoring in so many different authors, genres, topics, and time periods, there must naturally be some evidence of outright disparities and blatant contradictions within the text. How could such disparities be avoided unless there were some overall guiding hand, principle, or plan?

Suggesting quick, contemporary, or glib reconciliations between difficult passages only complicates the process of searching for real possible harmonizations. Therefore, not all that passes under the rubric of harmonizing can automatically be assumed to be reliable or methodologically commendable.

---

1. Samuel Taylor Coleridge, cited by Oswald T. Allis, *The Five Books of Moses*, 2nd ed. (Philadelphia: Presbyterian and Reformed, 1949), 125.

Nevertheless, the decision as to whether harmonization is possible is not all that difficult, nor is it all that novel in and of itself, for this process is seen in much of real life where contentions often arise over which scenario, or combination of scenarios, is closer to the actual facts in the case in question. Life itself calls for many types of daily reconciliations for all sorts of disparities. The job of the listener or adjudicator is to consider the evidence from all sides to see if a reasonable accounting for the facts of the case can be ascertained from what each party is presenting.

Let it be conceded, however, that part of the problem with biblical harmonization lies in the fact that work by conservatives has often ended up being more than a bit artificial and appearing contrived, despite the good intentions of those suggesting solutions. Nevertheless, poor practice is not enough reason for automatic rejection for the viability and legitimacy of the whole practice or of the possibility that real solutions exist for some, or even many, of the discrepancies in the biblical text.

"Harmonization," argued Raymond B. Dillard, "is the effort to provide scenarios by which two apparently contradictory statements, or one improbable statement, can be considered historically [or factually] accurate."[2] But this effort is not to be regarded as an automatic result, for as Carl F. H. Henry cautioned: "Evangelical scholars do not insist that historical realities conform to all of their proposals for harmonization; their intent, rather, is to show that their premises do not cancel the logical possibility of reconciling apparently divergent reports [in Scripture]."[3]

The Antiquity of the Practice of Harmonization

There is a long tradition of discussion on many of the more famous alleged discrepancies in the Bible. Among the early church fathers, one could list such writers as Eusebius, Chrysostom, Augustine, and Theodoret, who each devoted whole treatises, or parts of them, to alleged discrepancies.[4] The

> *Not all that passes under the rubric of harmonizing can automatically be assumed to be reliable or methodologically commendable.*

---

2. Raymond B. Dillard, "Harmonization: A Help and a Hindrance," in *Inerrancy and Hermeneutic: A Tradition, A Challenge, A Debate*, ed. Harvie M. Conn (Grand Rapids: Baker, 1988), 152. Additional essays on this topic by evangelical writers include Craig L. Blomberg, "The Legitimacy and Limits of Harmonization," in *Hermeneutics, Authority, and Canon*, ed. D. A. Carson and John D. Woodbridge (Grand Rapids: Zondervan, 1986), 139–74; Craig L. Blomberg, "The Unity and Diversity of Scripture," in the *New Dictionary of Biblical Theology*, ed. T. Desmond Alexander et al. (Downers Grove, Ill.: InterVarsity, 2000), 71–72; and Gleason L. Archer, *Encyclopedia of Bible Difficulties* (Grand Rapids: Zondervan, 1982), 27–44.
3. Carl F. H. Henry, *God, Revelation and Authority*. 6 vols. (Waco, Tex.: Word, 1976–83), 4:364, cited in Blomberg, "Legitimacy and Limits of Harmonization," 161.
4. For a history of those who worked in examining synopses of parallel historical passages in the Bible, see Ronald Youngblood, "From Tatian to Swanson, from Calvin to Ben David: The Harmonization of Biblical History," *Journal of the Evangelical Theological Society* 25 (1982): 414–23.

subject appears to have fallen out of favor, however, from the latter part of the fifth century AD to the beginning of the sixteenth century. Almost no extant works can be cited on the topic of alleged discrepancies from this time period. Fortunately for us, however, the Reformation supplied a new impetus to all aspects of the study of the Bible, with this area of concern being treated once again.

For example, a work in Latin by Andreas Althamer in 1527 dealt with some 160 alleged biblical discrepancies. This title went through sixteen editions. In 1662 Johannes Thaddaeus and Thomas Mann offered a publication from London with the title *The Reconciler of the Bible Inlarged* [sic], which dealt with more than 3,000 contradictions in both testaments. This work counted each problem twice; in earlier editions of this same work, only 1,050 cases were itemized. John W. Haley, in his magisterial 1874 offering entitled *An Examination of the Alleged Discrepancies of the Bible*,[5] cited some forty-two titles from the Reformation and Post-Reformation era that dealt with all sorts of biblical contradictions. Haley complained that the Thaddaeus and Mann volume included "a multitude of trivial discrepancies, and omit[ted] many of the more important [ones]." Haley dealt with approximately some 2,750 citations from both the Old and New Testaments under the rubric of the following three categories: doctrinal, ethical, and historical discrepancies.

Oliver St. John Cooper examined 57 instances of scriptural disagreements in his *Four Hundred Texts of Holy Scripture with Their Corresponding Passages Explained*, a 1791 London publication. Likewise, Samuel Davidson included 115 contradictions on pages 516–611 of his *Sacred Hermeneutics, Developed and Applied*, an 1843 Edinburgh text. The history of this discussion is filled with names of some of the great biblical scholars of earlier days.

In more recent times, M. R. DeHaan published his *Answers to Bible Questions* (Grand Rapids: Zondervan, 1952); a mixture of doctrinal, factual, and interpretive questions. In 1965 J. Carter Swaim contributed his *Answers to Your Questions about the Bible* (New York: Vanguard). This was followed in 1972 with a volume by F. F. Bruce entitled *Answers to Questions* (Zondervan) and in 1979 by Robert H. Mounce's *Answers to Questions about the Bible* (Grand Rapids: Baker). Paul R. Van Gorder

---

5. John W. Haley. *An Examination of the Alleged Discrepancies of the Bible* (Boston: Estes and Lauriat, 1874). This edition was reprinted with an introduction by Alvah Hovey, professor of Newton Theology Institution in Nashville (B. C. Goodpasture, 1951) and distributed by Baker Publishing Group, Grand Rapids. The list of forty-two titles from the Reformation and Post-Reformation era that dealt with biblical contradictions can be found on pp. 437–42.

added another text in 1980 called *Since You Asked* (Grand Rapids: Radio Bible Class), a text organized alphabetically by topic with scripture and subject indexes.

My former colleague, Gleason L. Archer, produced a fairly large tome in 1982 called *Encyclopedia of Bible Difficulties* (Zondervan), arranged canonically. The first of InterVarsity's Hard Sayings series appeared in 1983: F. F. Bruce's *The Hard Sayings of Jesus* (Downers Grove, Ill.: InterVarsity), which considered seventy sayings of Jesus that were considered "hard" to understand or reconcile with the message of the rest of the Bible. The second in this series came in 1988, which was my first contribution to this area of study. It was entitled *Hard Sayings of the Old Testament*, with another seventy problematic texts of Scripture, this time from the Old Testament. This was followed in 1989 by Manfred T. Brauch's *Hard Sayings of Paul*, with another similar list of sayings. In 1991 Peter H. Davids contributed to this same InterVarsity series his *More Hard Sayings of the New Testament*, and I added in 1992 *More Hard Sayings of the Old Testament*. All five volumes in this series were reedited, and in the case of the Old Testament, considerably enlarged with another seventy difficult sayings, into one large tome called *Hard Sayings of the Bible* (InterVarsity, 1996).

In the meantime, David C. Downing contributed *What You Know Might Not Be So: 220 Misinterpretations of Bible Texts Explained* (Baker, 1987). Also, Robert H. Stein had produced in 1988 his *Difficult Passages in the Epistles* (Baker), arranged under a fivefold division: understanding words, understanding grammar, understanding context, understanding content, and understanding pairs of difficult passages by using the comparative method.

This is by no means a comprehensive list of contributors to the subject of harmonization of biblical texts, but it does demonstrate that the subject has continued to arouse interest over the years.

Seven Possible Sources for Biblical Discrepancies

Because the Bible is such a significant book, inquirers have numerous questions about the harmonization of its content. How did these discrepancies arise, and to what causes should they be attributed? Why would a self-revealing God who wished to make himself known to mortals allow contradictions? If the premise is true that our Lord made sure that his word was accurately communicated to the original writers of Scripture, why did he not take as much care in maintaining that same degree of accuracy through-out the document in the copies that have come down to us in our day?

There is no denying that the Bible contains numerous examples of apparent discrepancies, which if taken at face value, seem to conflict with or contradict some other statement in the Scriptures. But a divine source does not guarantee that all human involvement in transcribing and reproducing copies of these texts will be miraculously free from error.

So what are the sources and types of errors the Bible exhibits? Can we trace what some of the possible causes or sources of these errors might be? To start our thinking on this process, let's look at the following seven examples.

1. Differences due to errors of transmission. Gleason Archer has provided a good example of a type of error that can be harmonized fairly easily — errors that occurred in the transmission of the text.[6] For example, the Hebrew text of Isaiah 9:2 (Eng., v. 3) read *l'* (*lamed aleph*), meaning "not," when it should have read *lw* (*lamed waw*), meaning "to it/him" as the Syriac Peshitta, the Aramaic Targum of Jonathan, and twenty medieval Hebrew manuscripts rendered it. Therefore, the KJV translation rendered it incorrectly with a strange reversal of thought, using the word "not" in this way: "Thou hast multiplied the nation *and* [the word 'and' is supplied but is not in the Hebrew] *not* increased the joy: they joy before thee according to the joy in harvest" (Isa. 9:3). Even the Masoretic scribes early on sensed that there was something wrong with the transmission of this text and indicated this in the margin of the Hebrew text.[7] The harmonized rendering, based on the aforementioned textual criticism, is "You have magnified the nation, *to it* you have given great joy ..." (my translation); the offending "not" was removed and sense and meaning were restored to this text in keeping with evidence preserved in early readings of the same text in other versions.

2. Differences based on alternative translation or understanding of a passage. My favorite example of a failure to understand contemporary usage is the meaning of the phrase "three days and three nights" in 1 Samuel 30:11–13 and Matthew 12:40.[8] Rather than viewing this as a total of seventy-two hours, or three full days, it is best to see it as a common expression in that day

---

6. Archer, *Encyclopedia of Bible Difficulties*, 33.
7. The Masoretes were a group of Jewish scribes who worked on the Hebrew text from about AD 500 to 1000, protecting it from textual inaccuracies and corruption.
8. E. W. Bullinger, *Figures of Speech Used in the Bible*, s.v., "Idioma" (1898, Eyre and Spottiswoode; repr., Grand Rapids: Baker, 1968), 845–47. It means "peculiar usage of words or phrases used in a common manner of speaking."

in which any part of a day or year could be referred to as all that day or year. Accordingly, in 1 Samuel 30:11–12, David and his men returned to Ziklag to learn that the Amalekites had raided that city during the absence of David and his troops, and that they had carried off as captives their women, children, and all their possessions from the city. As David pursued the raiders, they found an Egyptian servant who had been abandoned in the Amalekites' hasty retreat with their captives and loot. The Egyptian had not eaten any food or had any water for "three days and three nights" (v. 12). He added, "Today is the third day" (literal Hebrew rendering of v. 13c, *hayyom sheloshah*). It is clear in this example that the full formula of "three days and three nights" could routinely be used as a stereotypical expression if the period of time touched any part of those three days and three nights. This happens in other temporal references as well. Therefore our Lord was in the grave from late Friday afternoon to early Sunday morning, a total of some thirty-eight hours and not seventy-two, and the stereotypical formula "three days and three nights" was rightfully used to acknowledge that parts of all three days were involved.

In another instance, this time in a geographical reference, Jesus is said to have preached his famous sermon on a "mountainside" (Gk., *oros*) in one text (Matt. 5:1) but "on a level place" (Gk., *pedinou*) in another place (Luke 6:17). A few interpreters have argued that these passages refer to two entirely different occasions, but this strains one's credulity when they both have very similar introductions, conclusions, structure, and details. Blomberg pointed out that the Septuagintal usage apparently used both terms to indicate a higher elevation than the coast.[9] While this is a possible resolution, the final answer must await more evidence.

3. Differences based on theologically motivated writing. Usually what we find here are examples of what has more recently been called "redaction criticism." This term serves as a quick handle for scholars to refer to tasks that interpreters have been performing for years, namely, noting the distinctive purpose(s), motive(s), theme(s), and emphasis (emphases) one writer employs over against another writer who has written on the same topic(s) that bring out his own distinctive goals for writing what he did. The fact that the writers had freedom to select what they would write in light of the purpose each had for writing should not be a mark against the legitimacy of their reports. And we must remember that more may have been going on than

---

9. Blomberg, "Legitimacy and Limits of Harmonization," 147. He points to Josh. 9:1; 10:40; 2 Chron. 26:10; Isa. 13:2 (LXX); and Jer. 31:8.

any one writer chose to include; thus one writer may have covered some aspects of an event while another writer chose to cover other details. Craig L. Blomberg cites Lord Macaulay's words in this connection: "What is told in the fullest and most accurate annals bears an infinitely small proportion to what is suppressed."[10]

For example, Matthew reports Jesus asking the rich young ruler, "Why do you ask me about what is good?" (Matt. 19:17). Two other gospels report Jesus as asking, "Why do you call me good?" (Mark 10:18; Luke 18:19). A so-called "additive harmonization" simply says that Jesus asked both questions. Some point to the continuous force of the Greek word *eperota*, "asking," in Mark 10:17. Others feel that is too tenuous a solution; therefore they say Matthew wanted to avoid the danger that his readers might have wrongly inferred that Jesus denied his own deity and accordingly inserted his own word about the rich young ruler "asking" Jesus "about" "what is good." Today we usually put added words in square brackets to indicate that they are not in the original quotation. However, even without the literary convention of square brackets when the Bible was written, it was still possible to accomplish the same type of insertions. Good interpretation must understand that is what Matthew may well have been doing.

Will Matthew's change result in retaining the *ipsissima vox Jesu*? Some think the answer is no, since the added words did not come directly from the lips of our Lord. However, if Matthew's motive and purpose are taken into consideration, along with the device where we now use square brackets to show what was added, the answer is yes. This is especially true if Matthew was trying to answer the original question this young man had about what good thing he had to do to gain eternal life. Moreover, even the Greek *ti me legeis agathou* can be understood to refer to Matthew's, Mark's, or even Luke's use of the word "good."

4. Differences based on textual-critical solutions. In the case of the New Testament, what we now consider to be the original text has by now been well established, with not more than a mere small page or page and a half of the Greek text still waiting for resolution. However, instead of accepting any and all sorts of harmonizing variants as the original text, the choice usually goes to the *lectio difficilior*, that is, the "harder reading," unless that reading is also too hard.

---

10. Ibid., 143.

Craig Blomberg pointed to Matthew 7:11 and Luke 11:13, passages that raise the question: What did Jesus promise his heavenly Father would give to his children: good gifts or the Holy Spirit?[11] The two pericopes share so many verbal parallels, that to conclude they are two different sayings given at two different times does not seem to be a fair way of resolving this discrepancy. A Lukan variant attested in an early Greek manuscript called p[45] reads, *pneuma agathon*, "good Spirit." This is not a common biblical term, and it would account for Matthew's *agatha*, "good," and Luke's *pneuma hagion*, "Holy Spirit." Should other early manuscript evidence continue to sustain p[45], this solution would be rendered as most probable.

Another example of a place where textual criticism can help is found in John 14:17: "the Spirit of truth. The world cannot accept him, because it neither sees him nor knows him. But you know him, for he lives with you and *will be* in you" (emphasis added). Or should we translate it "*is in you*"? Which reading is to be preferred, *estin* or *estai*? Some early texts, such as p[66] and p[75] read, *menei ... estai*, that is, "he abides with you and *is* in you." The implications of this slight difference in textual readings are enormous, for the question is whether the Holy Spirit indwelt believers prior to our Lord's resurrection and ascension into heaven or occurred only after his resurrection and ascension. Given the fact that the text affirms that the Holy Spirit already "lives with you," and the fact that *estai* is the harder reading, the case of "is in you" is to be preferred. Therefore, the Holy Spirit also indwelt believers during the days of the Old Testament!

5. Differences based on the omission of words. There are two well-known types of transmissional errors: *homoeoteleuton*, meaning "having the same ending," where the copyist inadvertently drops some words or letters that have an identical ending with those that occur in nearby lines, and *homoeoarkton*, which means "that which has a similar beginning" and involves a loss of words as the eye of the scribe jumps from the beginning of one line to another similar beginning.

An outstanding example of homoeoteleuton occurs in Psalm 145, which is an alphabetic acrostic psalm. Each successive letter of the twenty-two-letter Hebrew alphabet appears in this twenty-one-verse psalm except the letter *nun* (*n*). The Masoretic Hebrew text of verse 13 (English 14) begins with a *mem* (*m*), which is the first letter of *malkuteka*, "your kingdom." Hebrew verse 14 (English 15) begins not with *nun*, which is the next letter

---

11. Blomberg, "Legitimacy and Limits of Harmonization," 145–46.

in the alphabet, but with *samekh* (*s*), which comes after *nun*: "The LORD upholds all those who fall" (*somek YHWH lekol-hannopelim*).

However, one Masoretic text in the Dead Sea Scrolls, along with the Syriac and the Septuagint, each retain what is probably the original verse that is missing in the alphabetic acrostic. It reads: "Faithful is Yahweh in all his promises and gracious in all he has made" (my translation of *ne'eman YHWH bekol-debarayw wehasid bekol-ma'asayw*). The reoccurrence of *YHWH bekol*, "Yahweh in all," so soon after *YHWH lekol*, "Yahweh to all," must have made the eye of the scribe skip, but the error is obvious, since it left an otherwise complete alphabet broken in the middle. Thus a whole missing verse can be restored in the Bible by this type of textual criticism detective work.

A possible example of homoeoarkton is in 1 Samuel 14:41. The Masoretic text reads, "Then Saul prayed to the LORD, the God of Israel, 'Grant a perfect one [Heb., *tamim*]." In this example, the eye of the scribe jumped from one beginning clause to another, because the consonantal spelling for "Thummim" (Heb., *tummim*) would have appeared to be the same at first glance, especially without the *dagesh forte* in the middle *mem*, as was common in unpointed Hebrew text. What was omitted was retained in the Septuagintal rendering of the Hebrew, which was as follows: "Why have you not answered your servant today? If the fault is in me or my son Jonathan, respond with the Urim, but if the men of Israel are at fault, respond with the Thummim."

The Septuagint is not able to help us with restorations of omissions that occurred before the third century BC, because it had not yet been translated. A famous example of this is 1 Samuel 13:1, where the Masoretic Hebrew text reads, "Saul was ... years old when he began to reign." The numeral has been completely omitted, and so far there has been no way of restoring what it was. A few late Septuagintal manuscripts supply the word "thirty" years old, but so far not one Hebrew manuscript has been found with a numeral in this position. This dilemma remains without even a good suggested solution.

6. Differences Based on the Transcription of Large Numbers. One area of harmonization is not so easily answered: the large numbers in the book of Chronicles as compared with those in Kings, for example. In general, many feel the need to reduce these numbers in some way.[12]

---

12. See J. Barton Payne, "The Validity of Numbers in Chronicles," *Bibliotheca Sacra* 136 (1979): 109–28, 206–20, with a chart summarizing his findings on p. 125; John Wenham, "Large Numbers in the Old Testament," *Tyndale Bulletin* 18 (1967): 19–53.

In recent times, some have pointed to the word for "thousand" (Heb. *'elph)*, which is also translated as a "clan," or a "unit" of a tribe, such as appears in Numbers 1:16; Judges 6:15; 1 Samuel 10:19–21; and Micah 5:2.[13] Thus large numbers that use the Hebrew word *'elph* would not amount to a "thousand" of whatever unit was noted, but to that *unit of clans* or *tribal entities*, thereby dropping the concept of a "thousand."

Payne divided all such numerical discrepancies into two groups: (1) those where no genuine difference occurs, and (2) those where there is a real difference. For those in the first group, Payne tended to explain the numerical differences by suggesting that there were different instances or different measures involved. Accordingly, 2 Samuel 24:24 notes that David gave 50 shekels of silver for Araunah's "threshing floor" and "oxen," whereas 1 Chronicles 21:25 has David paying 600 shekels of gold for "the site." Payne declared that this was no contradiction, for Samuel spoke of a fairly small parcel, while the chronicler's price was for the whole area on Mount Moriah that he was purchasing.[14] On the face of it, this seems like a fair reading of both texts.

The attempt to make *'elep* mean "clan" (as it surely does in Judg. 6:15) to solve the problem of such large numbers (e.g., in Chronicles) runs into difficulties, however, in Exodus 38:25–26. There a half shekel was to be given for each of the 603,550 warriors above the age of twenty years old, a total of "100 talents and 1,775 shekels" (*me'od kikkor we'elep useba' me'od wahamissah wesib'im sekel*). Since there are 3,000 shekels to a talent, that would come to 300,000, plus 1,775, for a total of 301,775, a number matching the number of troops at the end of the wilderness march in Numbers 26:51 and 1:46, since a half shekel was given for each man (301,775 times two equals 603,550)! The use of *'elep* in the shekel count proved to be real "thousands," and not a "clan" or "family unit" values as in the use of *'elph* here.

As already noted, the most notorious discrepancies in biblical numbers are to be found in the postexilic era, especially in Chronicles. Many scholars feel that several of these 629[15] numbers are impossibly high. The

13. G. E. Mendenhall, "The Census Lists of Numbers 1 and 26," *Journal of Biblical Literature* 77 (1958): 52–66.

14. See also Raymond Dillard, "David's Census: Perspectives on 2 Samuel 24 and 1 Chronicles 21," in *Through Christ's Word*, ed. Robert Godfrey and Jesse Boyd III (Phillipsburg, N.J.: Presbyterian and Reformed, 1985), 94–107.

15. This number comes from a conservative scholar, J. Barton Payne, "The Validity of the Numbers in Chronicles," *Bibliotheca Sacra* 136 (1979): 109–28; 206–20; J. Barton Payne, "The Validity of Numbers in Chronicles," *Near East Archaeological Society Bulletin*, New Series 11 (1978): 5–58. Also see Wenham, "Large Numbers," 19–53; and H. L. Allrik, "The Lists of Zerubbabel (Nehemiah 7 and Ezra 2) and the Hebrew Numerical Notation," *Bulletin of American Schools of Oriental Research* 136 (1954): 21–27. Also note Walter C. Kaiser Jr., "Aren't Many Old Testament Numbers Wrong?" in *Hard Sayings of the Bible*, ed. Walter C. Kaiser et al. (Downers Grove, Ill.: InterVarsity Press, 1996), 51–54.

most serious examples appear where we have parallel texts with figures. For example, 1 Chronicles 19:18 has David killing "7,000 charioteers of the Arameans and 40,000 foot soldiers," whereas 2 Samuel 10:18 has "700 charioteers" and "40,000 horsemen;" 2 Chronicles 9:25 claims that Solomon had "4,000 stalls for horses and chariots and 12,000 horsemen," but 1 Kings 4:26 says he had "40,000 stalls of horses for his chariots, and 12,000 horsemen" (all NASB). Second Chronicles 36:9 assures us that "Jehoiachin was eight years old when he became king" while 2 Kings 24:8 declares he was "eighteen years old when he became king" (both NASB). In these examples, it is almost certain that there is a transcriptional error that goes far back in the history of one or more families of manuscripts. J. Barton Payne found that "in the eleven cases of disagreement over numbers that have arisen between the MT [Masoretic Hebrew text] of Chronicles and of Samuel/Kings because of copyists' errors, Chronicles is found to be correct in [only] five, and one remains uncertain."[16]

One other notable example of differing numbers can be seen in the two parallel lists of Nehemiah 7 and Ezra 2 of the exiles who returned back to Israel. Thirty-three family units appear in both lists with 153 numbers, 29 of which are not the same in both lists. If a cipher notation was used with something like vertical strokes for units, horizontal strokes for tens, and stylized *mems* (the initial letter of the Hebrew word *me'ah*, "hundred") for hundreds, then the scribe miscopied a single stroke. But there is also the possibility that different circumstances affected the numbers in each count, for Ezra's list was composed while people were assembling in Babylon, while Nehemiah's count was drawn up in Judea after the walls of Jerusalem were rebuilt. In the interim, many could have changed their minds and others died. As H. L. Allrik concluded, "While at first glance these textual-numerical differences may seem detrimental, actually they greatly enhance the value of the lists, as they bring out much of their real nature and age."[17]

7. Differences based on famous historical contradictions. A problem arises with who gets credit for killing Goliath—David or Elhanan. From 1 Samuel 17:4, 7, and 50 we learn that David decapitated the giant Goliath after he felled him with a slingshot and stone. But 2 Samuel 21:19 in the Hebrew

---

16. J. Barton Payne, "1, 2 Chronicles," in *The Expositor's Bible Commentary*, vol. 4, ed. Frank E. Gabelein (Grand Rapids: Zondervan, 1988), 311. Note especially Payne's appendix A on p. 561, "Numbers in Chronicles That Disagree with Their Old Testament Parallels," and appendix B on p. 562, "Numbers Over 1,000 Unique to Chronicles."
17. Allrik, "Lists of Zerubbabel," 27.

Masoretic text states that "Elhanan, the son of Yaare-oregim the Bethlehemite, killed Goliath the Gittite, the shaft of whose spear was like a weaver's beam." As the text stands, it sure looks like two different persons are claiming the honor for the same incident.

Providentially, we do have another text, 1 Chronicles 20:5, that explains: "Elhanan son of Jair killed Lahmi the brother of Goliath the Gittite." It is possible now to see that 1 Chronicles 20:5 and 2 Samuel 21:19 are the true readings. The copyist of one of the earlier manuscripts made three errors: (1) he misread the direct object sign (*'et*), that comes just before "Lahmi" as a *bet*, and he got a new word: "Bethlehemite"; (2) he misread the word for "brother" (*'ahi*) as if it were the direct object sign, thereby making Goliath the object of "killed"; and (3) he misplaced the word for "weavers" right after "Elhanan," to give an unheard of patronymic of "the son of the forests of weavers!" Thus the errors of 2 Samuel are easily reconstructed from the parallel text preserved in 1 Chronicles 20:5. So David retains his conquest of Goliath, and Elhanan gets the credit for taking out Goliath's brother Lahmi.

Conclusion

While harmonization has enjoyed a rather long history with some outstanding contributions, there have also been some major debacles along the way, such as the attempt to coordinate Peter's denials of our Lord before the cock crowed twice, which in overworked harmonization amounted instead to six such denials.[18] Preferably, we must move only when the evidence is in, thereby avoiding facile harmonizations that often tend to be incorrect as the facts become available.

Enough progress has been made in the area of reconciling apparent contradictions that the case for the unity of the Bible can be sustained. This does not mean that all of the problems have been solved successfully or to the agreement of all scholars, but it does mean that enough principles are operating that provide us with a good measure of success and a sufficient confidence that the remaining issues can be remedied in similar ways as the ones that now rest securely within the enormous amount of material in the noncontradicted sections of the Bible.

18. Harold Lindsell, *The Battle for the Bible* (Grand Rapids: Zondervan, 1976), 174–76.

The Unity *of the* Hebrew Bible

Our sense that the moral stance of the Old Testament is simply chaotic derives largely from the fact that it is so much a part of our common Western heritage that we cannot stand far enough away to recognize the family likeness among its writings, and thus to see how markedly they differ, as a whole, from those of other major religious and ethical systems.

—John J. Barton[1]

I got the idea for the title and general thrust of this chapter some time ago while reading David Noel Freedman's book by the same name, *The Unity of the Hebrew Bible*.[2] Rather than pursuing some unitary or unifying theme found throughout the text of the Old Testament, Freedman was more concerned to determine the "organization, arrangement, and amalgamation of the different individual literary entities [and how they merged] into the whole that we call the Hebrew Bible—and the process by which that feat was achieved."[3]

In carrying out this objective, Freedman announced two principles: (1) the historical narratives generally come from the time of the author(s), and therefore they are roughly contemporary with the writer(s) of these stories (being completed in his judgment shortly after the last of the stories was finished); and (2) the primary indicator of the larger groupings within the

1. John J. Barton, "Approaches to Ethics in the Old Testament," in *Beginning Old Testament Study*, ed. J. Rogerson (London: SPCK, 1983), 126.
2. David Noel Freedman, *The Unity of the Hebrew Bible* (Ann Arbor, Mich.: University of Michigan Press, 1991).
3. Ibid., vi.

Hebrew Bible can be found in their "symmetry," which is defined by structures and numbers ("usually of a simple binary or bilateral kind")[4] as evidence of purposeful, deliberate decisions producing a unified whole.[5]

In Freedman's view, the first nine books of the Hebrew Bible are so organized and well assembled that they represented the work of a single mind (such as Ezra the scribe, Nehemiah, or a group of people who put the whole thing together). This Enneateuch (this "nine-book" collection from Genesis to 2 Kings) forms the core of the Hebrew Bible, for it tells the story that began at Babylon (the Tower of Babel in Gen. 11) and ends with the nation of Israel in captivity in Babylon (2 Kings 25) once again.

Freedman recognized that for many the Hebrew Bible is regarded as having a divine origin. But, he argued, since it is "entirely a human document,"[6] it is still proper to address the same questions of the Bible that one would address to any other work of literature, including such questions as who, what, when, where, why, and how.

Of course those questions are legitimate, even on the divine origin basis as well. But the answers to those questions will not always be limited to a strictly human level of argumentation, since the text will make higher divine claims for itself. Some of the very same data Freedman points to are equally applicable to God being the organizing mind behind the unity in these nine books as Ezra or Nehemiah—even though the story of Israel ends, for all intents and purposes, in the "Primary History" of the nine books with the Ezra-Nehemiah story.

The Overall Organization and Divisions of the Hebrew Bible

Jewish tradition divided the Hebrew Bible into three parts identified by the acronym TaNaK, in which the first division was designated by *T* for the Torah or Law (Genesis, Exodus, Leviticus, Numbers, and Deuteronomy); the second division was denoted by *N* for *Nebi'im*, the Prophets, both the Former Prophets (Joshua, Judges, Samuel, and Kings; the last two books were taken as one book each despite our English division of the books into 1 and 2 Samuel and 1 and 2 Kings) and the Latter Prophets (Isaiah, Jeremiah, Ezekiel, and the twelve Minor Prophets, which were all taken as one book); and the third division was marked by *K* for *Ketubim*, the Writings,

---

4. Ibid.
5. Ibid.
6. Ibid., 2.

which in turn were made up of the three poetical books (Psalms, Proverbs, and Job), the five Megillot, or Scrolls (Song of Songs, Ruth, Lamentations, Ecclesiastes, and Esther), and the Histories (Daniel, Ezra-Nehemiah, 1 and 2 Chronicles). (The two *a* vowels in TaNaK were supplied between the *T*, the *N*, and the *K* to help pronounce the acronym.)

Freedman noted the following distributions and proportions of these major divisions of the Hebrew Bible, consisting of 305,500 words in the Hebrew Bible, rounded off to 300,000:

Torah/Law	5 books	80,000 words	Primary History
Former Prophets	4 books	70,000 words	Primary History
Latter Prophets	4 books	72,000 words	
Writings	11 books	84,000 words	

What he labeled the "core Bible" of the Old Testament, or the "Primary History," comprises about 150,000 words, or one-half of the entire Hebrew Bible. In these nine books, the central content of the Bible can be found. From this perspective, the center or apex of the Hebrew Bible comes at the end of the Primary History—the point at which the story is told of the Babylonian captivity of the people of Judah, the loss of Israel's nationhood, and the complete destruction of the capital of Judah, Jerusalem.

Freedman argued that the same apex, or melancholy center, reappears in the whole corpus of the Latter Prophets, which comes at the end of the book of Jeremiah and the beginning of the book of Ezekiel. A similar center is posed for the *Ketubim*, the Writings, with the book of Lamentations, mourning the fall of Jerusalem, in the center of those eleven books as well. Thus the symmetrical pattern is played out three separate times, thereby reinforcing a definite purpose and pattern as to where the history of the nation of Israel was going and had gone.

However, while the fall of Jerusalem is the middle of the Bible, the middle of the Latter Prophets, and the middle of the Writings, this was not the midpoint of the Enneateuch ("nine-book" collection) or Primary History. That midpoint for the first nine books of the Hebrew Bible came in the book of Deuteronomy, where Moses, toward the end of his life, recites on Mount Sinai all that God has done for the nation, as found especially in his covenant with them and its commandments. It is true that this central event was also recorded in the book of Exodus, but the replication of this key event again at the center of the nine books, in Deuteronomy, must not be missed.

In Freedman's view, then, the story found in the first nine books of the Old Testament is:

> The first and perhaps the most important and influential prose narrative ever written, preceding, for example, Herodotus [484?–425? BC] and his *History of the Persian Wars* by at least a century[7] [was the Primary History]. The Primary History may be compared with such a historical work because it constitutes historical writing, although it is perhaps more credulous in some respects than modern historians require. In other words, although it is not history in the modern sense, it is clearly interested in real people, real places, and real events.[8]

The Decalogue

If the principle goal of the Primary History was to explain how it happened that the chosen people of Israel were at first rescued from their slavery in Egypt, given a home in the land of Canaan, and ended up in the Babylonian exile, as Freedman laid it out so succinctly, then at least nine of the Ten Commandments will play a large role in solving that conundrum. The same God who created and shaped Israel is the God who could discipline them when they failed to follow him. The covenant that God gave to Israel contained both promise and threat in it, as the farewell speeches of Moses (Deut. 33) and Joshua (Josh. 23–24) indicate.

So important was the Decalogue that it appeared near the start of Israel's exodus from Egypt (Ex. 20) and was repeated just before they entered the land of Canaan (Deut. 5). Moses himself is therefore the pivotal character who overshadows the first half of the story of this people and these nine books. Both in his role of reviewing their history and in his role of forecasting the future of the nation, his focus remained on the behavior of the nation of Israel.

The Ten Words, or Decalogue, is the epitome of God's covenant, Freedman argued. They appear at the exodus and in Deuteronomy, at the center of the nine books, and act as the pivot and apex of the nine books. This

---

7. That is assuming that Ezra or Nehemiah is the organizing editor of all these books, for which there is no collateral evidence. I believe there are better evidential grounds for placing it around 1400 BC.
8. Freedman, *Unity of the Hebrew Bible*, 9. I would not agree with his use of the word "credulous," but otherwise the statement is a great mark for a real history. He went on to qualify this statement a bit more, but the overall impact stands.

cannot be a "numerical accident" or a mere "coincidence,"[9] for both Moses and Joshua, in their valedictory speeches, focus on these words as the basis for what can be expected in their own day and in the future.

The organization of the nine books revolves around Israel's violation of nine of the Ten Commandments before the Babylonian exile ensued. One commandment and one violation appear in each book, Freedman observed, thereby showing how the future of the nation was progressively put in jeopardy and progressively teetered on the brink of disaster. Despite the intervention of one extraordinary leader after another throughout their history, causing God to relent time and again, finally in the end Yahweh's patience will have run out as nine of the Ten Commandments have been broken one after the other. This is the scenario Freedman proposed. He asked:

> What are the chances that such a pattern and sequence actually occur in the Primary History? And if they do occur, or any portion of them [falls into place], is that evidence of a guiding editorial hand?...
>
> There are Ten Commandments but only nine books.... So an adjustment will be necessary. The editor will have to dissolve or absorb one of the commandments along the way or otherwise account for the discrepancy.[10]

To be sure, there were covenants earlier than the Sinaitic covenant. There was the covenant with the seasons in Noah's day (Gen. 9), and the covenant with Abraham (Gen. 12, 15, 17), but those were not the covenants that Israel decided to break, according to Freedman's way of viewing the material. Therefore, Freedman began with the second book of the nine and doubled up two commandments in the book of Exodus.

One other problem appears before we can view the layout of Freedman's scenario: there are several different ways of numbering the commandments (Protestant, Jewish, Roman Catholic, and Lutheran). Freedman adopted what he called the consensus view that most scholars follow and untangled the order of commandments six though eight by appealing to the abbreviated order of the Decalogue that appears in Jeremiah's famous "temple gate message" in Jeremiah 7:8–11, where the order of the commandments given in verse 9 is 8 (stealing), 6 (murder), and 7 (adultery). The order in the Septuagint is 7, 8, 6; and the order of these same three commandments in the Nash Papyrus, Philo, and the New Testament (Luke 18:20; Rom. 13:9; and James 2:11) is 7, 6, 8. Hosea 4:2 has yet another order for these three: 6, 8, 7. When all of these variations are charted, they look like this:

9. Ibid., 15.
10. Ibid., 17.

Ex. 20; Deut. 5	Jer. 7:8–11	Septuagint	Nash, Philo, NT	Hos. 4:2
6	8	7	7	6
7	6	8	6	8
8	7	6	8	7

If the order in which these three violations take place in the Primary History is favored, then the order given in Jeremiah 7:8–11 is taken as normative. The result that follows from this decision is as follows:[11]

The Prohibitions			**The Violations**	
Exodus 20		Deuteronomy 5	Commandment Number	
Verse 3	Apostasy	Verse 7	1	Ex. 32
4	Idolatry	8	2	Ex. 32
7	Blasphemy	11	3	Lev. 24:10–16
8	Sabbath	12	4	Num. 15:32–36
12	Parents	16	5	Deut. 21:18–21
15	Stealing	19	8	Josh. 7
13	Killing	17	6	Judg. 19–21
14	Adultery	18	7	2 Sam. 11–12
16	False Witness	20	9	1 Kings 21
17	Coveting	21	10	?– – –

The first violation happened when Moses was absent from the Israelite camp while he was up on Mount Sinai. When Aaron made the golden calf, he violated both of the first two commandments: "You shall have no other gods before me" (Ex. 20:3); "You shall not make for yourself an idol in the

11. As presented by Freedman in ibid., 18–19.

form of anything" (v. 4). Tragically, it was no one less than Aaron, Moses' older brother, who declared of the golden calf, "These are your gods, O Israel, who brought you up out of Egypt" (Ex. 32:4). Thus, in one single event, we have a double violation of the first two commandments.

But this may not be as unusual as it seems, for what Freedman missed was that the final event in 1 Kings 21 likewise had a double violation, wherein both Queen Jezebel and King Ahab violated not just the ninth commandment against false witnesses by lying about a crime that Naboth did not commit, but King Ahab also violated the tenth commandment when he coveted Naboth's vineyard despite the fact that poor Naboth was not free to sell or exchange that property under any circumstances, since the Lord owned all the land and it was to stay in the family line in perpetuity (Lev. 25:23). Thus 1 Kings 21 forms an inclusion by ending the ninth book with a double violation, just as Israel began this series of ten violations of the Decalogue with a double offense.[12]

The third violation comes in the third book, noted Freedman. It involves a case of blasphemy, which Exodus 20:7 had cautioned against, "You shall not misuse the name of the Lord your God." But in Leviticus 24:10–16, an unnamed man, born to an Israelite woman from the tribe of Dan and an Egyptian man, got into a fight with another Israelite, in which he blasphemed the name of God. He was put into custody until the decision obtained from the Lord was that he should be taken outside the camp and be stoned by the entire congregation. As a result it was proclaimed that "if anyone curses his God, he will be held responsible; anyone who blasphemes the name of the Lord must be put to death" (Lev. 24:15–16).

The fourth commandment deals with the Sabbath: "Remember the Sabbath day by keeping it holy" (Ex. 20:8). Again, it is the fourth book of the nine, Numbers 15:32–36, where the story is told of a man who gathered sticks on the Sabbath, apparently not out of necessity, but in brazen and purposeful defiance (Heb., *beyad ramah*, "with a high hand") of God, thereby "blaspheming" (Heb., *megaddeph*) or "reviling the Lord." Such a person was to be cut off from his people. This offender also had to be put into custody until the Lord indicated what his punishment should be: "The man must die" (Num. 15:35). Both the third and the fourth violations of the Decalogue show how serious it is to challenge God's authority. The observance of the Sabbath continued to be a real issue for Israel's prophets, as can be seen in their continued use of it as an example of the people's lapsing

---

12. This paragraph is my suggestion that is to be added to Freedman's observations.

from the standards God had set before them (Isa. 56:2–6; 58:13–14; Jer. 17:21–27; Amos 8:5).

The fifth commandment exhorts, "Honor your father and your mother, so that you may live long in the land the LORD your God is giving you" (Ex. 20:12). True to plan, it was the fifth book of the nine that raised this issue; only this time it came in the form of a hypothetical case law in Deuteronomy 21:18–21. In this probable case of parental abuse, the son acted in stubborn rebellion and did not respond to any type of discipline. The son was to be brought to the elders of the city, and charges were to be laid against him. "He is a profligate and a drunkard" (Deut. 21:20). He, too, was to be stoned so that evil could be destroyed from Israel's midst (v. 21).

The sixth book, Joshua, actually picks up the eighth commandment, according to the numbering found in Jeremiah 7. The offense was one of thievery, and it was committed by Achan when he looted Jericho contrary to the injunction given by the Lord (Josh. 7). The whole city of Jericho had been put under what in Hebrew is called a *herem*, an "involuntary ban," in which anything that was not destroyed or burnt up in the capture of that city, such as iron, silver, or gold, was to be put into the tabernacle of God, dedicated to the Lord's exclusive use. In fact, the whole city was to be dedicated to the Lord. But Achan chose to disregard such instructions, which resulted in his death.

According to the order of Jeremiah 7, the probation against murder comes next, and the book that details this law is the book of Judges. Judges, of course, illustrates a number of killings (e.g., of Eglon by Ehud, of Sisera by Jael, and of the Philistines by Samson), but these generally were not violations of the decree of God, as judged by a divine decree to go into battle. The case described in Judges 19–21, however, is a different story. It involved a gang rape of the Levite's concubine and her "murder" (the same Hebrew word, *ratsach*, used in the Decalogue). So brutal and so appalling was this crime that the writer of Judges exclaimed: "Such a thing has never been seen or done, not since the day the Israelites came up out of Egypt. Think about it! Consider it! Tell us what to do!" (19:30).

The eighth book of the nine, Samuel, focuses on the prohibition against adultery. It concerns the case of King David committing adultery with Uriah the Hittite's wife, Bathsheba (1 Sam. 11–12). With this incident came the turning point in the life of the kingdom and David its king. From here on out the distaff side of David's line was consistently a source of real trouble.

Finally, 1 Kings 21 gives the account of the landowner Naboth who was deliberately set up for annihilation by a coveting king and by a complicitous queen who employed two downright liars to carry out her wishes to do away with Naboth and his sons so that King Ahab could fulfill his covetous desires on Naboth's vineyard. In so doing, the ninth and tenth commandments were broken, which completed the whole series of the Ten Commandments. The Primary History in the Enneateuch details, then, why God had to judge his people with an exile in Assyria and Babylon.

The Latter Prophets

Freedman went on to describe the linkage between the Latter Prophets and the Primary History as being one of a "supplement to the Primary History."[13] He argued that both sections were meant to be read together. But what the prophetic books did was to go beyond the Primary History, which warned of the coming exile in Babylon, along with the inevitable destruction of the commonwealth of Israel. The prophets reviewed the same coming destruction but went on to dramatically point, in chapters like Ezekiel 37 and Jeremiah 32, to the fact that Yahweh would restore the people to the land after they had been punished. He would see to it that the cities were rebuilt, that safety was guaranteed for the land, and that the temple was restored.

The Writings

In like manner, a similar case was made for the Writings. It focused more on the southern kingdom of Judah and the survival of that nation under Persian rule, for the northern kingdom had already long since been carried off into captivity. It emphasized the dynasty of David and Yahweh's commitment to the city of Jerusalem. The only book Freedman cannot easily put into this structure is the book of Daniel. His conclusion, in his own words, goes like this:

> I have presented a case for the unity of the Hebrew Bible—as a literary composite. Certainly there can be no argument for unitary authorship, since different parts and books arise from vastly different times and places. But we can speak about compilation and organization, what we mean by editing or redacting in the broad sense. From a study of the Bible's contents, style, lan-

---

13. Freedman, *Unity of the Hebrew Bible*, 42.

guage and literary features, I conclude that there is a pervasive unity, elements that tie individual components into a complex but unified structure.[14]

Freedman has given us a most creative and unusual approach to the question of the unity of the Old Testament. He has made a strong case for the unity of the message and plan of the Old Testament. As he centered his case for the unity of the Bible around the Decalogue, he showed how each of the books in what he calls the Primary History of the Bible illustrates one of the Ten Commandments after another in an order he also defends. I am convinced he has latched on to one of the Bible's integrating themes. What is so amazing is that he has opted to take what might be judged to be a more propositional and historical path than the contemporary culture would seem to tolerate, constantly affirming, as many evangelicals would, a "unitary authorship." Freedman's basic idea is ripe for further development. It is my hope that some will take up this challenge and carry his thesis forward in the future.

But the impact of Freedman's work also comes close to what G. Ernest Wright wanted as he argued for his "kerygmatic core" for the unity of the Bible.[15] However, Wright felt the concentration on history and Israel's life within that history would only lead to the wide spectrum of diversity rather than its unity. It would only be in this "confessional rehearsal of events interpreted as the redemptive activity of God" that certain inferences could be drawn out for the unity of the Hebrew Bible as far as G. Ernest Wright was concerned.[16] Therefore, while there was vast variety in the Old Testament, the unifying factor could be found in the recital of Israel's confession of God's saving and redemptive acts.

Legitimate Kinds of Diversity in the Old Testament

There is no doubt that the Old Testament does exhibit a good deal of diversity, but of what sort is it, and what do we mean by diversity? Is there, for example, a polarity in the theology of the Old Testament?

J. G. McConville agreed that there was a large amount of diversity in the Old Testament, but his caution was as follows:

---

14. Ibid., 98.
15. G. Ernest Wright, "Wherein Lies the Unity of the Bible?" *The Journal of Bible and Religion* 20, no. 3 (1952): 196.
16. Ibid., 197.

[Diversity] does not always have the kind of significance which some writers attribute to it.... The question still remaining is whether there is a kind of diversity in the Old Testament whose *essence* is discord or conflict. Are there competing beliefs, ideologies, attitudes among which we, as those who confess a biblical faith, are compelled to select some and reject others?... The answer [for solving this dilemma] lies in the direction of exegesis.[17]

That, of course, does not end the debate, for as McConville immediately noted, there are "sharp disagreements" in our exegetical results even among those who are in broad sympathy with each other and the text of Scripture, not to mention the wide spectrum of views found in the scholarly academy. McConville's way of resolving this dilemma is to note that "true biblical interpretation is a dialectic between understanding the letter (the jot and the tittle) and understanding the whole."[18] In McConville's view, the way out of this impasse, and the threat of subjectivity in interpretation, is to read the text "in terms of all of Scripture, even if that means modifying slightly what one believes 'Scripture says.' A canon which can in principle be abbreviated, on the other hand, leads to the postulation of 'diversities' which are in fact illusory."[19]

Just what McConville had in mind here is not clear. There is, of course, an organic connection in the theology of the whole canon, but how that would lead us to "modify slightly" what one believed the text said originally is beyond me. What in latter revelation would cause this distortion or "modification" of the earlier meaning of the words in the Old Testament? Nevertheless, I am still in partial agreement with McConville's overall approach. He went on to observe:

The approach to the Old Testament which stresses diversity (wherever, that is, it retains an interest in hearing and using Scripture confessionally) can end in a flattening and a uniformity ... [which] reduce[s biblical data] to the lowest common denominator.... In contrast, where the unity of the Old Testament is regarded as the primary hermeneutical datum, the real diversity of the material can emerge, to the richer benefit of the believing community. This is important, for the unity I am advocating is not a ground for pan-harmonization.... The unity I am concerned for is one which is in contrast to the idea of competing theologies or ideologies.[20]

---

17. J. G. McConville, "Using Scripture for Theology: Unity and Diversity in Old Testament Theology: The Old Testament as a Hermeneutical Problem," *Scottish Bulletin of Evangelical Theology* 5 (1987): 50.
18. Ibid., 51.
19. Ibid., 52.
20. Ibid., 53.

McConville summarized his approach to solving the issue of unity and diversity in the Old Testament by beginning his exegesis with a concept of unity rather than beginning with a postulate of diversity. To this principle, he would add three more elements:

A recognition of the forward movement, or historical character of the Old Testament revelation. However, he warned that biblical theologies that were rigidly systematic were at a great disadvantage, for the Old Testament covers too long a period of time not to be described chronologically.

A theological-unifying element. Eichrodt had such an element, but von Rad did not. For it to be theology, it must make statements about God, and in that sense it is a systematic theology. It is impossible to appropriate the Old Testament for Christian use without recognizing in some way its preparatory character and the way it fits in the life of the New Testament and the church.

An existential element. There is an aspect of the Old Testament that offers the experience of "nowness" yet is repeatable in numerous forms. This is what transposes this book into a higher key, for in Christ, Christians also have the same experience of salvation.[21]

Surely these elements are helpful in what they affirm. I personally would emphasize more the organic nature and connectivity of all the details of the older Scripture with the new, and not just the historicality and the existential and theologically proper aspects of the text. McConville finds the theme of "paradox" useful,[22] but I do not think we know enough to determine whether that is the best approach to the Old Testament and whether Scripture is indeed a paradox. He, too, is reluctant to speak of a "center" or a unifying concept to the Bible, such as I argue for in the "Promise-Plan of God" (chapter 11).

Overall I am satisfied that a number of strategies have been mapped out that direct us to legitimate ways that the Old Testament text can be seen as possessing a unifying plan from start to finish. This is a major gain after an absence for such strategies for the past half century.

21. Ibid., 54–57.
22. Ibid., 53.

The Unity *of the* New Testament

There is unity in the diverse theologies of the New Testament because each writing witnesses to God's self-revelation in Jesus Christ.

—Frank J. Matera[1]

In a recent essay, Andreas J. Köstenberger began his analysis on the subject this chapter aims to treat by saying: "The traditional emphasis on the unity of the NT (at least in conservative circles) has in recent years been all but supplanted by the critical consensus that the NT consists of a variety of theologies that, if not irreconcilable, at least stand in considerable tension with one another."[2]

Even though Walter Bauer, Rudolf Bultmann, Ernst Käsemann, and to some degree James Dunn, have had a major part in fostering such a claim, which emphasizes the New Testament's diversity at the expense of its unity, Köstenberger rightly points to such relatively conservative scholars as Peter Stuhlmacher, who likewise maintains that "the Bible contains diverse voices that do not merely complement but also contradict each other."[3] No longer

---

1. Frank J. Matera, *New Testament Theology: Exploring Diversity and Unity* (Louisville: Westminster, 2007), 423.
2. Andreas J. Köstenberger, "Diversity and Unity in the New Testament," in *Biblical Theology: Retrospect and Prospect*, ed. Scott J. Hafemann (Downers Grove, Ill.: InterVarsity, 2002), 144.
3. Ibid., 144, quoting Peter Stuhlmacher, "Der Kanon und seine Auslegung," in *Jesus Christus al die Mitte der Schrift. Studien zur Hermeneutik des Evangeliums*, ed. Christof Landmesser et al. (Berlin: De Gruyter, 1997), 287.

is the division on this subject of unity or diversity in the New Testament along liberal and conservative lines; the verdict that diversity reigns in the New Testament is almost universal among all biblical scholars, liberal and conservative alike!

But can such a claim be justified in light of our study of Scripture? The older conviction was that the Scriptures exhibited such a unity and cohesiveness that Christians over the centuries tended to appeal almost indiscriminately to different parts of the Bible in support of a certain doctrinal or ethical teaching. It would not have been unusual for scholars and Bible teachers in another day to make a sweep of the canon to further establish a doctrine or to illustrate the same point made in one or more texts to the same doctrine or to a similar representation found elsewhere in the Bible. But how could this have been anywhere near possible if there was such widespread evidence of diversity and discontinuity that such multitext appeals in different books of the Bible would almost inevitably lead to contrary, if not contradictory, points of view within the same Bible, according to the argument from a reigning diversity claim?

In order to pursue this question, we must ask where these points of tension and possible evidences of strong diversity arise to such a level as to present discord for a claim to finding a unifying wholeness in the New Testament. These nodule points of alleged tension will be the subject of this chapter. They may be listed as: (1) the relationship between Jesus and Paul, (2) the alleged tension between the Synoptic Gospels and the gospel of John, (3) the alleged differences between the Paul presented in the book of Acts and the Paul of the Epistles, and (4) the alleged differences between the apostle Paul and the book of James and other New Testament writers.[4] Only when these perceived tensions and roadblocks are adequately dealt with will it be possible for us to explore the possibility of an integrative theme that could bring cohesiveness to what otherwise would be a most assorted group of writings and ideas.

The Relationship between Jesus and Paul

Who is the founder of Christianity: Jesus or Paul? Much of contemporary scholarship wants to characterize Paul as the founder of the Christian faith. David Wenham argued that Paul deliberately built on the foundation that

---

4. Köstenberger's list in "Diversity and Unity in the New Testament," 145, is the main basis for organizing my approach to this subject.

had been laid by Jesus of Nazareth, even though Paul was not one of Jesus' disciples.[5] On the other hand, a good number of New Testament scholars depict the apostle Paul as having little knowledge of Jesus of Nazareth, with little interest in him, and proclaiming a theology that was radically different from what we find in the gospel presentations of Jesus.[6]

There are four or five terms, or themes, found in Paul's teaching that appear to be strikingly different from those of Jesus. First, some say Jesus' stress on the kingdom of God is lost in Paul in favor of an emphasis on justification. A second piece of evidence is that there are few references to Jesus' life and ministry in Paul. Paul preferred, it would appear, to appeal more openly and frequently to the Old Testament as his source of authority. A third argument for discontinuity between Jesus and Paul is that Paul failed to bolster his argument at several points by appealing to Jesus when he could have done so to his advantage. For example, when Paul gave his teaching of Christian giving in 2 Corinthians 8–9, he could have appealed with great advantage to Jesus' teaching about laying up treasures in heaven, but Paul did not do so. Paul also could have appealed to some of Jesus' parables on wealth, but he never did so. Paul could have cut to the chase in his arguments about clean and unclean foods by appealing to Mark 7:19 where "Jesus declared all foods 'clean,'"[7] but he did not do so. Another point of distinction was that while Jesus rarely mentioned the church (Matt. 16:18; 18:17), Paul developed the doctrine of the church in great detail in his epistles. Finally, some claim that Jesus concentrated his mission on Israel (Matt. 10:5–6; 15:24), whereas Paul wanted to announce the gospel to the ends of the earth (Acts 9:15; Rom. 16:26).

Nevertheless, the case for diversity and disunity between Jesus and Paul is rather weak. Of course Paul did use different terminology than Jesus, but that does not mean there is a total, or even a major, discontinuity between the two. For example, Paul occasionally did refer to the "kingdom of God" (1 Cor. 6:9, 10; Gal. 5:21) in ways that showed he was conversant with Jesus'

---

5. David Wenham, *Paul: Founder of Christianity or Follower of Jesus?* (Grand Rapids: Eerdmans, 1996); David Wenham, "Appendix: Unity and Diversity in the New Testament," in G. E. Ladd, *A Theology of the New Testament* (Grand Rapids: Eerdmans, 1993), 684–719, esp. 704–9.
6. Wenham, *Paul*, ch. 1, n. 56, cites V. P. Furnish, "The Jesus-Paul Debate: From Baur to Bultmann," *Bulletin of the John Rylands Library* 47 (1964–65): 342–81; A. J. M. Wedderburn, ed., *Paul and Jesus* (Sheffield: T. & T. Clark, 1989), 17–50; S. G. Wilson, "From Jesus to Paul: The Contours and Consequences of a Debate," in P. Richardson and J. C. Hurd, *From Jesus to Paul: Studies in Honour of Francis Wright Beare* (Waterloo, Iowa: Wilfred Laurier University Press, 1984), 1–21.
7. Hope Egan, *Holy Cow! Does God Care about What We Eat?* (Littleton, Colo.: First Fruits of Zion, 2005), 99–104, has called my attention to the fact that the Greek manuscripts of Mark 7:19 do not have the words: "Thus he [Jesus] declared," followed by the translation "all foods clean." But a better rendering of "all foods clean" can be seen in Jesus' point that the bread passed through the digestive system and left the body, and thereby we have the translation, "purging all foods."

usage.[8] Since Jesus stressed taking up the cross and following him, and the fact that his death was a "baptism" he had to undergo (Mark 8:34; 10:38, 39), Paul may have found the grounds for his emphasis in being baptized into Jesus' death and resurrection in this same Jesus tradition. Even the thought in Jesus' kingdom teaching is close to Paul's use of "righteousness" and "justification," for in Paul these terms are not narrowly conceived as pertaining only to individual salvation. Paul had in mind corporate and cosmic terms as he announced God's righteousness being revealed in Romans 1:16–17, possibly reflecting Isaiah 61:11, where "the LORD God will make righteousness and praise spring up before the nations."[9]

Certainly there are real differences in emphases between Jesus and Paul, but the reason is not that the message has changed, rather that Paul was facing different times and a different context. Moreover, Paul did include some explicit references to Jesus' teaching in his epistles. For example, in 1 Corinthians 7:10 Paul referred to Jesus' teaching on divorce. Again, in 1 Corinthians 9:14 Paul made reference to Jesus when he said that "those who preach the gospel should receive their living from the gospel," as found in Matthew 10:10 and in Jesus' parable in Luke 10:7. Even Paul's reference to a "thief" in 1 Thessalonians 5:4 may be an allusion to Jesus' teaching (Matt. 24:23). Add to this last reference the Pauline teaching on the second coming of Christ in 1 and 2 Thessalonians and Jesus' eschatological parables on the wise and foolish virgins, the watchman, and the steward, along with the thief just mentioned—all are possible themes that Paul easily could have drawn upon. Still, proving that he did *directly* draw on these themes from Jesus is not something easily accomplished. On one occasion, however, Paul did directly appeal to our Lord's teaching: "According to the Lord's own word, we tell you that we who are still alive, who are left till the coming of our Lord, will certainly not precede those who have fallen asleep" (1 Thess. 4:15). This, of course, is not a direct quote or even an allusion to the Gospels, but it seems to have come from a prophecy from the Lord preserved in the tradition, as Paul himself claimed.

Finally, in the 1 Corinthians 11:23–26 account of the Last Supper, Paul began with these words: "For I received from the Lord what I also passed on to you: The Lord Jesus, on the night he was betrayed, took bread, and when he had given thanks, he broke it and said, 'This is my body, which is for you; do this in remembrance of me.' " Paul was aware that he was

---

8. G. Johnston, "Kingdom of God Sayings in Paul's Letters," in Richardson and Hurd, *From Jesus to Paul*, 143–56.
9. A point made by Wenham, "Appendix: Unity and Diversity," 705–6.

"passing on," a tradition he had received from Jesus, one his disciples had followed as well.

Thus it is hard to make the case for a serious conflict between Jesus and Paul. Some may have wanted Paul to appeal to Jesus' prepassion ministry more frequently, but Paul did not witness that, and he had not been commissioned by the Holy Spirit to go over that same ground again. His call, apparently, was to take the messianic story preserved in the postpassion ministry of Christ, of his death, burial, and resurrection, to the ends of the earth. At times Paul recognized that his persuasion on a point came directly from the Lord Jesus, as in Romans 14:14, "I know and I am persuaded by the Lord Jesus, that nothing is common in itself" (translation mine). But at other times Paul knew he was adding to the progress of revelation under the urging of the Holy Spirit.

It is true that the apostle Paul strenuously argued that he was not at all dependent on any human sources for his message or authority in Galatians 1–2. What he had and what he taught had come to him by direct divine revelation (Gal. 1:12). So we conclude that Paul saw himself as a servant of Jesus Christ rather than as the one who was responsible for founding a new offshoot of the Jesus movement or as the one who was the founder of Christianity.

The Alleged Distinctions between the Synoptics and the Gospel of John

Andreas J. Köstenberger[10] noted that the criticisms of Bretschneider (1820) and D. F. Strauss (1835) impacted the case for the reliability of John's gospel and seriously compromised its message for decades. While recent studies have done much to reverse this negative judgment raised against John,[11] there remain a number of lingering issues that affect the discussion of the unity of the theology of the Synoptics and John. Some of these are as follows: (1) The Synoptics prefer to use shorter aphorisms, while John uses more extended discourses. (2) John's use of Jesus' miracles deemphasized

---

10. Andreas J. Köstenberger, "Early Doubts of the Apostolic Authorship of the Fourth Gospel in the History of Modern Biblical Criticism," in *Studies on John and Gender: A Decade of Scholarship* (New York: Peter Lang, 2001), 17–47.

11. See, e.g., Craig L. Blomberg, *The Historical Reliability of John's Gospel: Issues and Commentary* (Downers Grove, Ill.: InterVarsity Press, 2002); Martin Hengel, "Das Johannesevangelium als Quelle fur die Geschichte des antiken Judentums," in *Judaica, Hellenistica et Christiana: Kleine Schriften II*, Wissenschaftliche Untersuchungen zum Neuen Testament 109 (Tubingen: Mohr Siebeck, 1999), 295, 322.

their miraculous aspects and focused more on their function in pointing to Jesus as the Messiah. (3) The Synoptics put more emphasis on Jesus' exorcisms, while John saw Satan himself as the real agent to be dealt with. (4) Finally, the major block between the three Synoptics and John's gospel allegedly was their timing of the crucifixion.

Both John and the Synoptics present Jesus as eating the Passover meal on Thursday night followed by the crucifixion on Friday afternoon. Some have misunderstood John's reference to "the day of Preparation of Passover Week" (John 19:14) as the event that occurred on Wednesday night with the crucifixion taking place on Thursday afternoon. But the solution to this misunderstanding is that in John 19:31 Jesus' crucifixion took place on "the day of Preparation" followed by the very next day being "a special Sabbath" (i.e., the seventh day of Passover week, the traditional Sabbath of the Old Testament). Accordingly, John also placed the crucifixion on Friday as did the Synoptics. "The Day of Preparation" in John, similar to its use in Mark and Luke, did not refer to the preparation for the Passover, but to the preparation for the Sabbath (Mark 15:42; Luke 23:54). Köstenberger also pointed to Josephus's *Antiquities of the Jews* (16.163–64), while noting that the Passover lasted a full week along with the Feast of Unleavened Bread (Luke 22:1), thus "it was appropriate to speak of the day of preparation for the Sabbath as the day of Preparation of Passover Week" (though not of the Passover in a narrower sense; John 19:14).[12]

As for the other issues mentioned already, they represent but varying perspectives rather than straightforward discrepancies. John seems, instead, to present a familiarity with the Synoptic material and to complement rather than contradict them.

Is the Paul of the Book of Acts or the Paul of the Epistles the Real Paul?

James Dunn,[13] along with others, has argued that New Testament Christianity was made up of a number of separate streams, parties, or trajectories. Usually four such groups have been identified: (1) a strong Jewish Christianity grouped around Jerusalem, (2) a Hellenistic Christianity tending at times to Gnosticism, (3) an apocalyptic Christianity with its emphasis on an imminent end of history, and (4) a catholic Christianity.

---

12. Köstenberger, "Diversity and Unity in the New Testament," 147–48.
13. J. D. G. Dunn, *Unity and Diversity in the New Testament*, 2nd ed. (London: SCM Press, 1990).

The greatest stress seems to have been between the Jewish audience and the Hellenists.

The division between these two groups involved a practical as well as a theological problem. It is thought that Luke's record of Stephen's speech in Acts 7 tipped scholars off to the fact that Stephen was not very enthusiastic about the temple, which he demeaned by calling it "made by men" (Acts 7:48; Gk., *cheiropoietos*), a word, they say, was reserved for pagan idols elsewhere. This attitude belied an allegiance to the Hellenistic type of Christianity.

Thus, when the question of adherence to the Mosaic law came up, Paul appeared to emerge as the leader of the Hellenist party. Surely the book of Galatians attests to the sharp division that this topic raised, especially for the Jewish Christians, such as James, who was the leader of the church in Jerusalem. There were tensions, of course, but did these necessarily lead to a diversity or contradiction in the substance or teaching of the New Testament? If Matthew and James are thought to represent the conservative Jewish Christian point of view, both Paul and James appeal to the example of Abraham to show that he was justified by his faith, not by the works of the law. But contrary to this scenario, the book of Acts pictures no such radical divide between Jewish and Hellenistic Christianity. Paul, the supposed leading figure of the liberal Hellenistic party, and James, the supposed leader of the Jerusalem congregation, work together on the controversial issues presented in Acts 15 and 21.

Some historians are not satisfied, however. They see Acts as a Lukan cover-up, supposing that the doctor wished to emphasize the unity of the contending sides and therefore played down the divisions. They claim Luke wrote at the expense of historical accuracy, depicting Paul as being more open to the Jews and the Judaizers than what he was in reality (Acts 16:3; 21:20–26). This is supposed to be proven by the fact that Luke failed to note the offering Paul brought to Jerusalem, one that Paul thought important enough to mention often (Rom. 15; 1 Cor. 16, 2 Cor. 8–9). But how accurate is the case for a Lukan cover-up?

Every historical portrayal is partial, for it is not a complete transcript of all that took place during the period of time covered. Surely there were differences of emphases and practice, but the whole thesis that there was a radical split between Paul and Jerusalem seems to be exaggerated according to David Wenham's best estimate.[14] Even if Luke's depiction of Paul in the book of Acts pictures a more conciliatory Paul than the Paul of the Letters, this does not seem to be far from Paul's own estimate of himself.

14. Wenham, "Appendix: Unity and Diversity," 691.

Paul claimed that people found him strong and bold in his letters but rather timid and unimpressive in his person and preaching (2 Cor. 10:1, 16). Paul was especially jealous for the gospel's sake, and in the defense of the gospel he came alive with strong statements.

But there is a conciliatory side to Paul as well—he could become as a Jew for Jews, or to those outside the Law he could fit in with them just as well (1 Cor. 9:20–21). And if Luke smoothed things out for Paul in the book of Acts, why did he not follow that same course of action when he described how things went as Paul arrived in Jerusalem in Acts 21 and faced stiff opposition and suspicion from the Jews? No, there was no Lukan cover-up; the Paul of Acts is still the same Paul of the Epistles.

The Alleged Differences between Paul and James and Other New Testament Writers

---

Some claim there were other points of tension between Paul and Peter, Paul and John, and Paul and James. The most famous, of course, is that Paul stressed salvation as the free gift of God received by faith without any works necessary to earn it (Rom. 3:21–28; Phil. 3:9) while James described faith without works as being dead. In fact, James declared that a person is justified by his works and not by his faith alone (James 2:17, 24, 26). But he used the word "justified" to describe two different things. James spoke of validating (or "justifying") the claim that one had real faith in the Lord; Paul spoke of "justification" as a forensic act made by God, in which he declared a person righteous on account of their believing faith alone. James wanted people to demonstrate the reality of their faith by their works (James 2:18). And Paul commended the Thessalonians for their works, which were put into action by their faith (1 Thess. 1:3), and said that each individual act or work was "prompted by [their] faith" (2 Thess. 1:11).[15]

This discussion of points of tension could be extended to show that alleged differences between other writers of Scripture and Paul all turn out to be of the same sort of misunderstanding that we have just answered in James's and Paul's differing use of the word *justify*.

It is true, for example, that Paul had to publicly oppose and rebuke Peter (Gal. 2:11) for his double standard of eating with the Gentiles when the Jews were not around and then drawing back from doing so when those who

---

15. I was reminded of this argument by Andreas J. Köstenberger, "Diversity and Unity," 152–53.

belonged to the circumcision group came to Antioch. But this so-called tension was not a doctrinal matter; it was one of consistency of practice.

The Unity of the New Testament

It is one thing to show that one alleged contradiction after another in the New Testament books is without factual basis. But it is quite another to suggest what the integrating theme, or divine plan and purpose, is for the twenty-seven books we call the New Testament. A full and careful hearing of all the various theological contributions of all the writers must be taken into account so that the full weight of both the diversity and the unity of the testament are brought to bear on this suggested case for unity.

For some, "the pursuit of a [single] center is chimerical."[16] These scholars only hope to get a cluster of some broad themes; therefore they have abandoned the search for any unifying theme or single center that would demonstrate a single organizing concept behind the whole project.

In place of the "promise-plan of God" that I am suggesting as the unifying theme of the whole Bible, others have proposed the search for "integrating motifs," such as C. H. Dodd suggested as early as 1936.[17] Dodd set up two criteria: (1) the integrative motif must be found in all the major books of the New Testament, and (2) any proposed theme must be a foundational belief that is shared by Jesus and the early church.[18]

Köstenberger thought three New Testament motifs would fit these two criteria. First, there was the motif of the "one God," as confirmed by the thirteen hundred New Testament references to *theos*. Surely that number of references ought to signal that he was of central significance.

Second, the abundant references to "Jesus the Christ, the exalted Lord" would seem to make the case for a second integrative motif. He was the one foretold in the Old Testament and the one who was at the heart of the good news the first Christians, along with the apostle Paul, preached.

The third integrating motif was "the gospel," the good news that had already been announced in the Old Testament. It was this good news that

16. D. A. Carson, "NT Theology," in *Dictionary of the Later New Testament and Its Developments*, ed. R. P. Martin and P. H. Davids (Downers Grove, Ill.: InterVarsity, 1998), 810; and C. H. H. Scobie, "Structure of Biblical Theology," *Tyndale Bulletin* 42 (1991): 178–79.

17. C. H. Dodd, "The Present Task in New Testament Studies, an Inaugural Lecture Delivered in the Divinity School, Cambridge, on Tuesday, 2 June 1936." Later that year he published *The Apostolic Preaching and Its Developments* (London: Hodder & Stoughton, 1936).

18. I am beholden for this discussion and what follows to Andreas J. Köstenberger, "Diversity and Unity," 154–58.

called persons to repentance and to faith in Christ. This gospel, Kösten-berger thought, was best summarized in Acts 10:36, "You know the mes-sage of God sent to the people of Israel, telling the good news of peace through Jesus Christ, who is Lord of all."

These three themes certainly do meet most of Dodd's two criteria, and they surely are most significant as far as some of the main content that must go into the cohesiveness of the testament. But in the main, they merely tell what the subjects are in the unifying plan. What is missing is the predicate. This repeats the mistake of Gerhard Hasel, who said that "Yahweh" was the center of the Old Testament, raising the questions, "Yahweh did what?" "Yahweh said what?" He too needed a predicate and an object. Only when those had been identified could a center or a unifying theme have been reached.

Conclusion

For all too many, the quest for some type of center in a comprehensive bibli-cal theology of the New Testament has been abandoned, and preference has been given to variations on some form of a multiperspectival approach. But I for one believe it is too soon to forfeit the case and abandon the cause.

The thing that still impresses me is this: If God the Father, Son, and Holy Spirit authored these books of the Bible, would you not think that his purpose and plan would be coordinated in such a way that it would be recognized as his master plan and strategy for planet Earth and its inhabitants? And if he cared enough to communicate with us about himself and what he had done for us (and he has), then would it not seem reasonable that out of that disclo-sure would arise the structure of his key objective(s) that made up the parts of his plan? That is what I have contended for in my *Promise-Plan of God.*[19]

Where most evangelicals agree, as Köstenberger put it so nicely, is that the whole of the New Testament is not "a disparate collection of ill-fitting parts, which together result in nothing more than a cacophony of voices, but a well-composed symphony, in which elements form a harmonious work that echoes into all the world to the glory of God and for the edification of those individuals who respond to the divine revelation in faith."[20]

19. Walter C. Kaiser Jr., *The Promise-Plan of God: A Biblical Theology of the Old and New Testaments* (Grand Rapids: Zondervan, 2008).
20. Köstenberger, "Diversity and Unity," 158.

The Unity *of the* Bible *in Its* Messianic Promises

I can no more understand Jesus apart from his Jewishness than I can understand Gandhi apart from his Indianness.

—Philip Yancey[1]

If the Old Testament's use of the language of prophecy, foretelling about the person, events, and claims of the coming Messiah, could only be recognized in hindsight — after the New Testament's (re)interpretation or enlargement of the words of the older testament into a deeper sense than they were originally intended, as all too many contend today — would there be any reason to think that the message of the two testaments was a unified message of a sure promise of a coming Messiah — much less any kind of foretelling of a personal Messiah and his works? Or put another way, did the Old Testament have an adequate picture of the person and work of the Messiah available so that the New Testament writers could appeal to it as a preexisting feature of the text? And if the answer is yes, but they had only a vague picture that would not have led anyone to anticipate the Messiah's arrival, then what happens to the frequent appeal of the New Testament writers by way of citations and allusions to the Old Testament? Why appeal to Old Testament texts that were already vacant and with little or

1. Philip Yancey, *The Jesus I Never Knew* (Grand Rapids: Zondervan, 1995), 51.

no apologetic value if it was only the New Testament that could offer the messianic meaning of most passages? Why, according to some, would the New Testament writers wish suddenly and belatedly to infuse those older texts with new higher values when such efforts would have been useless to say the least?

As Stanley Glen stated the problem, summarizing the negative point of view, "The first impression of the use [the New Testament writers] made of the Old Testament is one which suggests a *random selection* of quotations and allusions, and at times an *extreme form* of exegesis, including some of the *extravagant examples of rabbinical argument*, the total effect of which leaves us in doubt as to any kind of procedure in going from the one testament to the other."[2]

Glen went on to argue that the New Testament kerygma itself was the way in which the testaments were connected. But this example shows how serious the issue is for the search for any kind of coherence or connections between the Old and the New Testaments, or for any real anticipation of a personal Messiah in the older testament, according to this manner of viewing the text.

It is a legitimate observation, of course, that some overly zealous believers in Messiah have unadvisedly applied a number of Old Testament passages to Christ, which on closer examination prove to be incorrect and without any factual basis or merit in the Old Testament setting. On the other hand, many contemporary scholars have gone in the other direction by reducing the number of passages that did, as a matter of fact, anticipate the coming of the Messiah.

Indeed, the nineteenth century was especially strong in the number of works on messianic prophecy in the Old Testament. Among this long list one might mention the studies of E. W. Hengstenberg,[3] Franz Delitzsch,[4] Edward Riehm,[5] and R. Payne Smith.[6] Three other Hebrew Christian writers should be mentioned as belonging to that same century, all three of which came to faith in Christ as a result of a study of messianic prophecy: David Baron,[7] Alfred Edersheim,[8] and Adolph Saphir.[9]

2. J. Stanley Glen, "Jesus Christ and the Unity of the Bible," *Interpretation* 5, no. 3 (1950): 263 (emphasis added).
3. E. W. Hengstenberg, *Christology of the Old Testament* (repr., Grand Rapids: Kregel, 1970).
4. Franz Delitzsch, *Messianic Prophecies in Historical Succession* (New York: Scribner, 1891).
5. Edward Riehm, *Messianic Prophecy: Its Origin, Historical Growth, and Relation to the New Testament* (Edinburgh: T. & T. Clark, 1900).
6. R. Payne Smith, *The Scripture Testimony to the Messiah*, 6th ed. 2 vols. (Edinburgh: William Oliphant, 1871).
7. David Baron, *Rays of Messiah's Glory: Christ in the Old Testament* (1886; repr., Grand Rapids: Zondervan, n.d.).
8. Alfred Edersheim, *The Life and Times of Jesus the Messiah*, 2 vols. (London: Longmans, 1915).
9. Adolph Saphir, *The Divine Unity of Scripture* (London: Hodder and Stoughton, 1893).

The late twentieth and early twenty-first centuries have not seen a large number of works of great importance on the doctrine of the Messiah, with the possible exceptions of: Sigmund Mowinckel,[10] Joachim Becker,[11] Donald Juel,[12] Jacob Neusner,[13] and James H. Charlesworth.[14] Several evangelical works, in the meantime, have appeared, including Gerald van Groningen,[15] James E. Smith,[16] Christopher J. H. Wright,[17] and Walter C. Kaiser Jr.[18] Therefore, before this discussion begins, it is best to try to define our terms.

Definition of Messiah and the Messianic Times

Most will be surprised to discover that the term *Messiah*, used to designate Jesus, appears only twice in the New Testament: Andrew used the term in John 1:41, and the Samaritan woman used it in John 4:25 as she referred to Jesus as the *Messias*, a Grecianized form of the Hebrew *mashiach*. The verbal form of *mashach*, which is associated with Messiah, meant "to anoint," whether it was the anointing of the tabernacle, the altar, the laver, or individuals, such as priests and kings. Even though *mashiach* occurs thirty-nine times in the Old Testament, only nine of those instances have a possible reference to the coming Messiah (1 Sam. 2:10, 35; Pss. 2:2; 89:51; 132:10, 17; Dan. 9:25, 26; Hab. 3:13).

The term *messianic*, however, had a much wider range of meanings than merely those referring to a personal Messiah. Instead, it generally referred to the end-times of the coming new age when this Messiah, who was prophet, priest, and king, would introduce a time of peace and deliverance for all believing mortals and for the created order itself.

J. Barton Payne identified 1,239 prophetic predictions in the Old Testament that involved some 6,641 verses, or 28.5 percent of the total corpus of the older testament. In the New Testament he found some 578 predictions

10. Sigmund Mowinckel, *He That Cometh*. Trans. G. W. Anderson (New York: Abingdon, 1854).
11. Joachim Becker, *Messianic Expectations in the Old Testament*, trans. David Green (Philadelphia: Fortress, 1980).
12. Donald Juel, *Messianic Exegesis: Christological Interpretation of the Old Testament in Early Christianity* (Philadelphia: Fortress, 1988).
13. Jacob Neusner, *Messiah in Context: Israel's History and Destiny in Formative Judaism* (Philadelphia: Fortress, 1984).
14. James H. Charlesworth, *The Messiah: Developments in Earliest Judaism and Christianity* (Minneapolis: Fortress, 1992).
15. Gerald van Groningen, *Messianic Revelation in the Old Testament* (Grand Rapids: Baker, 1990).
16. James E. Smith, *What the Bible Teaches about the Promised Messiah* (Nashville: Thomas Nelson, 1993).
17. Christopher J. H. Wright, *Knowing Jesus through the Old Testament* (Downers Grove, Ill.: InterVarsity, 1992).
18. Walter C. Kaiser Jr., *The Messiah in the Old Testament* (Grand Rapids: Zondervan, 1995).

in 1,711 verses, or some 21.5 percent of that text.[19] Payne also found 127 personal messianic predictions in some 3,348 verses in the Old Testament, whereas Edersheim reported that the Jewish literature accumulated some 456 passages that were in general messianic in the Tanak (= the Old Testament) — 75 in the Pentateuch, 243 in the Prophets, and 138 in the Writings.[20] This later count, of course, was based on an expansive midrashic and rabbinical method of exegeting the text. Nevertheless, the Messiah and his times were more than passing phenomena. They were a central and most germane concept.

The Origin of the Messianic Hope

The search for the time and circumstances in which the concept of a Messiah and his times arose has created another large amount of scholarly effort. Perhaps, then, it would be best to follow the strategy suggested by Alfred Edersheim[21] and James Smith,[22] as they used a process of elimination to determine if we could locate the origin of this messianic hope.

First of all, we can be sure that this hope did not begin with the New Testament, for those writers repeatedly appealed to an existing state of expectation in the Old Testament. In like manner, we can say that this hope could not have arisen in the intertestamental era as, for example, Joachim Becker alleged. Becker's reason for locating this hope so late in time was based on his conclusion that "there is no evidence of true messianism until the second century B.C.... It is on the threshold of the New Testament that we encounter real messianism."[23] It must be noted, however, that the data from the intertestamental period for this hope is sparse indeed. Franz Delitzsch commented, "The development of the Messianic idea after the conclusion of the canon [of the Old Testament] remains ... far behind that which precedes in the time of Old Testament prophecy. It affords no progress, but rather regress."[24]

A third suggestion also has problems connected with it. Thus, to claim that the origins of the messianic hope began in the postexilic period runs the

---

19. J. Barton Payne, *Encyclopedia of Biblical Prophecy* (New York: Harper & Row, 1973), 675–76.
20. Edersheim, *Life and Times*, vol. 2, app. 9. These numbers include use of midrashic exegesis rather than a limitation of the methods of interpretation to grammatico-historical exegesis.
21. Alfred Edersheim, *Prophecy and History in Relation to the Messiah* (Grand Rapids: Baker, 1955), 5ff.
22. Smith, *What the Bible Teaches*, 14–19.
23. Becker, *Messianic Expectations*, 50, 87.
24. Delitzsch. *Messianic Prophecies*, 119.

risk of explaining why—at the time that the house of David lay in shambles at the hands of the resounding defeat of Jerusalem, and the Davidic line at the hands of the Babylonians—the postexilic community would find any hope in a message that offered a future ruler who would come from the house of David. The exilic prophets of Daniel and Ezekiel (sixth century BC), along with the postexilic prophet Zechariah (sixth century BC), upheld the prospect of a revived house of David, but to think that such an idea arose from the exiles themselves (fifth century BC), in the awkwardness of their situation in Babylon, is straining the limits of credulity. A revived Judean state or a house of David would need to be "played down," for it did not evidence the political realities of that day if the captives were to be the source for this messianic hope. The fortunes of David's line seemed to be at an all-time low.

Just as unrealistic were those solutions that suggested that this hope for a Messiah originated in circles outside of Israel. Unfortunately for this theory, the concept of a personal Messiah has no counterpart in the ancient Near Eastern milieu, according to E. Jenni,[25] for such a concept as the Messiah is not found among any ancient Near Eastern religions of that era. Likewise, all attempts to explain this concept from naturalistic explanations or from logical reasoning seemed to have ended in failure as well.

Finally, not even the claim that this hope arose out of Israel's faith gets at the truth of the matter; Israel's messianic hope originated in the revelation of God to his prophets of old. Right from the very start of the revelatory process, our Lord began to lay the foundations for this hope, promising one who would come from the "seed/descendant" of the woman Eve and would crush Satan's head (Gen. 3:15). Also, Yahweh himself would come and personally "dwell" in the tents of Shem (Gen. 9:27),[26] and through the Shemitic (later shortened through the Greek to "Semitic") peoples, he would name one from the "seed" of Abraham to be the avenue through whom all the world would be blessed (Gen. 12:3). Indeed, this would be the very essence of the "gospel" itself (Gal. 3:8). Moreover, the scepter (symbol of rule and authority) would be given to the tribe of Judah (Gen. 49:10), through whom would come security and abundance for all (Gen. 49:11–12). Judah was the fourth son in Jacob's line; Reuben, Simeon and Levi (sons one, two, and three) had all been bypassed in favor of Judah.

---

25. E. Jenni, "Messiah, Jewish," in *The Interpreter's Dictionary of the Bible*, vol. K–Q, ed. George Buttrick (New York: Abingdon, 1960), 362.
26. For a better subject of the verb "dwell" than "Japheth," see Walter C. Kaiser Jr., *The Promise-Plan of God: A Biblical Theology of the Old and New Testaments* (Grand Rapids: Zondervan, 2008), 44–46.

The Interpretation of Messianic Prophecy

There is no royal road to interpreting prophecy, as the strong divisions on how to interpret the messianic texts give evidence aplenty. All too many interpreters make a division between the meaning the prophets attached to their own utterances and the meaning God apparently had intended all along for these same words to include. To say, as is customary for many conservative interpreters when affirming this point, that "Scripture affirms that the writers themselves did not always *fully comprehend* their own utterances"[27] is to overload the principle. The words "fully" and "comprehend" make it a surefire principle to which all must agree, because only God has "comprehensive" knowledge and no mortal has "full" knowledge. Therefore, the principle wins general approval on a technicality. But aside from that important caveat, we must still ask, does Scripture somehow indicate that the writers were often in the dark about their meanings, especially ones about the future of the coming Messiah?

However, Acts 2:30–31 assures us that when David received the prophecy of Psalm 16:10 that "[God would] not abandon [him] to the grave, nor [would he] let [his] *Holy One* see decay" (emphasis added), because David was a "prophet," and furthermore, because he was "*seeing* what was ahead" (Acts 2:31, emphasis added), he "knew that God had promised him on oath that he would place one of his descendants on his throne" (Acts 2:30). That is why David "spoke of the resurrection of Christ, that he was not abandoned to the grave, nor did his [the Messiah's/Christ's] body see decay" (Acts 2:31). Now, unless we wish to make a special case for David the prophet apart from the other Old Testament prophets, it would be unfair to say that the prophet David "wrote better than he knew." How could David be without some understanding of Christ's resurrection when he wrote Psalm 16?[28] The text says that "[David] was a prophet" (Acts 2:30) and therefore he spoke as one who was "seeing what was ahead, he spoke of the resurrection of the Christ" (2:31). He wrote what had been revealed to him, and it concerned the resurrection of the Holy One (Heb.,

27. E.g., Smith, *What the Bible Teaches*, 21 (emphasis mine).
28. For a fuller discussion, see Walter C. Kaiser Jr., "The Promise to David in Psalm 16 and Its Application in Acts 2:25–33 and 13:32–37," *Journal of the Evangelical Theological Society* 23 (1980): 219–29; and its development in my article "Accurate and Authoritative Citations of the Old Testament by the New Testament," in *Counterpoints: Three Views on the New Testament Use of the Old Testament*, ed. Kenneth Berding and Jonathan Lunde (Grand Rapids: Zondervan, 2008). Also see Walter C. Kaiser Jr. and Moisés Silva, *An Introduction to Biblical Hermeneutics: The Search for Meaning*, 2nd ed. (Grand Rapids: Zondervan 2007), 95–106, 191–209.

hasid). The climax of the Davidic line would be in the glorified Messiah! By now the word *hasid*, "Holy One," was functioning as a technical term for the Messiah.

Nevertheless, some claim that 1 Peter 1:10–11 taught that the prophets were, in general, at a loss to understand their own prophecies. It must be admitted that, as the text teaches, the Old Testament prophets "searched intently and with the greatest care, trying to find out the time and circumstances [Gk., *eis tina e poion kairon*] to which the Spirit of Christ in them was pointing" when they received utterances. But it was only the time or the particular set of circumstances that was withheld from them, for the text of Peter goes on to claim five things the prophets realized about the revelations given to them. They knew (1) they were speaking about the Messiah, (2) the Messiah would have to suffer, (3) the Messiah would also experience "glory," (4) suffering would come first and glory would follow, and (5) their words had relevancy not only for themselves, but for later generations, such as the one Peter was addressing in the church.

To translate the clause "unto what *person* or what manner of time" would be self-defeating, because the text goes right on to say that it was in fact that very person (i.e., in "the sufferings of Christ") who had been revealed to them. He was the very one they were talking about! Several Greek grammarians are agreed that the expression *eis tina n poion kairon* is a "tautology for emphasis"[29] in which both *tina* and *poion* go with *kairon*, so the prophets were just as ignorant of the *time* factor in their prophecies as was the Son of Man, who did not know the time of the Second Coming, and as we are today on this same topic. Despite such clear teaching, there have been some in recent history who actually thought they knew the time of Christ's second advent and wrote books saying so, only to put them on sale after the event failed to materialize on the predicted date.

Others have taken an alternate route to finding meaning in these prophecies about the Messiah. For example, in 1927, Father André Fernandez coined the term *sensus plenior*,[30] which was popularized by Father

---

29. F. Blass and A. DeBrunner, *A Greek Grammar of the New Testament*, rev. and trans. Robert W. Funk (Chicago: University of Chicago Press, 1957), 155; A. T. Robertson, *A Grammar of the Greek New Testament in Light of Historical Research*, 4th ed. (Nashville: Broadman, 1923), 735–36; W. F. Arndt and F. W. Gingrich, *A Greek-English Lexicon of the New Testament* (Chicago: University of Chicago Press, 1957), 691; Charles Briggs. *International Critical Commentary on I Peter* (Edinburgh: T. & T. Clark), 107–8; and E. G. Selwyn, *The First Epistle of St. Peter* (London: Macmillan, 1955), 134–38. My former student Dr. Richard Schultz has called to my attention the same construction, though in reverse order, in Dionysius (or Longinus): *poia de kai tis aute*, "What and what manner of road is this?" (*On the Sublime*, 13.2 in the Loeb Classical Library; Aristotle 23:199 [Cambridge: Harvard University Press, 1995]).
30. F. André Fernandez, "Hermeneutica," *Institutiones Biblicae Scholis Accomodata*, 2nd ed. (Rome: Biblical Institute, 1927), 306.

Raymond E. Brown in his doctoral dissertation on this topic in 1955. Brown defined *sensus plenior* this way: "The *sensus plenior* is that additional, deeper meaning, intended by God, but not clearly intended by the human author, which is seen to exist in the words of a biblical text (or group of texts, or even a whole book) when they are studied in the light of further revelation or development in the understanding of revelation."[31]

This opened up the Old Testament text to say things that could not be pointed out by the usual method of grammatico-historical exegesis or the overall context of the Old Testament book or pericope. In fact, Louis Berkhof announced, "There is no truth in the assertion that the intent of the secondary authors [of Scripture, meaning the human writers], determined by grammatico-historical method, always ... represents in all its *fullness* the meaning of the Holy Spirit."[32] Again there is that weasel word "fullness" in another statement about interpreting messianic texts. But J. Barton Payne also generally agreed with this view, for he affirmed that "prophecy is transcendent as well as historical; and what its contemporaries [Biblical authors? Or readers?] may have thought must remain secondary to what God's inspiration may determinatively reveal as His primary intention."[33] But how would we distinguish between the two meanings, and where was the divine meaning tucked away among the grammar and syntax of the words before us?

In a rather brilliant review of this theory, coming from the same Roman Catholic side of the aisle as Raymond Brown represents, Bruce Vawter recognized *sensus plenior* as abandoning the old scholastic analogy of instrumental causality. He explained:

> If this fuller or deeper meaning was reserved by God to himself and did not enter into the writer's purview at all, do we not postulate a Biblical word effected outside the control of the human author's will and judgment.... and therefore not produced through a truly *human* instrumentality? If, as in scholastic definitions, Scripture is the *conscriptio* [writing together] of God and man, does not the acceptance of a *sensus plenior* deprive this alleged scriptural sense of one of its essential elements, to the extent that logically it cannot be called scriptural at all?[34]

---

31. Raymond E. Brown, *The Sensus Plenior of Sacred Scripture* (Baltimore: St. Mary's University, 1955), 92. Also see Raymond E. Brown, "The History and Development of the Theory of *Sensus Plenior*," *Catholic Biblical Quarterly* 15 (1953): 141–62.
32. Louis Berkhof, *Principles of Biblical Interpretation* (Grand Rapids: Baker, 1950), 60.
33. Payne, *Encyclopedia of Biblical Phrophecy*, 5 (emphasis added).
34. Bruce Vawter, *Biblical Inspiration*, Theological Resources (Philadelphia: Westminster, 1972), 115.

According to the view being critiqued here, the divine and human authors must each have gone their separate ways if there was no *concursus* as has been taught heretofore, each writing at his own level. But if this is true (and I do not think it is), then what happens to the concept of the divine use of the human instrumentality?

The effect of Vawter's argument was to declare that the *sensus plenior* meaning (despite its high claims for being a deeper meaning from God himself to the interpreter) simply was not "Scripture" in the sense that it came from what was "written" (Gk., *graphe*). That is to say, if the deeper meaning was one that was not located in the words, sentences, grammar, syntax, and paragraphs of the text, but instead was found by "reading between the lines" of Scripture, then it was not "Scripture"—that is, that which stands "written" in the text! Moreover, if this "fuller sense" opened up new vistas for the interpreter, how did it also escape the sacred writers of Scripture and the people whom that revelation was originally intended to help in Old Testament times? Could not the same process that, according to this theory, aided the interpreter likewise have aided those human authors of Scripture who were writing the words declared to be from God? Why the delay when the revealing source was the same Lord of all Scripture?

While the tendency in some of the modern scholarship has been to affirm that the New Testament authors used a type of *sensus plenior*, or some other form of Jewish exegetical methods of interpreting the text, such as *midrash* or *pesher* exegesis, leading to modifications in the straightforward meaning of the Old Testament text, already in 1885 Frederic Gardiner had anticipated many of these tendencies. He commented:

> In all quotations which are used argumentatively in order to establish any fact of doctrine, it is obviously necessary that the passage in question should be fairly cited according to its real interest and meaning, in order that the argument drawn from it may be valid. There has been much rash criticism ... that the Apostles and especially St. Paul, brought up in rabbinical schools of thought quoted Scriptures after a rabbinical and inconsequential fashion. A patient and careful examination of the passages themselves will remove such misapprehension.[35]

Gardiner said exactly what needed to be said on this topic. Nevertheless, on the evangelical side of the aisle, it is interesting to see how a slipperiness in interpretation has developed—one that slides from a search for "more

---

35. Frederic Gardiner, *The Old and New Testaments in Their Mutual Relations* (New York: James Pott, 1885), 317–18.

significance" in a text to eventually seeing this *significance* as one of the *new meanings*, albeit a deeper one, embodied somehow in the text. Graeme Goldsworthy was candid in his summing up his view on this matter. He opined:

> The *sensus plenior* of an OT text, or indeed of the whole OT, cannot be found by exegesis of the texts themselves. Exegesis aims at understanding what was intended by the author, the *sensus literalis*. But there is a deeper meaning in the mind of the divine author which emerges in further revelation, usually the NT. This approach embraces typology, but also addresses the question of how a text may have more than one meaning. While typology focuses upon historical events, which foreshadow later events, *sensus plenior* focuses on the use of words.[36]

Such statements are confusing. If this deeper meaning cannot be found in an exegesis of the Old Testament text, then how can it be found in the "words" vis-à-vis typology, which focuses on persons, events, or institutions? If the meaning of the words must await their further elaboration in the New Testament, then we have to answer two questions: (1) Were not the original audiences, to whom the Old Testament writers addressed these words, left out of these meanings, indeed, of any and all deeper meanings? And (2), if there is no signal from the original writers that more was stored in the words than appeared on the surface meaning, would this not be an example of what we call *eisegesis*, a reading backward into the Old Testament texts new meanings not discoverable by the rules of language and exegesis?

The alternative to using rabbinical methods of interpretation, or something like a *sensus plenior*, is simply to read the larger number of the messianic prophecies in the Old Testament in their natural, literal, or straightforward way. However, some voices, such as that of Alexander McCaul, continue to make additional kinds of objections to our vacillating evangelical practices. He complained:

> A mode of interpretation that is based upon two contradictory principles [a literal and a figurative or even a "deeper" interpretation] is necessarily false [from a Jewish point of view]. "You prove that Jesus is the Messiah ... by the grammatical principle [and then] ... you evade difficulties by the adoption of the figurative. Choose one of the two. [However,] [c]arry through the

---

36. Graeme Goldsworthy, "The Relationship of the Old Testament and New Testament," in *New Dictionary of Biblical Theology*, ed. T. Desmond Alexander, Brian S. Rosner, D. A. Carson, Graeme Goldsworthy, and Steve Carter (Downers Grove, Ill.: InterVarsity Press, 2000), 88.

figurative exposition, and then there is no suffering Messiah; carry through the literal, and a large portion of the prophecies are not yet fulfilled.

[Baron continued by responding that] the Jew's demand is reasonable, and his objections to this expository inconsistency [is] valid.... To receive those prophecies which foretell Messiah's humiliation and atoning death in their plain and literal sense [but not all as we have noticed above], and seek to allegorise [*sic*] those which deal with his glorious reign on the earth and over restored and blessed Israel, is to place an insurmountable stumbling-block before every Jew of common sense, and to hold up prophecy to scorn of the infidel.[37]

E. D. Hirsch's famous distinction between "meaning" and "significance" brought some immediate relief.[38] Hirsch declared that "meaning" was all that the human author expressed directly, indirectly, tacitly or allusively in his own words. But "significance" named a relationship, which we as readers drew as we associated what was said in the author's meaning with some other situation, person, institution, or the like. "Meaning" was unchanging, according to Hirsch; "significance" was changeable and must change, since the interests and questions asked relate the texts to many new situations, persons, institutions, and scores of other relationships and settings.

The question of the ignorance of the writers of Scripture with regard to their own meanings, which permits interpreters to find "deep meanings" embedded somehow within the text, or, better still, between the lines, or allows different senses than the grammar or syntax reveals, still persists. Hirsch once again addressed some of the most pressing questions:

How can an author mean something he did not mean? The answer to that question is simple. It is not possible to mean what one does not mean, though it is very possible to mean what one is not conscious of meaning. That is the entire issue in the argument based on authorial ignorance. That a man may not be conscious of all that he means is no more remarkable than that he may not be conscious of all he does. There is a difference between meaning and consciousness of meaning, and since meaning is an affair of the consciousness, one can say more precisely that there is a difference between consciousness and self-consciousness. Indeed, when an author's meaning is complicated, he cannot possibly at a given moment be paying attention to all its complexities.[39]

Even Hirsch seems to have contradicted himself, for he asserted that an author cannot mean something he did not mean, and yet that same author

---

37. Alexander McCaul, cited in Baron, *Rays of Messiah's Glory*, 81.
38. E. D. Hirsch, *Validity in Interpretation* (New Haven, Conn.: Yale University Press, 1967), xi, 8.
39. Ibid., 22.

can "mean what [he] is not conscious of meaning" and that about which he has no awareness. Which way did Hirsch wish to argue? And where would we allow room for divine revelation in that whole process? It is best, therefore, to conclude that only those meanings which we can validate on the basis of the writer's truth-assertions/intentions will be the basis for locating meaning in the Old Testament text. If the New Testament writers appeal to some alleged "deeper meaning," not discoverable by the methods of grammar, syntax, and the like, in passages where the New Testament writer is appealing to the old in a doctrinal or apologetic context, then that meaning cannot be allowed as having the predictive or apologetic values that the New Testament was thought to have discovered in the Old. In that case, it would be a new meaning foisted over the old that takes it in a different direction than its surface meaning—a process capable of self-destructing all possible communication, let alone all predictive prophecies about the Messiah!

The Apologetic Argument from Scripture

In many ways, it was Anthony Collins who, in the eighteenth century, started the modern debate that has continued to this very moment, to show that the use of the literal meaning of certain of the messianic so-called proof texts from the Old Testament did not support the messianic interpretation placed on them by the New Testament.[40] If this was the proper conclusion, then one of the strong reasons for asserting the unity between the testaments was gone. Collins argued that only the original sense (i.e., the literal sense) could be accepted as the valid and true meaning of the text. Spiritual fulfillments of these Old Testament texts, Collins warned, were no more than illustrations; they did not amount to specific "proofs" that Jesus was the Messiah. Interestingly enough, less than twenty years after Collins's first book appeared, George Handel's oratorio *The Messiah* had its first performance in 1742 and continues to have a large visibility to this day, incorporating a large number of Scriptures some would deny have any applicability to the Messiah.

---

40. Anthony Collins's two books were entitled *Discourse of the Grounds and Reasons for the Christian Religion* (1724) and *The Scheme of Literal Prophecy Considered* (1727). These references, those that follow in this discussion, were supplied to me from the article by Ronald E. Clements, "Messianic Prophecy or Messianic History?" *Horizons in Biblical Theology* 1 (1979): 87. Clements refers to J. O'Higgins, *Anthony Collins: The Man and His Works*, International Archives of the History of Ideas 35 (The Hague: Nijhoff, 1970), 155ff., for Collins's works on biblical prophecy.

In the meantime the debate over how best to understand the messianic references in the Old Testament continued to rage in earnest. Thomas Sherlock's *The Use and Intent of Prophecy* (London, 1732) argued for a type of dual meaning for these prophecies. To be sure, there was a literal meaning, but there also had to be a later, fuller meaning to which the messianic interpretation was attached.

J. G. Herder (1744–1803) and J. G. Eichhorn (1752–1827) concluded that the whole idea that the Old Testament contained a prediction of a coming Savior was merely a dogmatic imposition laid over Scripture. Prophecy had only a single meaning, which could not be maneuvered into depicting a coming Messiah. Both men felt that the end of the eighteenth century had erased the concept of Messiah from the Old Testament altogether.[41]

E. W. von Hengstenberg, however, mounted a massive attempt to stem the negative tide against a messianic interpretation of the Old Testament in a three-volume set that appeared from 1829 to 1835. A second edition, now in four volumes, appeared between 1854 and 1858, entitled *Christology of the Old Testament and a Commentary on the Messianic Predictions*.[42] Usually Hengstenberg treated the messianic idea in its chronological order and in its literal meaning; however, in difficult places he allowed the New Testament to be the final arbiter of its meaning and thus gave way, in part, to the dual meaning theory of some messianic prophecies. Hengstenberg, the conservative, inveighed against the "rationalistic" interpretations of others while they accused this successor and holder of the chair of the earlier higher critic, W. M. L. DeWette, of imposing a dogmatic scheme over the text without regard to its historical aspects.

Another conservative, Franz Delitzsch, broke with Hengstenberg's occasional use of the New Testament principle, noting that this dual meaning had failed to win the confidence of the scholarly community. Delitzsch wrote a work entitled *Messianic Prophecies in Historical Succession*.[43] He announced two criteria: (1) each prophecy had to be placed in the times and circumstances of the original prophet, and (2) only a single meaning was to be given to each prophecy without resorting to a typological or spiritual meaning in order to rescue the passage for messianic interpretation.

41. The work of Herder and Eichhorn on prophecy is recorded in E. Sehmsdorf. *Die Prophetenauslegung bei J. G. Eichhorn* (Göttingen: Vandenhoeck, 1971), 153–54, as cited by Clements, "Messianic Prophecy," 89.
42. Hengstenberg's first edition was published in Berlin, but the second edition was later translated into English by Reuel Keith and published in Alexandria by Morrison (1836–39). An abridged edition was completed by Thomas Kerchever Arnold (London: Francis and John Rivington, 1847), and reprinted by Kregel in Grand Rapids as *Christology of the Old Testament and a Commentary on the Messianic Predictions* (1970), with a foreword by Walter C. Kaiser Jr.
43. Franz Delitzsch, *Messianic Prophecies in Historical Succession* (Edinburgh: T. & T. Clark, 1891).

Delitzsch proposed the idea of development, which allowed Jesus to say *more* in a prophecy's fulfillment, though it was organically connected to the Old Testament in its basic seminal idea. This resulted in the fact that the earlier testament was seen to offer *less* on these same topics but was certainly in line with the general tenor and direction of a messianic expectation.

This battle has continued to seesaw back and forth in the nineteenth, twentieth, and twenty-first centuries. The single historical and grammatical meaning of the Old Testament was opposed by those who garnered the theological, spiritual dual meanings obtained from the New Testament and imposed these new meanings over the older so-called typological predictions. The battle would have been at a stalemate had not Willis J. Beecher arisen at the start of the twentieth century and given the Stone lectures at Princeton Seminary in 1902 on the relation of the promise-plan to the promise of the Messiah.[44]

The Promise-Plan of God

Instead of contending for a messianic interpretation that results from collecting a number of scattered predictions throughout the Old Testament and then proceeding to match each up with a New Testament fulfillment, the promise-plan method of interpreting messianic texts calls special attention to *what it was that connected*: (1) the ancient prediction and (2) the New Testament fulfillment. This view was first set forth by Beecher in his 1902 Stone lectures and then published as *The Prophets and the Promise*. He observed that attention had to be given to more than just the older prediction and the later fulfillment:

> [Considering only the two poles of prediction and fulfillment in prophecy, left out] the *means* employed for that purpose. The *promise* and the *means* and the *result* are all in mind at once.... If the promise involved a series of results, we might connect any one of the results with the foretelling clause as a fulfilled prediction.... But if we permanently confined our thought to these items in the fulfilled promise [i.e., just the older prediction and the newer fulfillment], we should be led to an inadequate and very likely a false idea of the promise and its fulfillment. To understand the predictive element aright, we must see it

---

44. See my chapter 11, which presents a fuller development of the promise-plan of God as a unitive factor in understanding the unity of the Bible.

in the light of other elements. Every fulfilled promise is a fulfilled prediction; but it is exceedingly important to look at it as a promise [and a historic means that carries the promise further] and not as a mere prediction.[45]

The point is that the promises of God are interrelated and usually connected in a *series* rather than found merely in a disconnected and heterogeneous group of sayings randomly and arbitrarily placed in the older testament until selected for use by the New Testament. Each new promise is *linked* in an ongoing stream of announcements that began in the prepatriarchal period of Genesis 1–11 and continued to be supplemented in the patriarchal, Mosaic, premonarchial, monarchial, and five prophetic periods in the preexilic, exilic, and postexilic times. Even though the promise is one, it is cumulative in its net effects. Rather than being a collection of assorted promises or predictions, God's messianic promises form one *continuous* pattern, purpose, and unified presentation of the Messiah and the messianic era.

As mentioned earlier, J. Barton Payne listed 127 personal messianic predictions involving 3,348 verses. But it was his list of *direct* personal messianic foretellings that came to a remarkable 574 verses[46] that interests us here. Payne found 103 *direct messianic* predictions in eighteen books of the Old Testament, including such high frequencies of usage as 25 in Isaiah, 24 in Psalms, and 20 in Zechariah. But these separate promises needed to be put into a cumulative and continuous pattern if the promise-plan of the Messiah was to be properly appreciated in the Old Testament.

The time sweep of this integrated promise-plan moved from the Garden of Eden in Genesis to the new heavens and new earth in Revelation. There were temporal enactments as part of this ongoing plan, but they in no way detracted from its climactic fulfillments in the first or second advents.

> *Rather than being a collection of assorted promises or predictions, God's messianic promises form one continuous pattern, purpose, and unified presentation of the Messiah and the messianic era.*

Conclusion

My conclusion is that the case for the unity of the promise of the Messiah is enormous, for the links between the promised prediction and the historic means by which God kept that word alive until it was fulfilled in part, or in the whole, were part and parcel of the doctrine of the Messiah. While the

45. Willis J. Beecher, *The Prophets and the Promise* (1905; repr., Grand Rapids: Baker, 1975), 376. See also Walter C. Kaiser Jr. *The Promise-Plan of God: A Biblical Theology of the Old and New Testaments* (Grand Rapids: Zondervan, 2008).
46. Payne, *Encyclopedia of Biblical Prophecy*, 667–68.

Messiah was at the heart of the promise-plan of God, the promise-plan was interconnected with the ongoing stream of events in the historic process that embraced the story from Eve, Noah, Shem, Abraham, Isaac, Jacob, Moses, David, and his whole reigning line. That is the means by which God kept the promise alive until Jesus came as a baby in Bethlehem.

The Unity *of the* Bible
between the Two Testaments

The God of the Old Testament and the New

> To use [the New Testament] alone is like taking the roofs and towers of a great cathedral in isolation and suggesting that the walls exist only that they may bear the roof.
>
> — H. L. Ellison[1]

From its earliest days, the Christian church has claimed the thirty-nine books of the Old Testament as an essential part of the sacred text. In fact, those books functioned as the sole source of authority for the early church from c. AD 30 to somewhere near AD 45–48, prior to the development of the New Testament canon. The first books of the New Testament began to appear around AD 45. And subsequent to that time, the first thirty-nine books remained as equal partners with the twenty-seven books of the New Testament, which were completed around AD 85–95. Upon the completion of the New Testament, the early church fathers witnessed to the unity of the canon of sixty-six books by according to both groups of texts full theological, ecclesiastical, and liturgical authority in their usage and citations.

But this unity was not without its challenges. After all, it seems almost impossible from a human point of view to think there could naturally have been any kind of unity in a series of books written in three different lan-

---

1. H. L. Ellison, *The Message of the Old Testament* (Grand Rapids: Eerdmans, 1969), 11.

guages (Hebrew, Aramaic, and Koine Greek) by some forty different authors representing three continents (Asia, Africa, and Europe) and almost every walk of life (shepherd, judge, king, prophet, priest, physician, tax collector, et al.) and spanning almost sixteen hundred years (approximately fifty some generations). When one adds to this mix the extraordinary variety of literary types (lists, narratives, law codes, poetry, parable, allegory, lament, apocalyptic, etc.) and the history of the nation of Israel and the early beginnings of the church, it seems incredible to suppose that there could be any kind of unity and coherence in such a pluralistic assortment—at least as judged from a human point of view.

Especially vulnerable to any kinds of claims of unity was the link between the two testaments. Often objections were raised against the older testament even by those who professed to believe in the later testament. How could there be any kind of harmony between the two testaments when there seemed to be serious contradictions and discontinuities present? Heading the list of objections against granting to the Old Testament equal status with the new was the way God was depicted in the Old Testament. Other ethical objections followed. Each of these objections must be examined if any case for unity is to be made. Therefore, let us take up in the first place those objections that claim that the God of the Old Testament can hardly be linked or equated with the God of the New Testament.

The God of the Old Testament Is a God of Wrath and Anger

Many people suppose that the God depicted in the Old Testament is miles away in quality and character from the deity represented in the New Testament. For example, some claim that whereas in the new covenant God is one who exhibits love and is full of mercy and tenderness, the old covenant deity appears to be full of wrath and anger. Should this charge prove true, it would be a fatal blow to any suggestions of continuity or unity.

Usually this discussion begins with the name Marcion, a prominent, wealthy ship owner who came to Rome just before AD 140. At first he was part of the believing community, but by AD 144 his views had become so strident that he was excommunicated by the church for labeling the God of the Old Testament as a fickle, hateful demiurge (i.e., a secondary deity, even though Marcion had admitted that same God had made the world). This also led Marcion to reduce the New Testament to a total of only ten

Pauline books, since so much of the New Testament quoted or alluded to the Old Testament.

Similar to this sharp dualistic system was that of Manichaeism, which likewise found the Old Testament to contain offensive morality and an inferior deity. This same line of thought would appear later in the twelfth Christian century among the Catharists ("the pure ones").

Accordingly, Marcion was not the last one in history to be offended by the way Yahweh was presented and appeared to act in the Old Testament. In fact, still today some assert that Yahweh is accurately depicted as a fickle, hateful, deceptive, and revengeful deity in the first thirty-nine books, a picture that cannot be harmonized with the way the later twenty-seven books paint our Lord.

Loving Jacob and hating Esau. The most notorious example of Yahweh's alleged hatefulness is found in the line, "Jacob I loved, but Esau I hated" (Rom. 9:13; cf. Mal. 1:2–3). Also prominent among God's hates and dislikes were hypocritical worship (Isa. 1:14; Amos 5:21) and evil of all sorts (Prov. 6:16–19). But how could a deity claim he still loved the person but hated what he did? This would not accurately represent Jesus of Nazareth, would it?

Nevertheless, the same sinless Jesus, on occasions in the New Testament, was likewise filled with indignation and anger (Mark 3:5; 10:14; John 2:17; 11:33, 38). Therefore, hate is a proper emotion for disavowing all that stands opposed to God himself and all that is good. Only the one who truly and passionately loves can understand the need to strongly oppose with a burning hatred all that is wrong and evil. As a matter of fact, the antonyms of "love" (Heb., 'ahabah, "to love") and "hatred" (Heb., sin'ah, "to hate") are used in Deuteronomy 21:15–17 to distinguish between the one loved and the one unloved. That same antonymic use is found in the Greek New Testament in Matthew 6:24 and Luke 16:13 where the terms mean "to prefer" one over the other, or to "love [one] more than" the other (see Matt. 10:37; cf. with Luke 14:26). Thus, in the case of Jacob and Esau, Jacob was elected and called to service, whereas Esau was not. However, Esau was not the object of contempt, for he, too, would realize God's promises in the present (Gen. 36:7), and his descendants would receive deliverance in the end-times (Amos 9:12; Obad. 19–21).

The case of Pharaoh. No less dramatic in this regard is the case of Pharaoh in the time of the exodus. Actually, the text repeatedly claimed that Yahweh's purpose in sending the plagues was evangelistic: "so that you [Pharaoh] may know [personally and experientially] that I am the LORD (Ex. 7:5, 17; 8:10[6], 22[18]; 9:14, 16, 29; 10:2; 14:4, 18). But the gift of God's mercy had no effect on Pharaoh, and only a remnant of the Egyptians responded in belief and joined Israel in their exit from the land with a "mixed multitude" (Ex. 12:38 NASB). Moreover, it was Pharaoh who repeatedly *hardened his own heart* ten times during the first five plagues (Ex. 7:13, 14, 22; 8:15[11], 19[15], 32[28]; 9:7, 34, 35; 13:15), before Yahweh seconded, as it were, Pharaoh's motion and hardened Pharaoh's heart ten times during the plagues six (Ex. 9:12) and eight through ten as well as in the pursuit of Israel to the sea (Ex. 10:1, 20, 27; 11:10; 13:15; 14:4, 8, 17). And all of this happened exactly as God had announced even prior to the unleashing of the plagues in Exodus 4:21; 7:3.

Note, however, the conditionality of such predictions in these contexts. God may produce hardness in one of two ways: permissive hardness or effective hardness. That is, God may withdraw from a person and leave that individual alone to go his or her own way, or he may order these actions after the person's time of grace has expired.

The anger or wrath of God. The question of divine anger (*ira Dei*) has had a long history with some extremely sharp debate even in the Christian church. The question became one of divine passibility (i.e., whether God had the capacity to feel, suffer, or be angry) or impassibility (i.e., the denial of God's capacity for these emotional qualities), and it raged on for quite a length of time. Gnosticism took strong exception to any and every claim that God could experience anger, feelings, pain, or sufferings of any kind.

Here again, it was Marcion who brought things to a head, for Marcion said that God was entirely apathetic and free of all affections and the ability to get angry, experience feelings, or suffer. It fell to the church father Lactantius in the last half of the third century AD to address this question in his famous *De Ira Dei*. As Lactantius beautifully reasoned, God must be moved by the presence of wickedness and sin of those who were in a covenant relationship with him, just as he is moved to love those who please him. Therefore he argued: "He who loves the good by this very fact hates evil; and he who does not hate evil, does not love the good; because the love of goodness issues directly out of the hatred of evil, and the hatred of evil issues directly out of the love of goodness. No one can love life without abhorring death; and no one can have an appetency for light without an antipathy to darkness."[2]

---

2. Lanctantius, *De Ira Dei*, 51.

Part of the problem is with the way we define *anger.* All too often we define it as Aristotle did: "the desire for retaliation,"[3] or the burning need to get revenge, or "to get even," for some slight or harm that was done to us. But Lactantius defined anger not as a "brief madness,"[4] but as "a motion of the soul rousing itself to curb sin."[5] That places a whole new perspective on its presence in the Godhead.

It is only when anger and wrath are left unchecked and uncontrolled that they become evils that need to be dealt with. But God's anger is never explosive, unreasonable, or unexplainable. Instead, it is his firm displeasure with our wickedness. Rather than anger controlling God, he uses it as an instrument of his will, thereby assuring us that his anger never shuts off his mercy and compassion toward us (Ps. 77:9). His anger, indeed, marked the end of his indifference to that evil, for he cannot, neither would he, remain neutral or impartial to the presence of evil (Isa. 26:20; 54:7–8; 57:16–19), for his love remains despite our rebellion (Jer. 31:3; Hos. 2:19).

It is a shame that some have depicted the wrath of God as bordering on that which is capricious, demonic, or evidence of some green-eyed monster of jealousy. The Jewish scholar Abraham Heschel explained how embarrassment over these emotional aspects in the biblical materials induced the historical-critical school to adopt an evolutionary scheme for explaining the character of God as he emerged from a terrible, mysterious force exhibiting the demonic and the primitive to a good and loving deity. They tended to transfer all the sinister forms of the demonic over to earliest expressions of God in the Old Testament, following an emerging path of social evolutionary thought. Heschel responded:

> This view, which is neither true to fact nor in line with the fundamental biblical outlook, arises from the failure to understand the meaning of the God of pathos and particularly the meaning of anger as a mode of pathos. "Pathos," like its Latin equivalent *passio, from pati* (to suffer), means a state or condition in which something happens to man [*sic*], something of which it is a passive victim ... emotions of pain or pleasure. We must not forget that the God of Israel is sublime rather than sentimental, nor should we associate the kind with the apathetic, the intense with the sinister, the dynamic with the demonic.[6]

---

3. Aristotle, *De Anima* 1.1. In this connection, see the superb discussion of this whole topic in Abraham Heschel, *The Prophets*, 2 vols. (New York: Harper & Row, 1962), 2:1–86, esp. 60n4.
4. Horace, *Epistolae* 1.2.62; also see J. C. Hardwick, "The Wrath of God and the Wrath of Man," *The Hibbert Journal* 39 (1940–41): 251–61.
5. Lactantius, cited by Heschel, *Prophets*, 2:82.
6. Heschel, *Prophets* 2:27–28, 84.

God's anger is a most awesome reality in both testaments, for Jesus called the Sadducees a "brood of vipers" (Matt. 3:7), just as John the Baptist called those coming out to be baptized by him a "brood of vipers" (Luke 3:7). In John 3 the wrath of God abides with all who do not believe on the Son of God (v. 18). Paul likewise warned of "the wrath to come" at the coming of our Lord Jesus Christ (1 Thess. 2:16; 5:9). In a similar manner the book of Revelation depicts the wrath of God that will be poured out on the wicked at the time of the second coming of Jesus (Rev. 14:10; 15:1).

The God of the Old Testament Is Deceptive

A divine sponsor of falsehood? Some find the claim that Yahweh of the Old Testament is a God of truth to be a misrepresentation of the facts, for he, say they, is all too often presented as a sponsor of falsehood by inspiring prophets to bring false messages, as in 1 Kings 22:2–23; Jeremiah 4:10; and Ezekiel 14:9.

What cannot be shown is that God was the efficient cause of the deceptions that took place. Instead, God is depicted as allowing a lying spirit to go and deceive King Ahab in 1 Kings 22:2–33 with the message that the king wanted to hear. R. J. Rushdoony, in a misplaced effort to rescue the lying of Rahab to save the spies that had snuck into Jericho (Josh. 2:2–7), and the lying midwives in Pharaoh's court (Ex. 1:18–19), argued against absolute truth telling by vindicating his position with the story about Ahab's lying prophets, which he declared taught that God placed a lying spirit in the mouths of these prophets![7] But W. B. Greene Jr. had a better understanding of the account:

> God is represented as having deceived Ahab ... only because the popular mind does not discriminate between what one does and what he only permits and also because it overlooks the great difference between the sovereign God's relation to the permission of evil and ours. It is true that in I Kgs xxii God seems to do more than simply permit the deception.... What else, however, does this mean than that, as God's eternal plan contemplates both the existence and the development of evil, so it provides for its accomplishment by the foreordained permission of evil on the occasions when and in the ways in which evil can by its own working serve the divine purpose? ... This is not saying that He takes evil *already* here, evil actually in manifestation, evil

---

7. R. J. Rushdoony, *The Institutes of Biblical Law* (Nutley, N.J.: Craig, 1973), 548.

that, if left uncontrolled by Him, would of itself hinder the good; and then so overrules the tendency of this evil that of itself, though contrary to its own intention, it advances truth.[8]

When King Ahab abandoned Yahweh as his Lord and determined to use prophecy for his own purposes, God allowed him to be ruined by the very instrument Ahab sought to prostitute. Rather than using the surrounding nations as the divine instrument of chastisement (Isa. 10:5), "The LORD ... poured into [the false prophets] a spirit of dizziness" (19:14).

Is God deceptive in what he promises? In the jeremiads offered by the prophet Jeremiah (4:10; 20:7), he mistook the promise of God's presence with his people and with the prophet himself as permanent insurance that no evil or derision would ever come on them. This confusion, however, is not a basis for saying that Yahweh had been deceptive or acted contrary to what he had promised. The promise-plan of God would always remain intact, but the people's continued enjoyment of its benefits rested in each generation on their obedience to the commands given in the revelation of God.

A similar comment could be made against the charge of divine deception in Ezekiel 14:9–10: "If the prophet is enticed to utter a prophecy, I the LORD have enticed that prophet, and I will stretch out my hand against him and destroy him from among my people Israel. They will bear their guilt—the prophet will be as guilty as the one who consults him."

What God permits, according to the usage of Scripture, is just as frequently attributed directly to God, for Scripture is not as concerned as we westerners are about secondary sources or causes. For example, Scripture says that "it was the LORD's will to crush [Jesus] and cause him to suffer" (Isa. 53:10), just as the apostle Peter preached on the day of Pentecost, "This man was handed over to you by God's set purpose and foreknowledge" (Acts 2:23). But Peter went on to say, "And you, with the help of wicked men [Jewish people and Romans], put him to death by nailing him to the cross." Therefore, the Jews and Romans both were the real culpable causes for Jesus' death, yet it pleased the Lord to bruise him. Consequently, it is fair to conclude that had God been the sole originating cause for the prophet's deception, that deception could not also be the object of his punishment, as Ezekiel 14:12–16 goes on to affirm.

---

8. William Brenton Greene Jr., "The Ethics of the Old Testament," *Princeton Theological Review* 27 (1929): 155–70; also in *Classical Evangelical Essays in Old Testament Interpretation*, ed. Walter C. Kaiser Jr. (Grand Rapids: Baker, 1972): 210–11.

In addition to the charges against blemishes in the character of God, other charges exist against the way God explicitly required acts that we would find repugnant or offensive. Four such alleged requirements must be examined.

The God of the Old Testament Ordered Human Sacrifice

One of the most startling requests ever made of a mortal by God is found in Genesis 22 where God orders Abraham, so it would seem, to commit murder by offering his only son Isaac up as a sacrifice. Confusingly, the later Mosaic law absolutely prohibits human sacrifice as it also scornfully rebukes those who offered their sons to the false god Molech (Lev. 18:21; 20:2).

However, in fairness, it must be remembered that we, the readers, are let in on the inside of what is about to happen by being told that the following command to Abraham was only to be a "test" (Heb., *nissah*, 22:1). While this announcement does indeed help us as the readers, it was totally unknown to Abraham; his experience was a genuine trial. Why God ordered the test is unknown to us; perhaps it was just as enigmatic to Abraham.

In eight other cases Elohim/Yahweh is called the "Tester." In six instances he tested Israel (Ex. 15:22–26; 16:4; 20:18–20; Deut. 8:2, 16; Judg. 2:21–22; 3:1–4), once he tested King Hezekiah (2 Chron. 32:31), and once he tested King David (Ps. 26:2). John I. Lawlor concluded in his study of the word *nissah*: "If the pattern seen in the use of the term *nissah*, when Yahweh/Elohim is said to be the 'tester,' can serve as a legitimate key for understanding its use in Gen. 22:1, then one may conclude that the reason Yahweh deemed it necessary to test Abraham was to know what was in his heart, to test his obedience to and fear of Yahweh when his promised and beloved son was at stake."[9]

Still unsatisfied, some will protest, "What kind of God would subject his follower to this type of ordeal?" But the answer depends on which part of the narrative is emphasized. If it is the command to sacrifice Isaac that is the focus of the inquiry, then the charge of divine deception looms large. But if the focus is on the intervention of God to stay the upraised hand of Abraham, then the conclusion reached would echo the conclusion of Roland de Vaux: "Any Israelite who heard this story would take it to mean that his race owed its existence to the mercy of God and its prosperity to the obedience of their ancestor."[10]

---

9. John I. Lawlor, "The Test of Abraham, Genesis 22:1–19," *Grace Theological Journal* 1 (1980): 28.
10. Roland de Vaux, *Ancient Israel* (New York: McGraw-Hill, 1965), 443, as cited in Lawlor, "Test of Abraham," 29.

Geerhardus Vos called us, however, to be cautious in our estimate of what was happening in God's command to sacrifice Isaac. His estimate of God's command to Abraham "distinctly implies in the abstract [that] the sacrifice of a human being cannot be condemned on principle. It is well to be cautious in committing one's self to that critical opinion, for it strikes at the very root of the atonement."[11] Vos concluded in that same place, "Not sacrifice of human life as such, but the sacrifice of average sinful human life is deprecated by the O.T."

Vos was correct to warn us against denying to God the voluntary sacrifice of his own Son, our Lord Jesus. And in the intervention of God, a substitute (a ram's life) was offered in place of a mortal's life. But I do not see how "average sinful life is deprecated," unless Vos meant no more than what I say when I refer to mortal life. The narrative, then, is one about "testing" and about divine intervention in providing as a ransom the life of a substitute in place of the life of a human being.

The God of the Old Testament Ordered "Borrowing" of Unreturnable Jewelry

In three passages in the Exodus record (3:21–22; 11:2–3; and 12:35–36), it appears as though God ordered the Israelites to despoil the Egyptians with no intent to return what they had "borrowed." But this moral difficulty is more a problem with modern translations than it is from the standpoint of the Hebrew text.

In each of the three texts, the same Hebrew verb is used as the Israelite women acquired the gold and silver jewelry. The Hebrew verb *sha'al* means "to ask" for something, as in Judges 8:24 and 1 Samuel 1:28. That is the way that the Septuagint and Vulgate rendered this verb (Gk., *aiteo*, and Lat., *postula*). However, this same Hebrew verb can mean "to borrow" in texts like Exodus 22:14[13] and 2 Kings 4:3; 6:5.

Since the Hebrew verb can be rendered either as "to ask" in an outright manner, or "to borrow," attention must be directed to the piel form of the Hebrew verb *natsal* in Exodus 3:22 and 12:36, meaning "You shall plunder the Egyptians." *Natsal* is a military metaphor that could mean taking something away by force, but never by fraud, as, for example, it is used as a military metaphor of the spoils after the battle in 2 Chronicles 20:25.

---

11. Geerhardus Vos, *Biblical Theology: Old and New Testaments* (Grand Rapids: Eerdmans, 1954), 106.

The background for what happened in Egypt must revert to some six hundred years before this "asking" event, where God had promised in Genesis 15:14 that after Israel had served four hundred years as strangers in another country, "they [would] come out with great possessions" (Heb., *birkush gadol*), and they would "not go empty-handed" (Ex. 3:20–21).

Nowhere does the text say or imply that the request was for a temporary period of time or that the Egyptians were coerced or unwilling contributors. In fact, it actually states the reverse: "I will make the Egyptians favorably disposed toward this people, so that when you leave you will not go empty-handed" (Ex. 3:21). God seemed to have softened the hearts of the Egyptians in that they began to complain against Pharaoh's stubbornness: "How long will this man be a snare to us? Let the people go, so they may worship the LORD their God. Do you not realize that Egypt is ruined?" (Ex. 10:7). Accordingly, as the people asked, God strangely and wondrously moved the hearts of the populace to respond generously and lavishly as Israel was given favor in the eyes of the sympathetic Egyptians, who by now took pity on how brutally the Israelites had suffered under the imperial hand of Pharaoh.

The God of the Old Testament Approved of Tricky Requests

Moses' request of Pharaoh to have permission to go for three days into the wilderness in order to worship Yahweh with sacrifices, which would have been offensive to the Egyptians if done in the land of Egypt, appears to some to be a ruse on Moses' part to get a three-day head start on Israel's escape from Egypt (Ex. 3:18–20; 5:1–3; 8:25–26; 10:9–10). But is this an example of a partial truth and a tricky ruse to get away—only to announce once safely outside of Egypt's borders, "Last one into Canaan is 'it': run for your lives"? Indeed, Rashi had glossed this example by citing Psalm 18:26, "To the crooked you show yourself shrewd." I seriously doubt that is the correct exegesis of this text or situation.

The matter is better represented by Augustine and the fifteenth-century Spanish exegete Abarbanel. They observed that God deliberately graded his requests of Pharaoh from an easier permission (a three-day journey with an agreed obligation to return) to a more difficult request (the total release of an enslaved people) in order to give Pharaoh every possible assistance in making an admittedly difficult political and economic decision. They argued that had Pharaoh acceded to this more modest request, Israel would have been under obligation to return to Egypt after the three-day worship retreat in the wilderness.[12] That request would then be followed, it is conjectured, by an increasingly more difficult series of requests leading to the final goal of a total release.

Since God reveals his "secret" (Heb., *sod*) to his servants (Amos 3:7), Moses was warned ahead of time of Pharaoh's recalcitrance, as he turned down an even more moderate request. As Greene commented:

> So far from God's course being the tricky one that many have tried to make it out to be, it was prompted by both justice and mercy. Mercy disposed Him to cause the favor asked of Pharaoh in the first instance to be moderate, that he could easily have granted it, had he chosen to do so and thus have disciplined himself to accede to the request for the release of the whole nation, a request which, if made at first, would have been too much for him.[13]

Greene continued by noting, "The favor asked of Pharaoh [was deliberately designed by God] to be so reasonable that his obduracy might appear so much more glaring, and might have no excuse."[14]

The God of the Old Testament Ordered the Extermination of Pagans

One of the most frequently raised objections to depicting the God of the Old Testament as a just, loving, and merciful God is his command to wipe off the face of the earth all the Canaanite men, women, and children. That is why Israel had been warned in Leviticus 18:28 that "if [they] defile[d] the land, it [would] vomit [them] out as it vomited out the nations before [them]." Nothing in this challenge was new to Israel, for God had reminded Israel that the land Moab now occupied had once belonged to the Emites, just as Ammon, also on the eastern side of the Jordan River, had once belonged to the Zamzummites; but God drove out these previous inhabitants of the land and gave it to Moab and Ammon. Likewise, God drove out the Avvites from the land of Esau. When the moral cup of a nation filled with iniquity to overflowing its brim (Gen. 15:16), the land vomited the old nation out of that territory as God gave it to the new occupants. That principle is still true to this day.

It is now possible for us to show in more detail the depths to which Canaanite culture had sunk from the remarkable archaeological finds that

---

12. Walter C. Kaiser Jr., "Exodus," in *Expositor's Bible Commentary*, 13 vols., 2nd ed. (Grand Rapids: Zondervan, 2008), 2:334–561.
13 Greene, *Classical Evangelical Essays*, 218–19.
14 Ibid., 219.

began in 1929 at the Syrian site of Ras Shamra, also known as ancient Ugarit. The language of Ugarit was so similar to biblical Hebrew that we have profited as much from the linguistic help we received from the enormous number of tablets found there as we have from the Canaanites' own depictions of their society's religion and morals. These texts, dated from about the time of Moses and Joshua in 1400–1300 BC, contain a number of the Canaanite myths about their gods and goddesses. The whole cult seems to have been based around a young god of rain, dew, thunder, and fertility named Baal. It is against this deity that Israel struggled so unsuccessfully for most of their history in Canaan. His actions in the myths were crude and lewd. And Israel must have eventually reasoned, *When in Canaan, do as the Canaanites do*—especially if you want to see your household, your crops, and your livestock and herds evidence abundant fertility. But God would have none of it.

Instead, God demanded that when they came into the land of Canaan, they were to "totally destroy" the nations living there: the Hittites, Girgashites, Amorites, Canaanites, Perizzites, Hivites, and Jebusites (Deut. 7:1–2). The term for "totally destroy" is the technical term *herem*, meaning "to take a forced dedication for [total] destruction" of that culture and nation. The word comes from the corresponding Hebrew verb *haram*, meaning "to separate." In Arabic a *harem* was the enclosure or courtyard that surrounded the women set aside as the king's harem. In Akkadian it was the term used for a prostitute. This word *herem*, or "ban," is used some eighty times in the Old Testament. While it has not been found in Ugaritic as yet, it was used in lines 14 to 17 of the famous Moabite Stone, which records that Mesha, king of Moab, "devoted (*harem*) seven thousand inhabitants of the city of Nebo to his god Chemosh."

The point remains that Canaan, similar to the other nations on the other side of the Jordan, had over the centuries (even millennia) exasperated the patience and goodness of God. Israel was not permitted to treat other nations the same way, as Deuteronomy 20:10–18 explains: "When you march up to attack a city, make its people an offer of peace…. However, in the cities of the nations the LORD your God is giving to you as an inheritance, do not leave alive anything that breathes. Completely destroy (*harem*) them…. Otherwise, they will teach you to follow all the detestable things they do in worshiping their gods, and you will sin against the LORD your God."

Lest Israel thought they were better than those other nations, they were bluntly reminded: "It is not because of your righteousness or your integrity that you are going to take possession of their land; but on account of the wickedness of these nations, the LORD your God will drive them out before you, to accomplish what he swore to your fathers, to Abraham, Isaac and Jacob" (Deut. 9:5).

The Canaanites' list of loathsome practices is long indeed, including burning their own children to honor their gods (Lev. 18:21), practicing sodomy, bestiality, and every brand of deviant sexuality (Lev. 18:23, 24; 20:3).

Some may still wonder, *Yes, I can see why the national political and cultic leaders were liable to divine punishment, but why include individuals who may have been innocent?* Greene counseled in this regard:

> We may not object to God's doing immediately and personally what we do not object to His doing mediately, through providence. Now nothing is more certain than that providence is administered on the principle that individuals share in the life of the family and of the nation to which they belong; and that, consequently it is right that they should participate in its punishments as in its rewards.... Though many innocent persons could not but suffer, it is *right*, because of the relation in which they stood to the guilty, that this should be so.[15]

The destruction of the Canaanites was on the same principle as Noah's flood, or the obliteration of the five cities of the plain (including Sodom and Gomorrah), or even the annihilation of Pharaoh's army. Usually the objections made to these punishments from God end up being from the same persons who find the doctrine of eternal punishment of all unrepentant wicked to be below the honor, majesty, and mercy of a loving God.

Conclusion

The objections made to the character of God in the Old Testament turn out to be unfairly leveled against God in that they have little or no appreciation for the full context of the passage or the culture. Moreover, if the objectors persist in their complaints, often they will find that what they have identified as an exclusive Old Testament problem also turns up as a problem in the New Testament. It is not as if there are two separate deities in the Bible, as Marcion wanted to explain it; he is the same Lord in both testaments.

Therefore, the unity of the Bible is not to be forfeited on this account, for Scripture depicts our Lord in the same manner in both divisions of the sixty-six books.

15. Ibid., 221–22.

The Unity *of the* Bible:
Two Testaments

The Morally Offensive Character and Acts of
Old Testament Men and Women

Divine approval of an individual in one aspect or area of his [or her] life does not entail and must not be extended to mean that there is a divine approval of that individual in all aspects of his character or conduct.

—Walter Kaiser[1]

The unity of the Bible appears to be badly broken when it presents to us a number of heroes such as Abraham, Moses, David, and Solomon, whose lives were anything but exemplary in at least one or more noticeable areas! If the Old Testament intended to introduce these leading characters to us merely as descriptors of persons whose character and conduct the New Testament sensitivities would later find reprehensible, wherein can any coherence or unity be found between the testaments? Rather than noting that the New Testament supplemented and carried the Old Testament further in the progress of revelation, it surely would in that case supplant it, thereby highlighting the New Testament's opposition to and divergence from the older testament.

For example, David, the Old Testament text assured us, was "a man after God's own heart," yet he committed adultery with Bathsheba. Abraham is likewise presented as the paragon of faith, so why did he lie to Pharaoh about his wife being his sister? And one could think of a thousand reasons why Solomon would need to be divinely rebuked, yet he was called by the Lord

---

1. Walter C. Kaiser Jr., *Toward Old Testament Ethics* (Grand Rapids: Zondervan, 1983), 270–71.

Jedidiah, "Loved by the LORD" (2 Sam 12:25). Either the men and women God chose to represent him in the areas of politics and religion were especially poor choices, or this was the best God had to work with during those earlier generations. But, if all this was so, how could there be any type of unity between the "people of God" in that testament and their counterparts in the New Testament? Surely, the failures, particularly in the lives of those in the Old Testament, present some of the best examples of inconsistencies from the standard raised in the New Testament. How could one argue for any kind of unity and coherence of message and morality given these aberrations?

Accordingly, we must examine a sampling of some of the charges against the character traits of the Old Testament women and men before we turn to scrutinize the conduct of those older generations as well. However, prior to looking at specific charges, perhaps no principle of moral hermeneutics is more important than a proper estimate of what is *normative* and what is purely *descriptive* as a narrative recorded of the character and conduct of these Old Testament worthies. Stated more formally, here is that important principle: God's approbation of an individual must be strictly limited to that portion of their characteristics or acts that were *textually* singled out beyond the mere recording of the narrative itself. Put more formally, divine approval of one area of a person's life is not a blanket approval of all areas of that person's life. This principle will be extremely significant as we identify what is normative and what is descriptive in the lives and characteristics of the Old Testament worthies. Therefore, let us take the charges up one at a time.

They Were Liars

On two separate occasions Abraham was caught red-handed lying as a human expedient or, as he claimed, to save his beautiful wife from the clutches of two lustful monarchs, Pharaoh and the Philistine king Abimelech (Gen. 12:10–20; 20:1–18). He declared, "She [i.e., his wife, Sarah] is my sister" (Gen. 12:13; 20:2).

Of course it was partly true, because Sarah was his half sister, and it was true that in that culture it was possible for a "sistership contract" to be written along with a marriage contract, which gave the wife greater protection.[2] But the subtleties of such rationalizations were apparently lost to

2. See Ephraim A. Speiser, "The Wife-Sister Motif in the Patriarchal Narratives," in *Biblical and Other Studies*, ed. A. Altman (Garden City, N.Y.: Doubleday, 1963), 15–28; and Ephraim A. Speiser, *Anchor Bible Commentary*, vol. 1 (Garden City, N.Y.: Doubleday, 1964), 91–94.

some, even to those who lived in their own culture, if indeed they ever had been presented to either of these monarchs in nearby cultures. Both of them complained that they had not been duly apprised that Sarah was indeed Abraham's wife. Neither a half-truth nor a so-called sistership document could be given as an excuse for the truth. Clearly Abraham lied, but neither did the Old Testament excuse him either!

Abraham may have evidenced great faith as he left Ur of the Chaldees (Gen. 12:1), as he looked up to the heavens and was told that his descendants would be as numerous as the stars (Gen. 15:5–6), and even as he trusted God and willingly offered up his son Isaac as a sacrifice (Gen. 22), but he surely is not to be commended for trusting God with the safekeeping of his wife—or for his ability to tell the truth! Indeed, like father, like son, for Isaac used the same type of ruse as Abraham in Genesis 26:6–11.

It is this same type of lying that we find in the Hebrew midwives (Ex. 1:17–21) and Rahab the Jericho harlot (Josh. 2:1–14; 6:25). Both were rewarded by God, but not because they lied; rather, it was because they feared God more than they feared Pharaoh or the king of Jericho. Therefore, they exhibit our principle extremely well; approval of a character in one area is not an approval in all areas of his or her life. The Bible does not make plastic saints out of its mortals, but describes them warts and all.

Their cases of prevarication, however, are altogether different from the case of Samuel, who wanted to know from God "How can I go?" to anoint David as king when Saul was so jealous for his position as king (1 Sam. 16:2)? Saul, the prophet feared, would kill Samuel out of fear for any rival for his throne. In this instance, God instructed Samuel to "take a ... sacrifice" (v. 2) and say that he had come to make a sacrifice to God without disclosing any other tasks the Lord had also assigned him to do—namely, anointing David as king. King Saul, by his actions in the latter part of his reign, had yielded his right to know some things; Samuel was under obligation to speak truthfully, but he was not at all obligated to tell everything he knew. John Murray concluded, "Without question, here is divine authority for [a type of] concealment by means of a statement other than that which would have disclosed the main purpose of Samuel's visit to Jesse."[3]

Somewhat similar to this case is King Zedekiah's warning Jeremiah not to reveal the full extent of their conversation to the princes when they found out the king had met with the imprisoned prophet and asked what they had talked about. Jeremiah was simply to tell them that he had petitioned the

---

3. John Murray, *Principles of Conduct* (Grand Rapids: Eerdmans, 1957), 139.

king not to send him back to Jonathan's house, which was accurate as far as it went but did not disclose the rest of their conversation (Jer. 38:15–16, 27). What then is a proper definition of a lie?

A lie must have three ingredients, explained Ezekiel Hopkins, following Augustine's lead: "[1] There must be the speaking of an untruth; [2] It must be known to us to be an untruth; and [3] it must be with a will and intent to deceive him to whom we speak it, and to lead him into error."[4]

What about the situation of Elisha? Did he not lead the Syrian army outside of Dothan to inside the walls of Samaria as the army was smitten with blindness in answer to Elijah's prayer? (2 Kings 6:8–23). Is this an example of the so-called "dutiful lie" (*mendacio officiosum*)? Again, the answer seems to be no, for he was under no obligation to announce to them that he was the man they sought. And when he told them that Dothan was not the city they were looking for, he was correct. But true to his word, he led them to the man they were looking for—no one less than himself—but within the walls of Samaria!

We have already noted that commendation of a person for one character trait is not a total endorsement of all that person is or does. The truth is not at all what is in question here, but the extent to which we are under obligation to reveal everything connected with a situation to every person who demands of us anything that even comes close to a full disclosure. Are we as truth-tellers obligated to reveal everything we know to whosoever asks it of us? According to the principles of 1 Samuel 16, we are never permitted to say anything untruthful, but neither are we obligated to always tell everything we know, especially when some, by the nature of what they might plan to do, have disqualified themselves from coming into possession of this information.

They Were Murderers

Three examples may be handled under this charge: (1) the actions of Judge Ehud against King Eglon of Moab (Judg. 3:15–26), (2) Jael's assassination of Captain Sisera (Judg. 4:17–21), and (3) David's advice to Solomon about the need for avenging the earlier attacks against him by Joab and Shimei (1 Kings 2:5–8). Here again caution is recommended, for we must distinguish between the mere *description*, or report, of what was taking place or about to be done and the actual *approval* of that action.

---

4. Ezekiel Hopkins, "Exposition of the Ten Commandments," in *The Whole Works of Ezekiel Hopkins* (1701; repr., Edinburgh: A. & C. Black, 1841), 134.

Interpreters are divided on many of these cases. For example, A. R. Fausset saw Judge Ehud's work as a "treacherous assassination" that did not "emanate from the Spirit of God." Fausset argued that while God accepted Ehud's courage, patriotism, and faith, his murder of Eglon, king of Moab, was "defective."[5] The nineteenth-century commentator George Bush came to the opposite conclusion. He argued that Ehud's act was vindicated on the grounds that God had raised him up as a deliverer for the country (Judg. 3:15). To clinch his argument, he asked, "Have we not eulogized Brutus for stabbing Caesar and ridding the country of that tyrant?"[6] This, however, sounds like teleological reasoning (rather than a deontological, duty-based ethic) that says the end justifies the means.

Thus Bush appears to have moved too easily from Ehud being given authority for a task to legitimizing all the ways that he carried out the job. Fausset had the better part of this argument, for Ehud is a case of the right man trying to do the right thing in the wrong way. Moab gives no evidence of being at war with Israel at this time; thus Eglon would not be expecting any sort of subversive activity. His act must be condemned when it is set against the rest of the revelation of God in both testaments.

In the case of Jael, the nation was at war. Jael was a relative by blood (the Kenites or Midianites were descendants from Abraham) to the nation of Israel, now under attack from Jabin, king of the Canaanites, in Hazor. She acts almost in the sense of an avenger of the blood of a relative. It is for this reason that she is eulogized as "most blessed of women" (Judg. 5:24). Of course there was deceit in her inviting Sisera into her tent, but the conditions of war should have alerted Sisera to this potentiality as well.

To use another comparison, when a Christian joins a sports team and is told to make a fake run off to the side to attract the opposition away from the real ball carrier, he cannot say, "I cannot do that! I am a Christian. Give me the ball and let me run with it, but I would be lying if I pretended to have the ball when it was not in my possession! I do not want to lose my testimony over a faked run around the end of the line of scrimmage in a football game!" The objection is groundless, for the rules of athletic contests lead us to expect just that type of activity. The same rules apply to diversionary tactics in the conduct of war.

The matter of Joab and Shimei is different (1 Kings 2:5–8). Even though Joab had committed a murder, David felt it would endanger the tranquility

5. A. R. Fausett, *A Critical and Expository Commentary on the Book of Judges* (1885; repr., Minneapolis: James and Klock, 1977), 69.
6. George Bush, *Notes on Judges* (1852; repr., Minneapolis: James & Klock, 1976), 37–39.

of the nation had he moved then and there against Joab and required his life. His hands at the moment were tied. But when these conditions changed, Joab's act of murder had to be dealt with by the state as the law required. Shimei, however, though given a reprieve on his death sentence for his insolent behavior against David when David was being chased from his throne by his own son, had his fate resting in his own hands as he was given terms for a stay of punishment. When Shimei violated the terms of his reprieve, he became responsible for his own punishment.

They Were Adulterers

David may have been called "a man after [God's] own heart" (1 Sam. 13:14), but his nefarious affair with Bathsheba was outside the bounds of that estimate. Only those who continue to do the will of God can be called persons after God's own heart, as Eli the priest was instructed (1 Sam. 2:35). Moreover, this expression seems to be a reference not so much to a person's moral conduct, but to one's official duties in office and the promotion of worship and service to God. David numbered the troops (which usually means a mustering of them for a war that was not declared by Yahweh), thereby projecting some unauthorized conquest into some foreign territory (2 Sam. 24).

Given the fact that David also had his adulterous affair with Bathsheba (2 Sam. 11), it is noteworthy that nevertheless his conscience was made tender toward God and he sincerely repented of both reckless acts (Pss. 32, 51). Neither act comes with divine approval or a commendation that would merit imitation. God never approved of adultery in any of his subjects, nor did he approve of military action simply to enlarge one's territory.

They Cursed Children

Those who know very little about the Bible seem to have heard the story of Elisha cursing the forty-two children (2 Kings 2:23–25). Robert Ingersoll, an atheistic rabble-rouser of another century, loved to play this number for all it was worth in his public lectures. As he told the story: "There was an old gentleman a little short of the article of hair. And as he was going through the town a number of little children cried out to him, 'Go up, thou baldhead.' And this man of God turned and cursed them.... And two bears came out of the woods and tore to pieces forty-two children."[7]

First, note that the so-called "little children" are hardly small kids who mouthed off what they had heard their older siblings or parents mockingly say about the prophet, unaware of what it meant at their tender age. The Hebrew *na'ar* ranges from an "infant" (Ex. 2:6; 2 Sam 12:16) all the way up to mature Absalom in revolt against his father's kingdom (2 Sam 14:21; 18:5). If this root is also related to a South Arabic verbal form "to instigate rebellion," then the word might be rendered here as "young toughs" or "teenage rowdies."[8]

Another surprise in this passage is that the prophet was not an old bald-headed, crotchety eccentric who had lost all patience with the younger generation, but was quite a young man who had had this encounter shortly after his ordination to the prophetic ministry. Since he lived almost sixty years after this experience, he could hardly have been more than twenty or twenty-five years old. The Bethel toughs castigated him with the epithet of old "bald-head" because it may have been a well-known curse used in those days. Surely, when they cried, "Go up, go up," they were alluding to and mockingly demeaning the ascension to heaven of Elisha's mentor, Elijah, suggesting that Elisha, too, might just as well "blast off" and "get off this earth and out of their way."

But did the prophet really lose his temper? He cursed these young toughs in the name of Yahweh, but it was not the prophet who brought the bears, but the sins of this city of Bethel, which had become the center for worshiping the bull calf. Why, then, was there so serious an indictment? It was because of the direct attack on God himself and his miraculous removal of Elijah from this earth. That town had substituted bull calves in place of the living God as well as joined in scoffing at God's messenger (cf. 2 Chron. 36:16). Elisha did not specify that it must be by the paws of a bear; nor did he spell out how many bears would be needed to do the job—all that was permissively in the hands of God; he sent the bears.

They Married Harlots

It is not unusual for readers of Scripture to be taken aback when they read that the prophet Hosea was commanded by God to "take to yourself an

7. Robert Ingersoll, *Ingersoll's 44 Lectures* (Chicago: J. Regan & Co., n.d.), 244.
8. Milton Fisher, "*Na'ar*," *Theological Wordbook of the Old Testament* (Chicago: Moody, 1981), 2:585–86.

adulterous wife" (Hos. 1:2). Rationalizations for God's actions have ranged from the command being only a vision form, or an allegory, to being a real historical event. Despite the attempts to rescue God from being involved in what he clearly condemned in other passages, neither the *allegorical* views of Calvin, Luther, Osiander, van Hoonacker or Gressman, nor the claims that this was only an *internal* vision, such as those held by C. F. Keil, E. W. Hengstenberg, nor the Jewish commentators Maimonites, Eben Ezra, or Kimchi, have offered much help in solving this dilemma. All these views fail to notice that the woman who is restored in Hosea 3 is the same as the woman Gomer whom Hosea married in chapter 1!

Therefore preference must be given to the real or historical view. But Gomer was not a harlot *at the time* Hosea married her. The sign that helps us to know that more is going on than meets the eye is that there is a grammatical construction here that uses a *zeugma*. A zeugma is a word used to modify two or more words in such a manner that it applies to each in a different sense or makes sense with only one. The Hebrew idiom for getting married is "to go and take for yourself a wife." In this context, however, the full statement with the use of modern square brackets would read as follows: "Go and take for yourself a[n adulterous] wife [and children of unfaithfulness]" (Hosea 1:2; see Gen. 4:19; 6:2; 19:14; Ex. 21:10; 34:16; and 1 Sam. 25:43 for other examples). If this is the correct reading, and I believe it is, then the command to get married applies only to the wife and not the children.

If an ellipsis were to be supplied, another verb would be needed, such as "and *beget* children of harlotry." The children are secondarily called "children of harlotry" after the fact because of their mother's subsequent reputation. But the text clearly claims that Hosea was the father of the children, since in the case of the first child, it specifically says, "she bore him [i.e., Hosea] a son" (Hos. 1:3), and in the case of all three children, Hosea personally named them (1:4, 6, 9)—a right reserved for the real father.

If I have correctly interpreted the details found in the text itself, then it is equally true that the same designation, "wife of harlotry" was given to Gomer by way of condensing both God's original command and what subsequently happened into a single statement. This type of construction, in which a result is put for what appears to be a purpose statement, is not unknown in Scripture, as E. P. Heavenor pointed out about Isaiah 6:9–12.[9]

---

9. E. S. P. Heavenor, "Hosea, Book of," in *The New Bible Dictionary*, ed. J. D. Douglas (London: Inter-Varsity, 1962): 540–41.

The same type of construction can be seen in Jesus' use of parables (Mark 4:11–12) and the hardening of Pharaoh's heart (Ex. 10:1; 11:10; 14:4). Our modern use of square brackets in the original divine command is a recent literary convention, but it is clear that it would be possible to intend the same effect even without them. We cannot impose our literary conventions on that ancient day, but we can be aware of their need to say in exactly that same manner what we now do by the literary convention of square brackets.

What Hosea did not know before he married Gomer became evident after she bore three children to him. Thus God did not command Hosea to marry a sexually promiscuous woman and thereby post an exception to the high view of marriage in the rest of the Bible. His command was to marry Gomer, but it was Gomer who later exhibited her penchant for adultery and abandonment of her home.

This same Lord, however, did tell Hosea to "Go, show your love to your wife again" (Hosea 3:1). The Hebrew word 'od, "again," goes with the word "Go," and not with "Yahweh said *again*." This is seen in the way the Hebrew conjunctive and disjunctive accents appear in the Masoretic punctuation (indicating that the word "again" goes with "go" and not with "said") and in the way the LXX, Syriac, and Vulgate handled this text. Thus the marriage between Hosea and Gomer was restored after the requisite period of purification ended, as the text notes.

They Committed Incest

Years ago while I, as a college student, was doing visitation among the parents of the Sunday school students I was teaching in South Chicago, a man told me bold-facedly that he was sleeping carnally with his daughters. When I mentioned to him that the Scriptures would not approve of that, he had a ready answer: Lot slept with his two daughters (Gen. 19:30–38). When I tried to draw the distinction for him between what the Bible *records* and what it *approves*, that nuance was lost on him. He repeatedly announced that he was doing exactly what was biblical, and that was that! No amount of hermeneutical explanation was going to convince him that what he was doing was not "biblical."

Seldom does the Bible stop to moralize on a point after it has described some of the questionable things God's people did. There is not a summons in our Bibles that asks after it has recorded one of these moral or ethically marginal episodes: "Dear reader, did you hear what that text of Scripture just said? Do you agree or disagree? Record your feelings here in the margins of your Bible." It is assumed that the Bible will be read contextually and therefore that certain actions will be condemned because they are out of keeping with what is taught elsewhere in the Scriptures. This type of harmonistic reading of the Bible is no more out of keeping with the normal rules of communicating than what we carry out in daily conversations.

They Were at Times Totally Lawless

The period of the Judges in the Bible was one of Israel's sorriest moments. "In those days Israel had no king; everyone did as he saw fit" (Judg. 17:6; 18:1; 19:1; 21:25). There was the idol-making Micah (Judg. 18), who was robbed of his idol by the tribe of Dan. Then there was the bigamous Levite (Judg. 19) who hacked up the corpse of his sexually abused concubine so as to arouse the wrath of the rest of the eleven tribes against an unrepentant tribe of Benjamin. This action resulted in the near demise of the tribe of Benjamin. The military action and the oath taken by the other eleven tribes to come against Benjamin for its intransigence and evil (Judg. 21) almost cost Israel one whole tribe in that nation, not to mention a future King Saul or an apostle Paul!

Gideon, in refusing the invitation to be their king, correctly stated, "The LORD will rule over you" (Judg. 8:23), but some in the nation opted for Gideon's son by a concubine, Abimelech, who brought tragedy on himself as well as on the men of Shechem and its villages (Judg. 9–10). Yes, all of this is described in the Bible, but nowhere does the text indicate that any of it was normative for that day or for ours. Only the purpose theme of the book of Judges alerts us to the fact that this, too, was an illustration of the fact that everyone was doing what seemed right in his own eyes.

They Sought Revenge

Two examples of the charge of God's people seeking revenge are generally given. One is Samuel's action in hewing Agag, king of the Amalekites, into pieces (1 Sam. 15:33). The other features David delivering seven of Saul's descendants into the hands of the Gibeonites because Saul broke the oath he had given to them (2 Sam. 21:1–9). At first these appear to be situations where unnecessary revenge was taken out on others.

Agag, however, was put to death as a leader of enemy forces that had been vanquished by Israel and not as some sort of placation of someone's emotions or personal hostilities. Moreover, it was not a vigilante action of a person acting alone; it was done by one in authority in Israel.

Part of the explanation in the case of Saul's seven relatives is found in the phenomenon known as "corporate solidarity." In this case, the *one* (Saul) is seen as the representative of the *many* (his seven relatives). Since their representative leader erred badly, the entire group was under the curse he brought upon them.

Nowhere does the Old Testament approve of any vendetta or revenge of any kind. Persons were not allowed to strike back tit for tat or take an eye for an eye or a tooth for a tooth. The *lex talionis*, or "Law of the Tooth," was nothing more than a stereotypical expression given as a general rule for the "judges" (and not to individuals) in the covenant code of Exodus 21–23. They were to "make the punishment fit the crime" — that is, as we would say today, "bumper for bumper" — without trying, as it often done in our day, to get a trumped-up whiplash payment out of it as well so as to pay off one's tuition for the next year in school.

Conclusion

The men and women we have just read about were involved in matters the biblical text as a whole disapproved of in a most vigorous way. The approval of a certain area of a person's life did not serve as a blanket endorsement of all that a person did. Thus it is important to separate what the Bible reports from what the Bible approves. Only in this fashion are we able to see continuity between the moral and ethical demands of both testaments.

The Unity *of the* Bible *and the* People *of* God

The idea of the "people of God" stands as one of the central messages of the Bible. It is prominently featured as the middle affirmation of the oft-repeated three parts of the tripartite formula for the promise-plan of God: "I will be your God, *you shall be my people*, and I will dwell in the midst of you."[1] This tripartite formula begins in Genesis (17:7) and stretches all the way to the next to the last chapter of the book of Revelation (21:4) in the New Testament. God will adopt a people to be his very own in a very distinctive way.

This formula for the promise-plan of God occurs some fifty times across both testaments. It is one of the most important confessional statements in the entire Bible. It would seem, at first glance, that both Israel in the Old Testament and the believing church in the New Testament are declared to form one continuous body, since the identical term, "people of God," is used of both Israel and the church in both testaments.[2] The term "people

1. D. J. A. Clines, in "The Theme of the Pentateuch," Journal for the Study of the Old Testament Supplement 10 (Sheffield, UK: JSOT, 1978), 29, affirmed that "the promise has three elements: posterity, divine-human relationship, and land. The posterity-element ... is dominant in Genesis 12–50, the relationship-element in Exodus and Leviticus, and the land-element [is dominant] in Numbers and Deuteronomy."
2. A good portion of the ideas used here are those reworked and expanded from my essay "Israel as the People of God," in *The People of God: Essays on the Believers' Church*, ed. Paul Basden and David S.

of God," then, is the continuity term for the unified people of God across both testaments.

But this topic also raises one of the major theological issues in the continuity question between the two testaments: what is the relationship between Israel and the church? Are Israel and the church in any sense part of the same "people of God"? And even if they did share a sense of community or some kind of continuity, how could that be in a partnership since Israel rejected Jesus' claim to be the nation's Messiah? Consequently, would that not mean that Jesus would need to found a new community with the twelve apostles, perhaps mimicking the twelve tribes of Israel, to establish a new "people of God," with Israel being replaced or left out of the picture altogether?

The People of God

The biblical idea of the "people of God" finds its first formal expression in the book of Exodus. Previously in the patriarchal narratives God had revealed himself as "being in the character of" (based on the grammatical use of the *beth essentiae* before the name for God) El Shaddai (i.e., the God of miracle-working power; Ex. 6:3). But now in the exodus and wilderness experience, as the enlarged family of Jacob prepared for nationhood, God would reveal himself "in the character of Yahweh" (the God who would be there, Ex. 6:3).[3]

Already God had announced that he would be a personal deity to Israel (Gen. 17:7). This affirmation was repeated in Exodus 6:3, as God associated the names of Abraham, Isaac, and Jacob with the fact that he was the one who originally appeared to them and announced his name as the great "I am."

From all of this we learn that the idea of the "people of God" is at the heart of biblical faith. Not only did God declare, "I am the LORD," but with five "I wills," he said that he would be the same one who would intervene for them (Ex. 6:6–7). The Lord enumerated these five divine acts:

I will bring you [Israel] out from under the yoke of the Egyptians.
I will free you from being slaves to them, and
I will redeem you with an outstretched arm and with mighty acts....
I will take you as my own people, and
I will be your God.

Dockery (Nashville: Broadman, 1991), 99–108.
3. For an enlarged discussion of the name "Yahweh," see Walter C. Kaiser Jr., "Exodus," in *The Expositor's Bible Commentary*, 13 vols., 2nd ed. (Grand Rapids: Zondervan, 2008), 2:391–94.

Already in Exodus 4:22–23, Israel was declared to be God's "son"; in fact, Israel was his "firstborn son." "Firstborn" in this context could not refer to "first" in chronology or birth order, for "Jacob," "Israel's" old name, was second in the line of birth after Esau. Rather, the term "firstborn" in this context would mean "first in rank," "first in preeminence," and "first in esteem," just as it would later mean in Colossians 1:15 and Revelation 1:5 when the word "firstborn" was used of Jesus as well. The Arians and Jehovah Witnesses got it wrong when they pressed "firstborn" to mean that Jesus was *chronologically* the first to be created in the universe and hence was not eternal. Rather, the claim is that Jesus is first in preeminence, not first in birth order.

To claim Israel as God's "firstborn" fits very nicely with another one of the peoplehood texts found in Exodus 19:5–6. If Israel would obey God, then they would be designated God's "treasured possession." The term used here is the Hebrew word *segullah* (Ex. 19:5), which pointed to Israel as God's "movable treasure" as opposed to real estate that could not be moved around like jewels and other treasures.[4]

Moreover, this uniquely owned people who had preeminence and pride of possession with God were destined to become a "kingdom of priests" and a "holy nation" (Ex. 19:6). It is surprising, however, that these words are not repeated anywhere else in the Old Testament. We do not hear of their announcement until 1 Peter 2:9–10, probably because Israel drew back from the awesomeness of hearing and seeing the evidences of God's powerful presence in the fire and thunder on the mountain, and accordingly they turned down any immediate role as a priesthood of believers. This role would only be delayed, however, not rescinded. The same concept, which would be reinstated among the people of God later in 1 Peter 2:9 and Revelation 1:6; 5:10, would designate those who accept the Savior as "the priesthood of all believers." However, even in Israel's day, the whole congregation was destined originally to be kings and priests to God and a nation set apart to God as "holy." Indeed, Psalm 24:1 would later teach that the whole world belongs to the Lord and everything in it, yet Israel was being invested with a special responsibility in the service of God, which they disrespectfully declined to accept at that time. Thus the concept of the priesthood of all believers was shelved until New Testament times due to Israel's refusal to hear God's word directly from heaven. They complained that it was too awesome!

4. See Kaiser, "Exodus," 2:472–73, and 473n5 on *segullah*. Also see Walter C. Kaiser Jr., *Toward an Old Testament Theology* (Grand Rapids: Zondervan, 1978), 101–11, on the people of promise.

Nevertheless, the idea of Israel's election for divine favor, evidenced by the increase of their numbers, by the covenant God who would walk with them, is again expanded in Leviticus 26:9–13. Once again God promised: "I will put my dwelling place among you ... I will walk among you and be your God, and you will be my people" (vv. 11–12). So, as Goldingay noted, the people of God "is not merely a natural entity. A special act of God creates it.... It is not even that God makes an already existent people his own; he brings a people into being. They only exist as a people because of an act of God."[5]

This relationship between God and his people, whom he has called together, is called a "covenant" (Heb., *berit*). Two different types of divine-human covenants emerge in the Old Testament: the first type is the "covenant of promise" (or what M. Weinfeld called "Covenant of Grant," or a "royal grant," made by a king to a loyal servant),[6] and the second is the "covenant of obligation." There are two outstanding examples of the "covenant of promise" in Genesis: one in 15:7–21 and the other in 17:1–22.

God made a covenant with Abram in Genesis 15 after the patriarch had cut a heifer, a goat, and a ram in half and laid the halves out to form an aisle down the middle (for the word for "make a covenant" is literally "to cut a covenant," Heb. *karat*). Abram fell into a deep sleep accompanied by an awful darkness, and God came to him in a vision. In the aisle set up by Abram, God, by himself, walked between the cut pieces as a "smoking firepot with a blazing torch," thereby taking an oath on himself alone that if he himself did not keep what he was now promising, especially about the *land*, he would become just like the animals he passed between: he would be dead!

In Genesis 17 this covenant of promise was again repeated, only this time the emphasis fell on the *posterity* that was to come (vv. 2, 5, 6, 16, 19, 21). God promised that he would have a personal relationship with Abraham and with his "descendants after [him]" (vv. 7, 8). In both of these examples, it is most important to note that God alone obligated himself, and he did not require that Abraham follow a certain lifestyle if he and his lineage were to enjoy this promise!

Despite the fact that the concept of "the people of God" referred predominantly to the Israelites throughout the Old Testament, it was by no means limited to them alone. In messianic times, "Many nations will be

---

5. J. Goldingay, *Theological Diversity and the Authority of the Old Testament* (Grand Rapids: Eerdmans, 1987), 62.
6. M. Weinfeld, "The Covenant of Grant in the OT and the Ancient Near East," *Journal of the American Oriental Society* 90 (1970): 184–203.

joined with the LORD . . . and will become my people," the Lord taught through the prophet Zechariah (2:11). In like manner, Isaiah had taught that the Lord himself would say, "Blessed be Egypt, my people, Assyria my handiwork, and Israel my inheritance" (Isa. 19:24–25). And was this not what Solomon had prayed for at the dedication of the temple—that "all the peoples of the earth may know your name and fear you, as do your own people Israel" (1 Kings 8:43; cf. Isa. 56:6–8). Thus, even before New Testament times, the concept of the people of God encompassed both believing Israel and believing Gentiles outside that nation.

What had begun as a promise to Abram that God would make him into a "great nation" (Heb., *legoy gadol*) continued to that climactic moment at Mount Sinai during "the day of assembly," when God formally constituted Israel as his people (Ex. 19:5–6; cf. Deut. 9:10; 10:4), a "holy nation" (Heb., *goy qadosh*). But most of all, Israel was God's "people" (Heb. *'am*; Gen. 17:5–6; cf. Deut. 4:27).

Israel is called the "people of God" about ten times. In another three hundred instances, the "people" appear with the pronominal suffix "my" (Heb., *'ammi*). Likewise, Yahweh is also called the "God of Israel."[7] This concept was well on its way to being one of the hallmarks of continuity in the developing collection of books known later as the Old Testament.

Other Old Testament Metaphors for the People of God

The wife of God. Frequently the prophets described the people of God as "God's wife" or "bride" (Isa. 54:5–8; 62:5; Jer. 2:2). This same metaphor carries through to the New Testament where Jesus characterizes himself as the "bridegroom" (Mark 2:18–20) and John regularly reflects on the nature of the church as the "bride of Christ," a figure that carries all the way through until the end of the book of Revelation (21:2, 9; 22:17).

The family of God. Another domestic figure for the people of God is the "family of God." Thus Israel was called Yahweh's "son" (Hos. 11:1). And in Matthew 2:15 that "son" climaxes in Jesus himself. Had anything happened to Israel as they crossed the Red Sea, Christmas and Easter would have been canceled immediately! This familial figure carried through to the church as well, for Jesus described the community of God as the

---

7. H. Bietenhard, "People," in Colin Brown, ed., *The New International Dictionary of New Testament Theology*, 3 vols. (Grand Rapids: Zondervan, 1976), 2:796.

"family of God" (Matt. 12:49–50), just as Paul exhorted Timothy to treat the members of the local church as family (1 Tim. 5:1–2). Other images for this Old Testament family of God are the "flock of God" (Pss. 80:1; 95:7; 100:3; Ezek. 34:15), also found in the New Testament (John 10:1–30; Acts 20:28; Heb. 13:20; 1 Peter 5:2–4), along with the "vineyard of God" (Ps. 80:8–19; Isa. 5:1–7), which is picked up in Mark 12:1–12 and John 15:1–8.

Names of children. Most memorable of all the images are the names that the prophet Hosea gave to his children: his daughter, his second child, was "Lo-Ruhamah" (meaning "no mercy"; Hos. 1:6), and his youngest son was "Lo-Ammi" (meaning "not my people"; v. 9). Peter used those same children's names to make his point of continuity in the New Testament: "Once you were not a people, but now you are the people of God; once you had not received mercy, but now you have received mercy" (1 Peter 2:10).

Some have contended that when the apostle Paul used Hosea 1:10 and 2:23 in Romans 9:24–29, he "replace[d] Israel with the Gentiles,... [for] Paul was a *Replacement* theologian."[8] But in the Hosean context, God had promised to restore the nation of Israel both spiritually and physically. Paul, having noted this, did not eliminate Israel from the action of God, but rather enlarged it by introducing the quotations from Hosea with "What if God ... did this [preparing for destruction] to make the riches of his glory known to the objects of his mercy ... even us, whom he also called, not only from the Jews but also from the Gentiles?" (Rom. 9:22–24). It would be too restrictive for Paul to argue that God had now concluded his patience and work with Israel and was turning completely and solely to the Gentiles. Romans 9:27–29 would be left dangling in the air, for Isaiah cried out in 1:9 and 10:22–23 concerning Israel that there still was a "remnant" of that nation who would believe and not become as Sodom and Gomorrah. In the Isaiah context, the prophet had predicted that "in that day" the survivors of the house of Jacob would rely only on the Lord and not on the one who struck them down. Paul taught that the people of God would include both Jews and Gentiles,[9] which agreed with the ancient word that God gave Abraham in Genesis 12:3.

8. Steve Lehrer, *New Covenant Theology: Questions Answered* (privately published, 2006), 236.
9. Ibid., 235–36, goes on to contrast the original meaning of the Old Testament texts with Paul's understanding in which God's original plan to save a small part of Israel from physical and spiritual destruction was reinterpreted by Paul to mean that the physical part was dropped in favor of a tiny remnant from ethnic Israel who would gain spiritual life while the nation as a whole would be replaced with a new people of God, the church.

A People from the Gentiles

From the few citations we have already shared between the two testaments, we have seen that there is a very real way in which believing Israel shared with the believing church its unique status of peoplehood. However, these believing Gentiles no more ceased being *ethne*, "Gentiles," than the Jewish believers ceased being "Jewish," when they, too, believed. Both, as we will see, were incorporated into one single, continuous body and family called "the church."

Even though the "middle wall of partition" had been broken down in Christ (Eph. 2:14 KJV), this did not mean that it was impossible to determine who was Jewish or who was Gentile, any more than it made it impossible to determine who was male or who was female. The point was that these designations no longer mattered or were areas of contention between the two groups of believers. The fact was that now the Gentiles would be heirs together with Israel. In Greek the equality that the Gentiles now enjoyed as part of the people of God is stressed by the prefix *sun*: "heirs *together* with Israel, members *together of one body*, and sharers *together in the promise* in Christ Jesus" (Eph. 3:6, emphasis added). This whole new discovery was a "mystery," taught Paul, which "was not made known to men in other generations as it now has been revealed" (v. 5). Abbot, in his International Critical Commentary, correctly noted that the "as" meant "not with such clarity as now."[10] This doctrine, then, was not mysterious, or a previous secret, but a revelation not known *to the degree* it was now being announced.

The Jerusalem Council. Nowhere did this issue of Israel and the church reach a higher pitch than at the Jerusalem Council in Acts 15. The dispute between the exclusivistic forces, who wanted people to adhere to circumcision and key features of the Mosaic customs in order to be part of the one family of God, and the inclusivistic defenders, who wanted to make room for the newly converted Gentiles without requiring all the trappings of the Torah, was sharp and acrimonious. At first it seemed as if no one was going to be able to harness this dispute at the Jerusalem Council. Peter, for example, tried to explain how his preparatory vision and his subsequent meeting with Cornelius, a Roman centurion, who on other grounds would have attracted

---

10. As cited by Daniel P. Fuller, *The Unity of the Bible: Unfolding God's Plan for humanity* (Grand Rapids: Zondervan, 1992), 434.

a natural antipathy from any respectable Jewish person, were completely unplanned and altogether new to him. However, when Peter saw that the power of the Holy Spirit fell on that small crowd in Cornelius's Gentile home as it had fallen on the Jewish crowd previously, he changed his mind, for God was surely no respecter of persons, rank, or ethnicity — the Holy Spirit fell on them just as he had fallen on those at Pentecost (Acts 15:8). Barnabas and Paul added what they had witnessed up in Asia Minor among the Gentiles, but the attitudes of those present at this council remained unchanged. Experiential theology was not going to be as convincing as the Word itself was.

Finally, James spoke up and quoted from Amos 9:11 – 12, settling the debate abruptly and conclusively, for Scripture signaled that what they were experiencing in this Jewish-Gentile issue was exactly what had been in the promise-plan of God all along — surprisingly as a part of the Davidic covenant!

What was so dramatic about James's citation of this Amos passage was the teaching it contained about the *extent* of the kingdom of God. That is how James introduced this quotation from Amos 9:11 – 12 in Acts 15:14 – 18 — Gentiles had been part of the promise given not only to Abraham, but also part of the promise given to the house of David.

> Simon [the apostle Peter] has described to us how God at first showed his concern by taking from the Gentiles a people for himself. The words of the [Old Testament] prophets are in agreement with this, as it is written:
>
>> "After this I will return
>>   and rebuild David's fallen tent.
>> Its ruins I will rebuild,
>>   and I will restore it,
>> that the remnant of men may seek the Lord,
>>   and all the Gentiles who bear my name,
>> says the Lord, who does these things"
>>   that have been known for ages.

The house of David. The prophet Amos had clearly argued in the eighth century BC that the reestablishment of the house of David (2 Sam. 7) from its later dilapidated and crumbling status as a "tent," "hut," or "booth" (rather than a "house" or dynasty) would have a real impact on the question of Jews and Gentiles in the one family and house of God. Not only would the ten northern tribes be reunited with the two Israelite southern tribes (note Amos's feminine plural suffix on "its/their broken places"; Heb., *pirtseyhen*, which can only refer to an inferred feminine noun, "kingdom," denoting the northern and southern kingdoms of Israel) and restore the new David, the Messiah, on the throne (note Amos's masculine singular suffix on "its/his ruins"; Heb., *harisotayw*, which has to look to David for an antecedent), but the former house of David, now looking like a collapsing, temporary "booth/shelter" (note the feminine singular suffix on "build it/her" in Amos; Heb. *benitiah*) would be reinstalled in all its former glory. All this will be done by the Lord himself in order that "the remnant of men [might] seek the Lord, [yes even] all the Gentiles who [would] bear [his] name" (Acts 15:17).[11]

When the Lord placed his name over anything, whether cities (2 Sam. 12:28; Jer. 25:29; Dan. 9:18–19), the temple (1 Kings 8:43; Jer. 7:10), or men or women (2 Chron. 7:14; Isa. 4:1; Jer. 14:9), it meant that they were owned by him and were a part of his movable treasure. In this situation, James affirmed that it had been God's design all along to make the Gentiles a part of his holy possession. In fact, as early as the promise made with Abraham in Genesis 12:3, God would bless that patriarch, but it would be for the express purpose that in his seed "all the nations of the earth would be blessed." From the beginning God intended that all the remnant of humanity would share in the spiritual benefits that would be offered through Israel.

No less significant in this whole plan to include the Gentiles as part of the people of God was the Davidic covenant. Second Samuel 7:19 declared that what had been given to David was a "charter for all humanity" (Heb. *wezo'at torat ha'adam*).[12] Thus, when one puts together, even as a minimum, the Abrahamic and Davidic covenants with the predicted word in Amos 9:11–12, it is clear that James was on good theological grounds as he tried to help that conflicted congregation see that what they were experiencing was not a shot out of the blue, but one that was deeply embedded in the plan of God from the start.[13]

James spoke of the saving work of God as he took from the nations/Gentiles a "people" (Gk., *laos*; Heb., *'am*) for himself just as he had promised

> *From the beginning God intended that all the remnant of humanity would share in the spiritual benefits that would be offered through Israel.*

11. For a discussion of the differences in the Hebrew, Greek, and Dead Sea Scroll rendering of the Amos passage, see Walter C. Kaiser Jr., "Including the Gentiles in the Plan of God: Amos 9:9–15," in *The Uses of the Old Testament in the New* (Chicago: Moody, 1985), 177–96, based on an article by the same title that appeared in *The Journal of the Evangelical Theological Society* 20 (1977): 97–111,
12. See Walter C. Kaiser Jr., "The Blessing of David: The Charter for Humanity," in *The Law and the Prophets: Old Testament Studies Prepared in Honor of Oswald Thompson Allis*, ed. John H. Skilton (Nutley, N.J.: Presbyterian and Reformed, 1974), 298–318.
13. See O. Palmer Robertson's extended use of Amos 9:11–15 in his essay "Hermeneutics of Continuity," in *Continuity and Discontinuity: Perspectives on the Relationship between the Old and New Testaments: Essays in Honor of S. Lewis Johnson Jr.*, ed. John S. Feinberg (Westchester, Ill.: Crossway, 1988), 89–108.

in the Abrahamic and Davidic promises. This too was part of raising up the dilapidated tent of David once more.

The Future for Jewish Israel

Did that mean that the fortunes and promises made to Israel were now jettisoned? While some may think that the question for a future Jewish Israel is primarily about the political fortunes of the modern state of Israel, it is instead the following issue above all others: Does God's original covenant with Israel, especially concerning the scope and identity of his "seed," still hold for Israel as well as for the nations? Can the Jewish people legitimately claim, at this present time, any of the promises made to the patriarchs, to David, and to the prophets about themselves and their future, or have some or all of them long since been forfeited and reinvested with other people groups?

It is impossible to talk about the biblical doctrine of salvation without seriously involving the Jewish-Gentile problem at the very center of that doctrine all the way through the biblical canon. All too frequently Romans 9–11 is treated as if it were a parenthesis in the plan and purpose of God, in the middle of Paul's great tractate on soteriology. But that point of view has failed to note that from the very inception of the message of this book, the apostle Paul welded the fortunes of the Jews and Gentiles together, as he announced in Romans 1:16: "I am not ashamed of the gospel, because it is the power of God for the salvation of everyone who believes: first for the Jew, then for the Gentile." From there on Paul interlaced Jew and Gentile all through his argument in Romans (e.g., Rom. 2:9, 10, 17, 28, 29; 3:1, 9, 29; 15:8, 27); thus Romans 9–11 is not a break in his logic or purpose. But what he does do in Romans 9–11 is focus on the concept of Israel as the people of God and how that relates to the Gentiles.

In fact, the whole shape of things for Paul was in many ways very weird and counterintuitive. "How is it," he pondered out loud in Romans 9:30–33:

> That the Gentiles, who did not pursue righteousness, have obtained it, a righteousness that is by faith; but Israel, who pursued a law of righteousness [or made a law out of righteousness], has not attained it. Why not? Because they pursued it not by faith but as if it were by works. They stumbled over the "stumbling stone." As it is written:

"See, I lay in Zion a stone that causes men to stumble
 and a rock that makes them fall,
and the one who trusts in him will never be put to shame."

—(a quote from Isa. 8:14; 28:16)

All of this raises a number of issues. First, if the gospel offer is to the Jew first, then why is it that so few Jewish people are receiving salvation from their sins? Paul said that it was this very fact that caused him great sorrow and unceasing anguish (Rom. 9:2); nevertheless, he was still confident in the effectiveness of the promises of God. Had not God given to Israel "the adoption as sons," the "divine glory," the "covenants," the "Law," "the temple worship," and even the "promises" (9:4)? Where then was the problem? The problem could not have been with God's word (9:6). "God's gifts and his call are irrevocable" (11:29), and his covenant with the patriarchs and with David were unconditional and solely dependent on God. Not once had Abraham been asked to walk between the animal pieces; and never had David been asked to do something in order to get the great promise he had received. Obedience was the expression of their faith. Even if the royal line of David, much less any other Israelite, failed to believe in the coming Messiah, they still had to transmit the promise-plan of God to the next generation whether or not they personally participated in it by faith.

But Paul did not want them (or us) to give up, for there remained "an appointed time" (9:9) when this dilemma would be resolved, just as it was on the day when Isaac was born, which set this plan into action (Rom. 9:6–7).

A second question arose: If God had not as yet fulfilled his promises to Israel, how would the Gentiles come to know and trust him? One must not blame God, however, for the fault was Israel's. Remember that there had always been a Jewish "remnant" who did believe, even if it was not a vast number of the Jewish people (Rom. 9:8–9).

Then a third issue must be examined: Has the offer of the gospel to the Gentiles nullified all God's promises to Israel, and has the nation fallen so badly as never to recover again? (Rom. 11:11). Paul picked up the question he began to raise in Romans 9:30–33 and answered decisively, "Not at all!" (11:11). The reason God permitted Israel to stumble was so that the riches of salvation might be shared with the Gentile world. But the success of the Gentile mission would likewise provoke Israel to jealousy and help them turn back to the Savior once again (Rom. 11:14; cf. Deut. 32:21). Israel was to be cast away only for a time; but their return one day would be all the more spectacular.

Is Israel responsible for their rejection of God? (Rom. 9:30 – 10:21). Of course they are! Israel failed to obtain what the Gentiles received for three reasons. First, Israel did not seek a righteousness from God that comes by faith (9:30 – 10:4). Second, Israel did not put their faith and trust in the Messiah, known as the "Stone," or "Rock" (9:32 – 33). Instead, they tripped over the very Stone that could have been their salvation. Third, they refused to hear the good news of the gospel and rejected it (10:14 – 21), even though this message went throughout the whole world (10:18). Israel was obstinate and disobedient, while many of the Gentiles were just the opposite.

Israel's rejection is not complete (Rom. 11:1 – 10). Paul began this section with a "then" (Gk., *oun*), showing that despite the sad case of Israel's rejection of Christ just rehearsed in Romans 9:30 – 10:21, this was not the end for Israel or the end of the discussion. Was Israel finished as far as the plan of God was concerned? "Absolutely not," answered Paul. Paul used the example of his own former denial of Christ to show that there was indeed hope for Israel, just as there was for him. But how could one man, even if he was a Jew descended from the tribe of Benjamin, solve the problem?

Paul restated the question from chapter 11, verse 1 as an affirmation in verse 2: "God did not reject his people, whom he foreknew." But that only begs the question, who are his people? Are "his people" the nation of Israel in a general sense, the elect within the nation, or someone else? This is a more difficult question, because the whole context is about the status of the nation as a whole (9:30 – 10:21), the ones who are enemies of the gospel at this stage (11:28). However, just as likely is the view that it is a remnant from Israel, because Paul had said that not all Israel is Israel (9:6 – 8). However, in support of the remnant thesis was the example of Elijah and the seven thousand who did not bow their knees to Baal (11:2 – 4) and the contrast between the election of grace and those who were hardened (11:5, 7). So the remnant theme seemed to win out for Paul, Elijah, and the seven thousand from Elijah's day who were like the remnant in Paul's day, who were not hardened like those in Deuteronomy 29:4 and Isaiah 29:10 (Rom. 11:8) and Psalm 69:22 – 23 (LXX 68:23 – 24; Rom. 11:9 – 10).

Israel's rejection is not final (Rom. 11:11 – 15). Is Israel's stumbling so severe that it is beyond any hope of recovery (v. 11)? Again, Paul is adamant, "Absolutely not!" (Gk., *me genoito*). God will use Israel's rejection as an opportunity for the "fullness" of salvation to come to the Gentiles (v. 12;

Gk., *pleroma*), eventually to make the Jewish people "envious" of what was originally theirs (v. 14).

Israel's rejection will open the opportunity for the reconciliation of the world and their acceptance of the Messiah. It will also mean "life from the dead" (v. 15). Rather than taking this to mean a general resurrection in the end-times when Christ returns to bring in the messianic age (*zon ek nekron* [v. 15] is never used as being equal to *anastasis ton vekron* [Rom. 1:4; 1 Cor. 15:12–13, 21, 42], which does refer to the end-time resurrection), it refers to the great blessing God will bring to the whole world just as texts such as Psalm 67:1–2 promised.

The Theology of the Olive Tree

Few illustrations are as decisive as the olive tree figure in Romans 11:16–24 in demonstrating that there is a unity to the people of God while both Israel and the church retain their identities. The connecting "for" in verse 21 provides us with the reason for believing in a future national restoration of the nation Israel.

The sap of the olive roots is to be found in the covenantal promise made to the forefathers Abraham, Isaac, and Jacob. This nation had been set aside and consecrated to God. The principle, based on Numbers 15:17–21, is that the holiness, or consecration, of the firstfruits and the root is passed on to the branches, which in this case are the Israelites. Accordingly, just as the offering of the firstfruits consecrates the whole harvest, so the Abrahamic covenant consecrated Israel and anticipated a harvest that would come some day.

Amazingly, the natural branches were lopped off and the wild olive branches of the Gentiles were grafted in (even though in the real realm of botany, cultivated branches are grafted on to a wild stump, which Paul said he realized but deliberately changed for the purposes of his illustration). But out of this unnatural illustration God would bring blessing to both the Jewish people and to the Gentiles.

Gentiles would become partakers with the Jewish people in the blessing of Abraham and David (Eph. 3:1–6, 11–16). But Gentiles would have to beware lest they think they had earned their salvation or somehow merited their place in the tree or program of God. They would have to resist vaunting themselves over the Jewish people, for if it were not for the roots in the patriarchal promise, the Davidic covenant, and the trunk of the tree Israel,

Just as the offering of the firstfruits consecrates the whole harvest, so the Abrahamic covenant consecrated Israel and anticipated a harvest that would come some day.

the church would have no rootage, no grounding, no anchoring or any source of its being; it would merely float in the air with no beginnings and no previous unifying factors or linkage to the past or future.

Paul pressed the argument for Israel's eventual restoration in Romans 11:23–26. God is able to finish his work, and he will graft back into the olive tree the natural branches of believing Israel once again. This partial hardness of Israel would continue, but only "until the full number of the Gentiles has come in" (11:25). The "mystery" of verse 25 was not that the salvation of the Gentiles or Israel had not been revealed in the Old Testament; rather, it was that the partial and temporary hardness of Israel would last only until the "full number" of the Gentile conversions had been reached.

The "covenant" mentioned in verse 27 is none other than the "new covenant" spoken of in Jeremiah 31:31–34 and some sixteen other places in the Old Testament under other names.[14]

While the wild engrafted branches could well be Gentile Christians, the parallel in the passage may be Gentile Christendom, though the text does not mention Christendom itself. More to the point, however, is the fact that if the cultivated branches were cut off because of unbelief, we may presume a regrafting in of the original branches when faith is present in those natural branches again.

The temporariness of Israel's "hardness" is to be "until that time when" (Gk., *archi hou*) the fullness of the Gentiles should be completed. Even though the term "fullness" is difficult and usually refers to a qualitative sense, here it seems best to take it in a quantitative sense since Paul has already spoken of a "fullness" in verse 12 (Gk., *pleroma*).

Israel's future restoration is spoken of in 11:26–27. It is introduced with "And so," (Gk., *hotos*). This expression in Greek is never rendered temporally, meaning "And then" (or as if it meant "after this"); rather, it is best rendered as "In this way." But what is the antecedent in that case? And why was there a change in the Greek tenses from the perfect and aorist in verse 25 to the future in verse 26? The antecedent appears to be the logical consequence of Israel's hardening until the fullness of the Gentiles comes in. Although the expression "And so" is not temporally understood, the context is temporally conditioned because it happens after the fullness of the Gentiles takes place. Nestle's edition of the Greek text on Romans 11:25 points to Luke 21:24, which says that "Jerusalem will be trampled on by

---

14. Walter C. Kaiser Jr., "The Old Promise and the New Covenant: Jeremiah 31:31–34," *Journal of the Evangelical Theological Society* 15 (1972): 11–23, reprinted in *The Bible in Its Literary Milieu,* ed. John Maier and Vincent Tollers (Grand Rapids: Eerdmans, 1979): 106–20.

the Gentiles until the times of the Gentiles are fulfilled." In like manner, we could render Romans 11:25, "a hardening has come upon part of Israel, until the fullness of the times of the Gentiles has come."[15]

Conclusion

The biblical writers could not have put the thesis that there is only one people of God any clearer than they have. To be sure, there still are distinguishing aspects of diversity, such as male, female, slave, free, Jew, Gentile, and the like. But the fact that there is one olive tree—notice, not one "vine," but one olive tree (also the ubiquitous symbol of Athens and the Gentile world)—should help us to sense the unitary features of the assorted groups of believers throughout the Scriptures.

The contemporary doctrine of the church must be anchored in the unity and singularity of the people of God of all ages. The gifts and calling that this people of God have are from God. Therefore, all attempts to isolate Israel from the church in every sense runs counter to the direct challenge of Scripture. On the other hand, all reports of Israel's death and demise as the people of God in every sense are, as Mark Twain quipped in another connection, certainly premature—and I might add, nonbiblical!

15. For this idea, see Hendrikus Berkhof, *Christ the Meaning of History* (Richmond: John Knox, 1962), 144.

The Unity *of the* Bible *and Its* Program

The Kingdom of God

> "The kingdom of this world has become the kingdom of our Lord and of his Christ, and he will reign for ever and ever."
>
> —Revelation 11:15

Two major lines of expectation filled the Old Testament: the hope that the Messiah would come and that there would be a "day of the Lord," in which the Messiah would rule triumphantly over a restored Israel, indeed, over all the earth. The ultimate purpose for Messiah's coming in the day of the Lord would be to establish the kingdom of God finally and completely on earth as it is in heaven as the initial part of the eternal state. Indeed, the announcement of the inauguration of that kingdom is how the gospel of Mark began with Jesus proclaiming, "The time has come. The kingdom of God is near. Repent and believe the good news!" (Mark 1:14–15).

But what was this kingdom of God?[1] John Bright called this to our attention:

> But for all his repeated mention of the kingdom of God, Jesus never once paused to define it. Nor did any hearer ever interrupt him to ask, "Master; what do these words, 'kingdom of God,' which you use so often, mean?" On

---

1. For many aspects of this chapter, I return to a chapter I wrote some years ago, "Kingdom Promises as Spiritual and National," in *Continuity and Discontinuity: Perspectives on the Relationship between the Old and New Testaments*, ed. John S. Feinberg (Westchester, Ill.: Crossway, 1988), 289–307.

the contrary, Jesus used the term as if assured it would be understood, and indeed it was. The kingdom of God lay within the vocabulary of every Jew. It was something they understood and longed for desperately.[2]

But what makes this all the more startling is that if we therefore assume there are a large number of references to the kingdom of God in the Old Testament, making the linguistic phenomena our sole guide, we find that is not so. The fact is that the expression "kingdom of God" does not appear even once. True, there are nine references to the kingdom over which Yahweh rules,[3] and some forty references to Yahweh as "King,"[4] but that is the sum of the matter. When we come to the New Testament, however, the frequency of the use of this term rises immediately. According to R. T. France's count,[5] there are some sixty instances in the teaching of Jesus (not counting the parallel passages) in the Synoptic Gospels, where this phrase of the kingdom of God points to the heart of his mission. Following the three gospels, the frequent use of this term surprisingly drops off once again as the book of Acts uses "kingdom" and "kingdom of God" only eight times.[6] The same conservative usage of kingdom terms continues from Romans through Jude, with a mere eighteen instances and only four more uses of the cognate verb "to reign" and two uses of the word "king."

Nevertheless, it would be wrong to conclude that the concept of the kingdom of God was quiescent and a rather minor theme in the Bible. We must respect Jesus' own summary of the burden of his mission. In like manner the apostles

- "preached the good news of the kingdom of God and the name of Jesus Christ" (Acts 8:12)
- "argu[ed] persuasively about the kingdom of God" (Acts 19:8)
- "testif[ied] to the *gospel* of God's grace.... [Paul declared] I have gone about preaching the *kingdom*.... For I have not hesitated to proclaim to you the *whole will of God*" (Acts 20:24–27; emphasis added; note "gospel" is paralleled by "the kingdom" and "the whole will of God")

---

2. John Bright, *The Kingdom of God: The Biblical Concept and Its Meaning for the Church* (Nashville: Abingdon, 1953), 17–18.
3. Three Hebrew terms are used for "kingdom": *malkut*, in Pss. 103:19; 145:11–13; Dan. 4:3, 34; *melukah*, in Obad. 21; Ps. 22:28; and *mamlakah*, in 1 Chron. 29:11.
4. Some of these references include Ex. 15:18; 1 Sam. 12:12; Pss. 145:11–13; 146:10; Isa. 6:5.
5. R. T. France, "The Church and the Kingdom of God: Some Hermeneutical Issues," *Biblical Interpretation and the Church: The Problem of Contextualization*, ed. D. A. Carson (Nashville: Thomas Nelson, 1985), 34.
6. This is all the more surprising since Luke uses the terms some thirty-three times in his gospel.

- "explained and declared to them the kingdom of God and tried to convince them about Jesus from the Law of Moses and from the Prophets" (Acts 28:23)
- "Boldly and without hindrance ... preached the kingdom of God and taught about the Lord Jesus Christ" (Acts 28:31)

The Kingdom in the Promise-Plan of God

Where, how, and under what circumstances, then, did the concept of the kingdom of God begin in the Bible? The answer is that the kingdom of God, as with many other doctrines, has a strong connection with the promise-plan of God. As Willis J. Beecher observed: "The most prominent [concept] in the New Testament is the proclamation of the kingdom and its anointed king. But it is on the basis of the divine promise that its preachers proclaim the kingdom, and when they appeal to the Old Testament in proof of Christian doctrine, they make the promise more prominent than the kingdom itself."[7]

This doctrine of the kingdom of God became quite well established with the promise made to King David that his kingdom would have a central place in the whole promise-plan of God. Thereafter the prophets picked up that theme and highlighted the promise of a personal king who would one day reign over Zion as sovereign over all the nations of the earth, both in the here and now, and especially in the day of the Lord that was to come.

Prelude to the King and Kingdom in the Prepatriarchal Era

Prior to the word given to the patriarchs, Yahweh was described as Creator and Maker of all that is. He it was who established all order in the world. At the apex of his work in creation he made the man and the woman in his own image (Gen. 1:26–27), and he turned over to them the task of ruling and subduing all that was on the earth. It was as if the Sovereign king turned over to vassal kings the stewardship of all that he had made on the earth. A faint hint of what was to come to the aid of fallen Adam and Eve was described in the prophecy of the "Seed" of the woman in Genesis 3:15 (NIV "offspring"). Nevertheless, humankind was not satisfied with this

---

7. Willis J. Beecher, *The Prophets and the Promise* (1905; repr., Grand Rapids: Baker, 1975), 178–79.

dominion over all that God had made; they wanted to raise up a "name," or "reputation," for themselves on two separate occasions (Gen. 6:4; 11:4). Both the autocratic movements of the presumptive kings, who saw themselves as "sons of the gods," and later as the tower builders, who feared global dispersion, were rejected by God for their selfish instincts. Their way was not to be the divine way. God would yet appoint his person and family and give them that very "name" all humanity had sought apart from his help or gifts.

The Origin of the King and the Kingdom Concept in the Patriarchal Era

And so God called a man named Abram from Ur in Mesopotamia and gave to him that great "name" that others had sought apart from the sovereign will of God (Gen. 12:2). Additionally, the promise of the "Seed" was repeated to this man and his lineage. But even more important, "kings" were promised from the line of Abraham, Sarah, and Jacob (Gen. 17:6, 16; 35:11).

Jacob's fourth son, Judah (not the eldest son, Reuben, or his second- and third-born sons, Simeon and Levi), was blessed by Jacob to be the princely tribe and leader of his people. To Judah was given the "scepter" and the "ruler's staff" of governing, which that tribe would hold as its own "until Shiloh comes" (Gen. 49:10 NASB). This enigmatic phrase has an enlarged explanation in Ezekiel 21:27, which reads, "until *he* comes *to whom it rightfully belongs*" (emphasis added to show words parallel to "Shiloh"). There would come in the Seed of Eve, Abraham, Isaac, Jacob, and later David, a Man of Promise who would be overwhelmingly successful. This coming king would rule and reign over all the peoples of the earth because it would be his right and destiny to do so.

The Concept of a King and the Kingdom in the Monarchical Era

The quest for having a king in Israel became a burning issue as the days of Samuel's judgeship began to come to an end. Samuel appointed his sons as judges in Israel, but his sons Joel and Abijah "did not walk in [Samuel's] ways. They turned aside after dishonest gain and accepted bribes and perverted justice" (1 Sam. 8:1–3). As a consequence, the elders came to Samuel and complained that his sons were no match for the job of leadership in

Israel; instead, the people demanded "a king to lead [them]" (v. 5). Samuel was deeply troubled by this rejection of himself and his own children. But the Lord interpreted it as a rejection of the Lord God himself as king over them (v. 7). The people's rationale was that they wanted to have a king over them so they could be just like the other nations (v. 5). So that is how the people got King Saul as their first king.

Prior to this, even Gideon had the good sense not to accept an earlier request to be a king over the people after his victory over the Midianites. Gideon replied: "I will not rule over you, nor will my son rule over you. The LORD will rule over you" (Judg. 8:22–23). Gideon's son Abimelech (born of Gideon's concubine), which means "My father [was/could have been][8] a king," was not as wise, for he assumed the kingship over Shechem and its environs only to be summarily killed by a woman (Judg. 9).

Yet, could it not be said that God had promised a king once they were settled in the land, just as Moses had described it in Deuteronomy 17:14–15? Yes, but a usurping ruler, such as Abimelech, was another false start and not what God had planned. To add to this bad experience, as it were, Israel now demanded a king to give them prestige among the nations.

God gave them King Saul, but that did not work out. He who began well did not end up well at all. So when Saul was rejected, God looked for "a man after his own heart" (1 Sam. 13:14), and David, the son of Jesse, was selected; at first anointed by the prophet Samuel (1 Sam. 16:13), then as king of Judah (2 Sam. 2:4), and finally as ruler over all Israel (2 Sam. 5:3).

In the Davidic promise in 2 Samuel 7, God promised to "establish [David's] kingdom" and "the throne of his kingdom forever" (2 Sam. 7:12–13, 16). Two psalms took up this theme and enlarged on it: Psalm 89:36 ("his line will continue forever and his throne [will] endure before me like the sun") and Psalm 72:8, the second of which described the extent of his kingdom in global terms ("[The king] will rule from sea to sea and from the River to the ends of the earth"). In fact, "All kings will bow down to him and all nations will serve him" (72:11), because "all nations will be blessed through him" (an obvious allusion to Gen. 12:3 in Ps. 72:17). David's throne, kingdom, and dynasty were nothing less than Yahweh's throne and kingdom, yet the end of the lineage of the Davidic line would be no one less than Messiah himself. That is why Psalm 45:6 could affirm: "Your throne, O God, will last for ever and ever; a scepter of justice will be the scepter of your kingdom."

8. Martin Buber, *Kingship of God*, 3rd rev. ed., trans. Richard Sheimann (New York: Harper & Row, 1967), 74, noticed that "to appoint a name" is never used in connection with giving a child a name at birth; rather, it implies that Gideon either gave his son a new name at the occasion of his victory over Midian or that this son of Gideon's maidservant "appointed himself" this name.

This future king would be no less than God's "Anointed One" (Ps. 2:2), Yahweh's "Son" (v. 7), and Yahweh's "King" (v. 6). The nations of the earth could plot and rage all they wanted to, but such a puny effort would not affect the outcome of God's success in the least. The Old Testament prophets saw "no end … of the increase of his government and peace" (Isa. 9:7).

The prophet Daniel described the "Anointed One" (Dan. 9:26) also as a "rock," not cut out of the mountain by human hands (2:34), and as "one like a son of man" (7:13). That Rock would come: "In the time of those kings [of Babylon, Medo-Persia, Greco-Macedonia, and Rome], the God of heaven will set up a kingdom that will never be destroyed, nor will it be left to another people. It will crush all those kingdoms and bring them to an end, but it will itself endure forever" (2:44).

To this same "son of man" was given by the Ancient of Days "authority, glory and sovereign power; all peoples, nations and men of every language worshiped him. His dominion is an everlasting dominion that will not pass away, and his kingdom is one that will never be destroyed" (Dan. 7:14).

All of this led believers to expect a future theophany when this Anointed One would come to receive from the Father, the Ancient of Days, the final manifestation of that kingdom in "that day" (beginning at Ex. 32:34, "when the time comes"). Discussion of this coming "day" was always an impending event that was forever "near." Five prophets in four different centuries declared that that day was "near" and about to happen (in the ninth century, Joel 1:15; 2:1; 3:14; and Obad. 15; in the eighth century, Isa. 12:6; in the seventh century, Zeph. 1:7, 14; and in the sixth century, Ezek. 30:3). Surely "that day" would usher in the victorious kingdom and universal reign and rule of Yahweh (Isa. 2:2; Mic. 4:1; Ezek. 38:8, 16).

But there was also a spiritual side to this kingdom. The Holy Spirit would be poured out on high (Isa. 32:15; Joel 2:28–29) and the Torah of God would be written on the hearts of believers (Jer. 31:33). Non-Jews would not be left out, for even though the Davidic dynasty (the promised Davidic "house," which was now faltering as a "dilapidated tent"; Amos 9:11) would surely go through a period of dormancy, nevertheless, God would once again raise it up to include "all the nations [or Gentiles] that bear my name" (Amos 9:12).

This national and spiritual kingdom, then, was the kingdom our Lord came preaching about (Mark 1:14–15). This was also the same kingdom the apostle Paul proclaimed and associated with the "gospel of God's grace" and with "the whole will [plan, counsel] of God" (Acts 20:24–27).

The Spiritual and Material Aspects of the Kingdom

So at what points does the controversy erupt when the topic of the kingdom of God is discussed (for that seems to have been the history of the idea in modern times)? Erich Sauer, some years ago noted that there were three areas of sharp dispute: (1) the extent to which the kingdom was enlarged and what it included, (2) the form God's rule would take, and (3) the time when God's kingdom would commence. These can be laid out more in detail as follows.

1. As to the degree of extension, we ask: what persons, nations, or land(s) are included in this concept of the kingdom of God?
2. As to its form, we ask: is the kingdom of God inward and spiritual? Or is it visible, material, historical, political, external? Or is it both at the same time?
3. As to its time, we ask: did the kingdom of God commence with Jesus' life and ministry here on earth, or did it begin with the ascension into heaven, or is it only to begin at a future parousia, epiphany, theophany of the returning Lord Jesus in connection with the days of his second advent?[9]

The most delicate of all theological moves is the one that attempts to integrate the eternal or universal kingdom ("his kingdom rules over all," Ps. 103:19) with what others are pleased to call his mediatorial or theocratic kingdom. Furthermore, the old dispensational distinction forced between the "kingdom of heaven," supposedly God's earthly kingdom, and the "kingdom of God," again allegedly the eternal spiritual kingdom of God, has long since been relinquished by almost all of the dispensationalists themselves. Both terms refer to the eternal kingdom (cf. Matt. 6:33 with 18:3–6; 7:21 and 19:14 with Mark 10:14). Both terms also refer to the present form of the kingdom (Matt. 13:11; Mark 4:11; Luke 8:10).[10]

At this point some critical hermeneutical principles come into play. For those who see only a mediatorial kingdom that is in line with salvation history that focuses on Christ and his redemption exclusively, three principles of interpretation are key: (1) a clear priority must be given to New Testament interpretations over the interpretation of the Old Testament; (2)

9. Erich Sauer, *From Eternity to Eternity* (Grand Rapids: Eerdmans, 1954), 185–86.
10. J. Dwight Pentecost, *Things to Come: A Study of Biblical Eschatology* (Grand Rapids: Zondervan, 1964), 433–34.

a priority must be given to spiritual illumination in the interpretive process over so-called scientific exegesis; and (3) Christ's prevailing over the forces of evil must come in the mediatorial mission of the church rather than in the days of a restored Israel or after the church has been "raptured" and removed from this earth.[11]

Over against these three suggested interpretive keys there are not two logics in the Bible: one in the Old Testament and another in the New. Nor should the classical rule *sacra scriptura sui ipsius interpres*, that is, "Sacred Scripture interprets itself" be made into a rule that says all later Scripture knows better than earlier texts on all subjects.[12] Nor can this rule be turned from saying that in the progress of doctrine, Scripture often enlarges on a topic it has raised in an earlier and more elementary way (as it often does) to say that the later Scriptures in the New Testament reinterpret the Old Testament sayings to give them a deeper or more spiritual or messianic meaning. But one should not go from the principle of the progress of revelation to say that the New Testament *reinterprets* the Old. It would not be helpful to cite texts like Matthew 11:25–27[13] or 16:17[14] to say that the same supernatural enlightenment that was given to those in Jesus' day to recognize the evidences for his divinity and Sonship were the same or equal to the gifts that are given to those of us who interpret God's Word. The veil that was over the minds of some in that former day was there because of unbelief (2 Cor. 3:15), not because the times have changed and now things that previously were not evident to any interpreter may yield new truths that were hidden or encoded in the text.

If that is so, why were the apostles still asking when our Lord would restore the national kingdom to Israel just prior to Pentecost (Acts 1:6)? Bruce Waltke says it was because they were guided by their own ignorance and therefore asked the wrong question.[15] He thinks that Jesus declined to correct their false assumption, just as he declined to straighten out the early church who assumed the apostle John would not die because of what Jesus had said in John 21:22–23 ("If I want him to remain alive until I return, what is that to you?"). Our Lord, of course, did not say John would not die;

---

11. Waltke, "Kingdom Promises as Spiritual," 264–66; 272–76.
12. See Walter C. Kaiser Jr. and Moisés Silva, *Introduction to Biblical Hermeneutics: The Search for Meaning*, 2nd ed. (Grand Rapids: Zondervan, 2007), 71–72; 246–49.
13. Matthew 11:25–27: "At that time Jesus said, 'I praise you, Father, Lord of heaven and earth, because you have hidden these things from the wise and learned, and revealed them to little children. Yes, Father, for this was your good pleasure.... No one knows the Father except the Son and those to whom the Son chooses to reveal him.'"
14. Matthew 16:17: "Jesus replied, 'Blessed are you, Simon son of Jonah, for this was not revealed to you by man, but by my Father in heaven.'"
15. Waltke, "Kingdom Promises as Spiritual," 273.

but then neither can Jesus' statement be maneuvered to say that his silence meant he disapproved of their question.

Today, mercifully, the old cleavage between amillennialism and premillennialism has narrowed considerably. At least two matters have helped this new relationship: (1) both sides now appeal to an "inaugurated eschatology" for the kingdom of God with its "already – not yet" hermeneutic, and (2) a fairly common understanding about the kingdom of God exists that allows for both a present realization in the life of the church as well as a future fulfillment of the kingdom of God in Israel, in real space and time. To be sure, the description of what that future entails is still under different assessments between these two positions. More recently an amillennialist tends to identify that future with the *new cosmos* while the historic premillennialist, or the progressive dispensationalist, will link that future with a restored Israel back in their land and a coming millennium.

The Future Earthly Kingdom and Israel

However, despite such great strides in many areas of agreement between these two schools, a large number of Christian interpreters claim that the fulfillment of the promise-plan of God does not include Israel as a race, for the blessing originally given to Israel, they conclude, has been lost through their disobedience and is now given instead to the Christian church. But as Willis J. Beecher said so boldly:

> But if the Christian interpreter persists in excluding the ethnical [sic] Israel from his conception of the fulfillment, or in regarding Israel's part in the matter as merely preparatory and not eternal [as the promise-plan has reiterated to the contrary so frequently], then he comes into conflict with the plain witness of both testaments. His interpretation is even less consistent with the text than is the exclusive Jewish conception. Rightly interpreted, the biblical statements include in the fulfillment both Israel the race, with whom the covenant is eternal, and also the personal Christ and his mission, with the whole spiritual Israel of the redeemed in all ages [and of all races].[16]

To be sure, our Lord anticipated Israel's disobedience and blindness. That was seen in his weeping over the city of Jerusalem as he said, "Look,

---

16. Beecher, *Prophets and the Promise*, 383.

your house is left desolate. For I tell you, you will not see me again until you say, "Blessed is he who comes in the name of the Lord" (Matt. 23:38–39).

Israel's house has remained desolate for some time, for "Jerusalem will be trampled on by the Gentiles until the times of the Gentiles are fulfilled" (Luke 21:24). But some future Israelites apparently would see the Lord once again. Of course the emphasis falls on Jerusalem's expected judgment, but what is taken matter-of-factly is that Jerusalem and Israel will still be in the picture once the "times of the Gentiles" are over.

That conclusion would accord with what the apostle Paul declared in Romans 11:12 about waiting until the time of the full inclusion of the Gentiles was over. Paul was straightforward about the fact that the promises made to ancient Israel had not failed, nor would they (Rom. 9:4–5). But we are even more startled by the fact that Israel's transgression would mean "riches for the world" (Rom. 11:12). The Gentile church should not be ignorant of this "mystery" (Rom. 11:25–26), lest it becomes conceited about its new position of preeminence.[17]

The Present Realm of God's Kingdom

One of the aspects of "mystery" connected with the formation of the church was that "many will come from the east and the west, and will take their places at the feast with Abraham, Isaac, and Jacob in the kingdom of heaven. But the subjects of the kingdom will be thrown outside, into the darkness, where there will be weeping and gnashing of teeth" (Matt. 8:11–12). And Jesus said in Matthew 21:43, "Therefore I tell you that the kingdom of God will be taken away from you and given to a people who will produce its fruit."

This mystery is unveiled more explicitly in Ephesians 3:1–13 (cf. Rom. 15:15–21). It is simply this: the Gentiles are to be heirs together with Israel, as emphasized by the repetition of the Greek prefix *sun*, "together," three times. They are to be "heirs together," "members together," and "sharers together" in the promise of God. This truth was not something that was a "mystery" or "mysterious" without any previous hints along these same lines, but it was a teaching that had not yet been revealed to the degree it now was announced.

---

17. For more detail, see Walter C. Kaiser Jr., "Jewish Evangelism in the New Millennium in Light of Israel's Future (Romans 9–11)," in *To the Jews First: The Case for Jewish Evangelism in Scripture and History*, ed. Darrell L. Bock and Mitch Glaser (Grand Rapids: Kregel, 2008), 40–52.

The Gentiles will have equal status with Israel in that future kingdom as Isaiah 56:6–8;[18] and 66:18–21[19] taught. Thus the Gentiles were called to a shared "inheritance" (Gal. 3:18), a shared "life" (Gal. 3:21; Rom. 4:17), and shared promise of the "Holy Spirit" (Gal. 3:14; Eph. 1:13) in the body of Christ, his church.

David's Throne, the Throne of God, and the Kingdom of God

John Walvoord asserted many years ago, "A search of the New Testament reveals that there is not one reference connecting the present session of Christ with the Davidic throne."[20] This was a failed attempt to separate David's occupancy of the throne from Christ's session at the Father's right hand, in order to maintain the *artificial distinction* that Israel must always be kept separate from the church.

As Darrell Bock showed, however, "Luke consistently associates the kingdom [pledged to King David] with Jesus' life and ministry."[21] God had promised to Mary that he would give to her child the throne of David, who would rule over the house of Jacob forever (Luke 1:32–33). Both Mary and Zechariah's hymns include spiritual, as well as national-political, aspects of the kingdom (Luke 1:51–55, 69–75, 78–79).

Moreover, the Greek perfect tense of the verb *engiken* in Luke 10:9 is better translated "to arrive," rather than "to approach," or "to draw near." Thus the timing of the arrival of the kingdom of God begins with Jesus' ministry and message, as well as that of the Seventy who were sent out. This timing for the inception of the kingdom is borne out in Luke 11:20, where the driving out of demons by Jesus is another signal that the kingdom "has come upon you" (NASB). The repetition of the spatial-temporal Greek preposition *epi*, "upon" (Luke 10:9; 11:20), along with the Greek aorist verb *ephthasen*, "to arrive," makes it clear that the kingdom is more than "near;" it has arrived—at least in its inception!

---

18. Isaiah 56:6–8: "'And foreigners who bind themselves to the LORD / to serve him, / to love the name of the LORD, / and to worship him, / all who keep the Sabbath without desecrating it, / and who hold fast to my covenant—/ these I will bring to my holy mountain / and give them joy in my house of prayer. / Their burnt offerings and sacrifices / will be accepted on my altar; / for my house will be called / a house of prayer for all nations.'
    "The Sovereign LORD declares—/ he who gathers the exiles of Israel: / 'I will gather still others to them / besides those already gathered.'"
19. Isaiah 66:18: "And I ... am about to come and gather all nations and tongues, and they will come and see my glory."
20. John Walvoord, "The Fulfillment of the Davidic Covenant," *Bibliotheca Sacra* 102 (1945): 163.
21. In what follows, I am beholden to Darrell L. Bock, "The Reign of the Lord Jesus," in *Dispensationalism, Israel and the Church*, ed. Craig Blaising and Darrell L. Bock (Grand Rapids: Zondervan, 1992), 38.

In the parable of the ten minas (in Luke 19:12), the nobleman, who probably portrays Jesus, went into a distant country "to receive a kingdom" (*labein heauto basileian*). His own countrymen, the Jewish people, did not want him to rule over them (v. 14). Nevertheless, the nobleman (Jesus) returned, "having received the kingdom" (*labonta ten basileian*). Notice that Jesus received this kingdom before he returned again! Bock is on the mark in these observations.

But all of this only intensifies the tension already in this topic of the kingdom: is the kingdom present or is the kingdom still to come? Luke answers that question in Acts 1:3–8. In the period of the forty days between Jesus' resurrection and his ascension, he "spoke about the kingdom of God" to eleven men (v. 3). In this context Luke does not say directly that he is speaking about a different form of the kingdom, but it is the apostles' question that tips us off that the topic of the kingdom has moved beyond where it had been in Luke's gospel. They were to wait for "the gift my Father promised" (v. 4). The apostles asked, "Lord, are you at this time going to restore the kingdom to Israel?" (v. 6). Jesus did not answer their question directly. That is why so many have taken his silence to mean that he repudiated and rejected their question and regarded it, according to that way of interpreting this text, as a sign of ignorance that was not worth answering. But this is not all that certain; for after all, the topic of discussion had been the "kingdom" during those forty days. Instead, Jesus promised his return in verse 11, which return is made a specific part of Peter's preaching in Acts 2–3.

The crucial link that further answers our question comes in Peter's clear statement in Acts 2:30, where God would make sure one of David's descendants would *kathisai* ("to sit") on his throne. Peter's allusion in that verse is to Psalm 132:11, argued Bock with clear insight, where that psalm directly reflects the promise that had been made to David in 2 Samuel 7—a psalm that was very nationalistic in tone. Peter linked the Davidic promise to Psalm 16, which was David's prediction of the resurrection of the Messiah. Accordingly, in Peter's preaching in Acts 2:31–35 being on David's throne is connected with being seated (*kathou*) at God's right hand.

Therefore, the counterclaim that David's throne is never connected with Jesus being seated at the Father's right hand can now be revised. Thus, whereas the Davidic throne in the infancy materials of the Gospels was viewed largely in an earthly, political connection, as it was for the most part in the Old Testament (2 Sam. 7; and Luke 1:46–55, 70–73), the rest of the gospel of Luke stresses that the kingdom of God had already arrived in the life and ministry of Jesus and the apostles.

The resulting picture of the kingdom is one in which there is a "now-already" aspect to the kingdom's appearance, as well as a "not yet" future part to that same kingdom. This should not surprise us, observed Bock, for that is how it is with our salvation: "I am saved/justified [already]" — but I am not yet saved/glorified." Bock went on to summarize the present situation: "But both the 'already' and the 'not yet' need careful defining, for covenant theologians of the past have tended to *over*emphasize the 'already' in their critiques of Dispensationalism, while *under*emphasizing the 'not yet.' Dispensationalists have tended to *under*emphasize the 'already,' minimizing what is presently fulfilled in God's program in an attempt to maintain distinctions [and put their stress on the 'not yet']."[22] Thus, while the King is not yet visible in his kingdom, the kingdom nevertheless has begun and is effectively and powerfully operating through Christ's disciples and his church.

Recall again the disciples' question in Acts 1:6, "Lord, are you at this time going to restore (*apokathistaneis*) the kingdom to Israel?" Here is another verbal linkage between this question from that forty-day seminar that Jesus gave his apostles and Peter's preaching in Acts 3:19, where it is said that Jesus must "remain in heaven until times of refreshing (*chronon apokatastaseos*) come from God, as he promised long ago through his holy prophets [Moses]" (v. 21, my translation). This speech of Peter's ends with three key references to the Torah, including Deuteronomy 18:15; Leviticus 23:29; and Genesis 12:3; 22:18; 26:4. Thus, for the sake of his Jewish audience, he makes a case for Jesus as the Messiah from the Torah itself. The word that the apostles used for the *time* for God to "restore" the kingdom of Israel, which Peter now repeats, is a technical term for God's political restoration of Israel (Ps. 16:5; Jer. 15:19; 16:15; 23:8; 24:6; Ezek. 16:55; 17:23; Hos. 11:11).[23] So, what the Torah and the Prophets promised Israel still remained in God's plan. These "times of restoration" of Acts 3:19 (my translation) would come when Jesus returned again. Bock goes on to distinguish between Jesus' reference to *chronous*, "times," and *kairoi*, "seasons." The "times" of "restoration" are connected with Jesus' return; the "seasons" of "refreshing" involve the current period included in the last days, in which sins are being wiped away as mortals repent and Jesus is still in heaven.

Five texts in the book of Revelation also make the same point as Luke has traced for us here. In Revelation 1:5–6 Jesus is called "the ruler of the

22. Ibid., 46 (emphasis added).
23. Ibid., 56. Cited from J. Carroll, *Response to the End of History: Eschatology and Situation in Luke-Acts* (Atlanta: Scholars, 1989), 146n124.

kings of the earth," which is an allusion to Psalm 89:27, a psalm about David's kingship and promise doctrine. Likewise, Revelation 1:9 emphasizes the same point.

Another text is Revelation 2:26–27, which speaks of the power of the disciples that comes from the Father and therefore recalls Psalm 2:9, a psalm that also depicts David's regal authority that is shared in the messianic line.

A fourth text from Revelation 3:7 mentioned the "key of David" that carried forward the Isaiah 22:22 allusion. The final text comes from Revelation 3:21, which again sees Jesus as finished with his conquering tasks and now seated on his throne. The allusion is once again to Psalm 110.

Some have tried to elude the forcefulness of this identification of David's throne with Jesus being seated on that same throne by trying to form an analogy between Jesus' current rule as one that was like David's during the time of Saul's rule. The idea is that Jesus now has authority but he does not use it, just as David could not exercise his authority during Saul's rule, despite the fact that he already had been anointed. But Jesus is not sitting passively until all his enemies are subdued, for Psalm 110 pictures Jesus as installed and as currently ruling and reigning. True, the Father tells Jesus to sit at his right hand "until" he has subdued all his enemies, but that does not mean Jesus is currently passive and waiting for a signal from the Father. Nor is it correct to suggest, noted Bock, whom we are following for this discussion, that the throne of Psalm 110 is a heavenly throne distinct from the Davidic earthly throne. The two thrones were equated in 1 Chronicles 29:23 and 2 Chronicles 9:8.[24]

Conclusion

The kingdom of God, therefore, is both present and future, as the "now-already" and "not yet" as these texts demonstrate. It also has spiritual and material aspects. It embraces the present work of the Christian church as well as the ancient promises made to the nation Israel. The kingdom of God is both a soteriological as well as an eschatological concept.

The concept of the program of God is a unified concept and a program that stretches from Genesis to Revelation. Here, then, is another argument for the unity of Scripture that manifests the single mind and purpose of God.

24. Ibid., 61–63.

The Unity *of the* Bible *and* *the* Promise-Plan *of* God

> God gave a promise to Abraham, and through him to mankind; a promise eternally ful-filled and fulfilling in the history of Israel; and chiefly fulfilled in Jesus Christ, he being that which is principal in the history of Israel.
>
> —Willis J. Beecher[1]

One of the great options for locating a unifying theological center for the whole Bible came from the pen of Willis J. Beecher (1838–1912) as a result of his Stone Lectures at Princeton Theological Seminary in 1902. These lectures were subsequently published in what became the frequently reprinted volume titled *The Prophets and the Promise.*[2]

The Definition of the Promise

Beecher argued for a single "promise" as the unifying center for the whole Bible. Rather than listing an assortment of random and scattered predictions from the Old Testament and then trying to identify the possible fulfillments in the New, he pointed to the integrating role that the doctrine

---

1. Willis J. Beecher, *The Prophets and the Promise* (1905; repr., Grand Rapids: Baker, 1975), 178.
2. Willis J. Beecher attended Auburn Theological Seminary in New York during the Civil War, was ordained as a Presbyterian minister in 1864, taught at Knox College in Illinois from 1865 to 1869, then returned to Auburn Seminary where he taught from 1871 to 1908. He was a contributor to the *Sunday School Times* and served as president of the Society of Biblical Literature in 1904.

of the promise played in both testaments. Thus, while systematic theology tended to separate promise from the prediction, as well as it generally omitted the threatening aspect of the judgments of God from the promise, the major fault Beecher found with systematic theology's presentation was that it overlooked the historic *means* by which God kept his word alive. These historic means connected the developing promise, with the ongoing partial fulfillments during the Old Testament days, and the final fulfillment in the New Testament and in the eschaton. These intermediate historic steps linked both the promising word with the continuous line of partial fulfillments until the final fulfillment in Jesus himself, whether at his first or second advent. Viewed in this manner, the promise was not simply a predictive word that remained inert and wrapped up only in its word form until the fulfillment reached its end point; it was a divine word that was maintained over the centuries in a continuous series of historic fulfillments that acted as down payments on that complete fulfillment that was still to come.[3]

Beecher defined this promise this way: "God gave a promise to Abraham, and through him to mankind; a promise eternally fulfilled and fulfilling in the history of Israel; and chiefly fulfilled in Jesus Christ, he being that which is principal in the history of Israel."[4] That single promise was the one given to Abraham and Israel (Rom. 4:13–17, 20; Heb. 6:13–15, 17; 11:9, 39–40). The New Testament writers regarded the development of this promise as a *single* promise (Gk., *epangelia*) that was repeated and unfolded through the centuries. So central was this article of faith that the apostle Paul, when on trial for his life, wrapped up his total life, ministry, and legal plea by claiming: "And now it is because of my hope in what God has *promised* our fathers that I am on trial here today. This is *the promise* our twelve tribes are hoping to see fulfilled as they earnestly serve God day and night ... that God raises the dead" (Acts 26:6–8, emphasis added).

The New Testament writers viewed this same promise they valued as the one made with Abram when he was called out of Ur of the Chaldeans. They, too, saw it to be not only a *single* promise, but also a *definite* promise. It often appeared with the article *the* in front of *promise*, and its content continued to grow even in their day.

---

3. In an article on *epangelia* and its related roots, Julius Schniewind and Gerhard Friedrich, in *Theological Dictionary of the New Testament*, ed. Gerhard Kittel, trans. Geoffrey W. Bromiley (Grand Rapids: Eerdmans, 1964), 2:579, said: "This word has no preliminary history in the OT. This is the more striking, because on the basis of Paul's teaching, we tend to consider the OT from the standpoint of promise."
4. Beecher, *Prophets and the Promise*, 178.

However, occasionally the one promise spread itself out into many specifications, and therefore the plural form, "promises," was used with reference to the numerous times it was unfolded as well as to the large number of doctrinal aspects it included. Thus Romans 9:4 and 15:8 – 9, for example, mention "the promises" that were made with the patriarchs and Israel. A brief sampling of the large number of specifications that were embraced in this one promise-plan of God included the kingdom of God, the ministry of the Holy Spirit, the resurrection of the Messiah, the outreach to the Gentiles, the gospel itself, the coming of the Messiah, and the like.

The writers of the Old Testament kept on claiming that the Messiah was the culminating fulfillment of this ancient promise, so that in preaching him they were preaching the promise as well. Accordingly, Paul preached at Pisidian Antioch: "We tell you the good news: What God promised our fathers he has fulfilled for us, their children, by raising up Jesus. As it is written in the second Psalm: 'You are my Son; today I have become your Father'" (Acts 13:32 – 33).

It is easy to see that these preachers clearly connected the promise with the gospel and the doctrine of redemption from sin and its consequences. Again, Paul made that clear in Galatians 3:8 by quoting from the promise given to Abraham in Genesis 12:3: "The Scripture foresaw that God would justify the Gentiles by faith, and announced the gospel in advance to Abraham: 'All nations will be blessed through you.'"

Even those who wandered through the wilderness for forty years had the same gospel preached to them, for Hebrews 4:2 taught: "For we also have had the gospel preached to us, just as they [the antecedent being 'whose bodies fell in the desert,' Heb. 3:17] did; but the message they heard was of no value to them, because those who heard it did not combine it with faith."

What, then, are the main lines in the Scriptures for the giving of and tracing the development of the promise-doctrine of God?

The Main Lines of the History of the Promise Doctrine

If the formal announcement of God's plan began with Abraham, then the ways in which it branched out and was fulfilled with an enlarged agenda and with other technical terms must be traced as it leads us into the New Testament. We will now follow it in several of the main historic epochs of biblical history.

The time of the patriarchs. In the history of Israel as recorded in the Old Testament, the call of Abram along with the promise provisions is singled out as the principal theme. It actually consists of a number of subordinate things and then of a more principal item.

There are, according to some counts, some seven subordinate items promised to Abraham, Isaac, and Jacob. They include: (1) "seed," that is, a posterity with a large number of descendants (Gen. 13:16; 15:5, 15–16; 26:4; 28:3–4; 35:11–12; 48:3–4); (2) a posterity that would become a "great nation" (Gen. 18:18; 35:11; 46:3); (3) descendants that would be or include "an assembly/community of nations" (Gen. 17:6, 16; 28:3; 35:11; 48:4); (4) "kings" who would arise from Abraham, Sarah, and Jacob (Gen. 17:6, 16; 35:11); (5) a posterity that would inherit the land of Canaan; (6) the possession of a "great name" (Gen. 12:2–3); and (7) a posterity that would "take possession of the cities of their enemies" (Gen. 22:17) in Canaan.

However, none of these features amounted to the principal item. The emphasis fell, instead, on that part of the "seed" that went all the way back to the *protoevangelium* in Genesis 3:15, where a male descendant from Eve's line would crush the head of "the serpent." But that was not all: through Abraham and that seed, "all the nations of the earth would be blessed." The passive form of the verb assured all that it would be God who would effect this, and not Abraham or his descendants. We can be sure that "the blessing of all the nations" was where the emphasis of this promise fell, for this aspect of the promise was repeated five times in Genesis (12:3; 18:18; 22:18; 26:4; 28:14), always in the climactic or culminating position in the list of promises.

Of special interest was the portion of the promise that referred to the "seed." Seed was not a plural word; instead, it was a collective noun. That is the way the apostle Paul read it as well. In Galatians 3:16, 19 Paul viewed the "Seed" as one that expressed a corporate solidarity, and one that had its culmination in none other than Jesus the Messiah.

The promises were spoken to Abraham and to his seed. The Scripture does not say "and to his seeds," meaning many people, but "and to your seed," meaning one person, who is Christ: "What, then, was the purpose of the law? It was added because of transgressions until the Seed to whom the promise referred had come" (Gal. 3:19).

God's covenant with Abraham was based on the promise with special reference to the Seed. It was God who initiated and who took all the responsibility for maintaining this covenant (Gen. 15:1–6).

One may question how far men like the patriarchs could have foreseen the future or understood what it was that was being promised to them. This much must have been clear to them: they and their descendants were being called eternally to be Yahweh's own people. Yahweh would be their God (Gen. 17:7–8; 28:21), and later he would add to this formula the two other parts—they would be his people, and he would come to dwell in the midst of them. In that they were told that the covenant was eternal (Gen. 17), they could expect that some of the events included in it would still be in progress beyond their times, even if they could not see as yet a person like Jesus arising to fulfill the heart of this promise. But they would also find the promise to be a religious doctrine that would hold the same place in their theology as the doctrine of Christ holds in our theology today. Therefore, they had certain things to believe, teach, and live out in everyday practice. In this way the promise was more than a prediction; it was a doctrine, and God's people were expected to believe and live according to it.

The time of the exodus. After the four hundred years between the time of the patriarchs and the events of the exodus, the promise of the covenant was freshly restated once again. It expressly perpetuated the offers given to Abraham (Ex. 2:24: "God heard their groaning and he remembered his covenant with Abraham, with Isaac and with Jacob"; also Ex. 3:13, 15–16; 6:3–5; Deut. 4:31). It was at this time that God took the Israelites "as [his] own people" (Ex. 6:7; 29:45; Lev. 11:45; 22:33; 25:38; 26:12, 45; Num. 15:41; Deut. 26:17–19; 29:12–13). In fact, God's intention was to make them all into a "kingdom of priests and a holy nation" (Ex. 19:5–6). Disappointingly, Israel shrunk back from this call to be a priesthood of believers and begged Moses instead to go into the presence of God to get God's Word, for the experience of having God speak to them from heaven was altogether too awesome and frightening—fire, lightning, thunder, and all! Thus, this mediatorial task of the whole body of the people was delayed until New Testament times (1 Peter 2:5, 9; Rev. 1:6; 5:10).

Nevertheless, Israel was to be Yahweh's "Son." This special relationship was not mentioned very often, but it was part of the same promise-plan (Ex. 4:22–23; Deut. 1:31; 32:6). Here again, the eternal and irrevocable aspects of the promise were stressed (Ex. 3:15; Deut. 4:40; 12:28). To be sure, *personal* participation in the promise covenant was conditioned on obedience (e.g., Deut. 4:40; 12:28), yet the promise itself was depicted as being irrevocable. In Leviticus 26:44–45 the Lord says: "Yet in spite of this, when they are in the land of their enemies, I will not reject them or abhor them so as to destroy them completely, breaking my covenant with them. I am the LORD their God. But for their sake I will remember the covenant with their ancestors whom I brought out of Egypt" (see also Deut. 4:30–31).

The time of David. In preparation for the throne of David to be set up, God began to give "rest" from all of Israel's enemies as he chose a "place" for his "name to dwell" among the people (Deut. 12:9–10, 14, 21; 25:19). This elusive "rest" was partially fulfilled at the time of the division of the land, as recorded in Deuteronomy 3:20, and in the work of the leader Joshua (Josh. 1:13). It is mentioned again in Psalm 95:11. This divine work of God was another link that connected the time of the exodus with that of David.

The classic passage that supplied the next advance in the promise-plan of God came in 2 Samuel 7, with its account of David's proposal to the prophet Nathan for building a temple for Yahweh. But instead of David building a "house" for Yahweh, God would make a "house," that is, a "dynasty," out of David (vv. 5, 10–11). The details in the promise seemed to be as numerous as they were in the promise given to Abraham. They included the following: (1) God would establish a "house" that consisted of a line of descendants that would come forth from David and sit on his throne (vv. 12, 16, 19, 25, 26, 29). (2) One of those descendants would build the temple for Yahweh that David had proposed. (3) The seed of David would reign in God's kingdom as a whole line of rulers who would succeed him (vv. 12, 13, 16). (4) This reign would extend into all eternity (vv. 13, 16, 25, 26, 29). (5) This promise to David was again declared to be irrevocable even if he sinned (vv. 14–15; cf. 1 Chron. 28:7; Ps. 132:12). (6) Finally, this promise was to be what I call a "charter for all humanity" (Heb., *torat ha'adam*) (v. 19), concluding exactly where the Abraham covenant climaxed with its "in your seed all the nations of the earth shall be blessed" — the missions aspect of the promise! This expression is often given strange translations in English texts, but what God was going to do would be a "law" or a "charter"[5] for everyone in the world to enjoy by faith, if they would. It, too, would act just as the climactic note in the Abrahamic covenant was aimed — a provision for all the nations.

The post-Davidic times. Up to this point, the view garnered from the earliest times to the times of David is that Yahweh has made Israel his distinctive

---

5. Bruce K. Waltke. *An Old Testament Theology: An Exegetical, Canonical, and Thematic Approach* (Grand Rapids: Zondervan, 2007), 692, where Waltke says, "Walt Kaiser plausibly interprets *torat ha'adam* (2 Sam. 7:19) in David's response to the covenant by 'a charter for humanity' that impacts all nations." Also see William J. Dumbrell, *Covenant and Creation: An Old Testament Covenantal Theology* (Exeter: Paternoster, 1984), 152.

people, and he has vested this relationship centrally in the royal line of David. Yahweh's purpose for doing this, however, was to bring blessing to all humanity. Added to this picture is the preaching of the prophets, who declared that this one promise was being fulfilled in their times; yet it also remained to be fulfilled largely in the future, in the person of the Messiah — a "now" and a "not yet" inaugurated eschatology.

The prophets spoke of Israel as the people of promise. While they could treat Israel merely as a nation or as a race of mortals, they could also distinguish a true Israel within Israel who had, like Abraham, believed in that coming Man of Promise. Moreover, all nations had an interest in the promise, for there was no other deliverance coming from any other source except through the promise God had given in this line established in Israel. This extension of the good news to all the nations could be seen in Solomon's prayer at the dedication of the temple (1 Kings 8:41–43; 2 Chron. 6:32–33), and in numerous formal repetitions in the Psalms and the Prophets (Ps. 72:17; Isa. 49:6–7; 65:16; Jer. 4:1–2; Zech. 14:16). But amazingly the promise was continuously declared to be eternal and irrevocable (1 Kings 11:36; 2 Chron. 21:7; Ps. 89:26–37; Isa. 59:20–21).

During the prophetic eras, certain words came to take on a partly technical usage in the teaching of the promise doctrine. The roots of several of these terms was often pre-Davidic, with strong development of them in the Psalms. The one surprising term, however, was *messiah*. This term appears some thirty-nine times in the older testament, yet in no more than nine of the thirty-nine instances does it possibly refer to the Messiah (1 Sam. 2:10, 35; Pss. 2:2; 20:6; 28:8; 84:9; Dan. 9:25, 26; Hab. 3:13). On the other hand, by all odds, the most prominent technical term for the special descendant of David was "the Servant of the LORD." It had been used in a nontechnical way of Moses, Caleb, Samson, and Nebuchadnezzar throughout Scripture, but it is with David that the term *servant* begins to take on a technical status. The term also is used of Israel (Isa. 41:8, 9; 44:1, 2, 21; 45:4; 48:20; 49:3). When the term *servant* is applied technically to Israel or to the line of David, it speaks of them either as the promise people or as the promise dynasty (Isa. 49:5–7; Rom. 9:6–8). Therefore we say that the servant is Israel, yet the servant is also Jesus, who is the highest disclosure of Yahweh himself, in and through the people of Israel.

Other technical terms can be added to "anointed one/Messiah" and "servant." We have already mentioned "Seed," "Son," and "firstborn." Add to these the "Chosen One," the "Holy One" (Heb., *hasid*), the "Branch" (Heb., *tsemah)*, "Shoot" (Heb., *netser*), the "lamp," and the "star" and the picture of Messiah in the Old Testament begins to broaden extensively.[6]

The times of fulfillment. No less certain were the New Testament writers that the single, definite promise from God was the theme not only of the older testament, but of the times of fulfillment as well. When Stephen stood before the Sanhedrin, he, too, traced that same path: "Brothers and fathers, listen to me! The God of glory appeared to our father Abraham while he was still in Mesopotamia, before he lived in Haran. 'Leave your country and your people,' God said, 'and go to the land I will show you.' ... As the time drew near for God to fulfill his promise to Abraham, the number of our people in Egypt greatly increased" (Acts 7:2–3, 17).

Despite the fact that the Old Testament does not use the term *promise*, it does possess the concept in a constellation of Hebrew terms, such as *blessing*, *oath*, *pledge*, and the like. Moreover, the writers of the New Testament adopted the Old Testament phraseology as their own way of expressing God's revelation to them. Routinely they appealed to concepts, such as "the last days," "the day of the Lord," "the Servant of the Lord," "my Holy One," "my Firstborn" and many others.

These New Testament writers also taught that the promise of God would operate eternally and irrevocably. Certainly "a hardening in part" had come over Israel (Rom. 11:25), but nevertheless, "God's gifts and his call [were] irrevocable" (Rom. 11:29). No less definitive was the announcement from the writer of the book of Hebrews:

> When God made his promise to Abraham, since there was no one greater for him to swear by, he swore by himself.... Because God wanted to make the unchanging nature of his purpose very clear to the heirs of what was promised, he confirmed it with an oath. God did this so that, by two unchangeable things [his word in Gen. 12 and his oath in Gen. 22] in which it is impossible for God to lie, we [the generations long after Abraham and his immediate heirs] who have fled to take hold of the hope offered to us may be greatly encouraged. (Heb. 6:13, 17–18)

This promise-plan of God exhibited strong connections with other doctrines throughout the New Testament. God had made it plain to Abraham that the benefits of this promise were not limited to him and his own people alone, but that he and his people were to be a channel through which the

---

6. Walter C. Kaiser Jr. *The Messiah in the Old Testament* (Grand Rapids: Zondervan, 1995), 136–230.

same benefits would come to the other nations as well. Paul taught in Galatians 3:6–8 three foundational truths: (1) Abraham received the gospel itself in advance of its fuller and later explication; (2) the substance of this gospel could be found in the words, "All nations will be blessed through you"; and (3) the gospel was the same one given to Abraham and the one by which all the Gentiles on earth were to be saved at the hearing of the name of Jesus. Paul put it this way: Abraham " 'believed God, and it was credited to him as righteousness.'" Understand, then, that those who believe are children of Abraham. Scripture foresaw that God would justify the Gentiles by faith, and announced the gospel in advance to Abraham: 'All nations will be blessed through you'" (Gal. 3:6–8).

Some may wonder why we have not declared as the unifying doctrine of the Bible the theme of "the kingdom of God," which Jesus came announcing. But, as Willis J. Beecher, whom we have been following in this presentation, commented: "The most prominent thing in the New Testament is the proclamation of the kingdom and its anointed king. But it is on the basis of the divine promise that its preachers proclaim the kingdom, and when they appeal to the Old Testament in proof of Christian doctrine, they make the promise more prominent than the kingdom itself."[7]

The time of the arrival of the promise. John the Baptist, more than any other person, prepared the way for the arrival of the fulfillment of the promise in Jesus the Messiah. John's record is found in all four gospels, amounting to 194 verses, which in its combined total exceeds the total number of verses in seventeen of the twenty-seven books of the New Testament, not to mention seven other allusions to John the Baptist in the book of Acts. John appeared on the scene as abruptly as did his earlier counterpart, Elijah, in 1 Kings 17:1. Despite the fact that there had not been any prophetic or written revelatory material for some four hundred years, suddenly a voice erupted out in the desert calling for men and women to repent and prepare the way of the Lord. Yet all of this should not have been all that surprising, for twice in the promise-plan it had been promised that he and his mission would precede the coming of the one in the Davidic line. John would point to Jesus as the Lamb of God who would take away the sin of the world (John 1:29). Jesus' estimate of John the Baptist would be that he was "more than a prophet" (Matt. 11:9). In fact, Jesus said, "Among those born of women there has not risen anyone greater than John the Baptist" (Matt. 11:11).

---

7. Beecher, *Prophets and the Promise*, 178–79.

Add to John's witness that of Zechariah the priest who, after nine months of speechlessness, broke out in an ecstatic paean of praise to God for keeping his promise to David, to Abraham, and to Zechariah himself, in sending John. Mary, the mother of our Lord, also had a song of praise to God that echoed the song of Hannah, for again God had accomplished what he had promised. Count among this watchful group also the elderly Simeon who, having seen Jesus when Mary and Joseph brought him to the temple for dedication, said that he had seen enough to satisfy him that the fulfillment of the Lord's promise was under way, and now he was ready to depart to be with his Lord. The content of the promise had been the substance of Israel's long-awaited hope.

The time of relating the gospel to the law. Between AD 46 and 48, the first two contributions to the New Testament were written: James and Galatians. Even though the Law of God, understood as that part that dealt with the ceremonies and rituals that were carried out by the priests in the temple, was now fulfilled, there was nevertheless an aspect of God's Law that remained, just as Jesus had taught in Matthew 5:17–20. Of course, Moses himself had cautioned at the time these ceremonies and rituals were revealed to him that they were merely a "copy" or a "model/pattern" of the real (Ex. 25:9, 40), while the real remained in heaven. When the real arrived in the Messiah, the copies, which were only shadows of the real, would become antiquated and replaced. So the rituals, sacrifices, and priesthood of the Old Testament were bound to be superseded and replaced.

James, the half brother of our Lord, wrote what is probably the earliest book of the New Testament. His themes and theology, at first glance, seem to be so random that some people thought his book exhibited about as much organization as the book of Proverbs. However, that first impression may need serious modification, for James may well be an exposition on Leviticus 19:12–18, as Luke T. Johnson has suggested.[8] Every verse from the holiness law of Leviticus 19:12–18 is commented on in the book of James except verse 14! James's emphasis, however, is on the royal law of love: "Love your neighbor as yourself."

James didn't see any opposition between the gospel and the law. One simply had to use the law properly; it was not an alternative route to eternal life. A person demonstrated genuine faith by obeying God's teaching.

---

8. Luke T. Johnson, "The Use of Leviticus 19 in the Letter of James," *Journal of Biblical Literature* 101 (1982): 391–401.

Galatians was written just before the Jerusalem Council in AD 50. Few chapters in the New Testament have as many references with such a strong emphasis on the "promise" as the third chapter of Galatians. Paul argued that the promise came 430 years before the law, therefore it took priority over the law.

The Judaizers, however, opposed such an emphasis on the promise of the gospel. Therefore their first line of attack was to go after Paul's apostolic authority. Paul easily demonstrated that he was beholden to no individual or group of persons for his message: it had come from God by divine revelation.

Paul's opponents also accused him of preaching a diminished message, for he denied that salvation could be obtained through works. The apostolic response was that mortals were justified by faith (Gal. 2:16; 3:8, 11, 24) and not by obedience to the law (2:16; 3:11).[9] The promise, however, was given to Abraham in advance so that all the nations of the earth could hear the message of grace.

The promise-plan and the mission of the church. The man who wanted to destroy the church (Acts 8:3) would be the one God would use to build it and to establish the body of Christ. In the AD 50s, 1 and 2 Thessalonians, 1 and 2 Corinthians, and Romans were written by the apostle Paul to these fledgling groups. In the letters to the church in Thessalonica, he focused on the Lord's second coming. In his letters to the young church at Corinth, this new commercial capital of Greece, he wrote to fix disorders in the believing body.

The church at Rome was different. No one knows when or how it started, but up to this point, Paul had never been there. Perhaps that is why Paul felt he had to give one of the fullest statements of the gospel as the righteousness of God found in any of his books. After showing how mortals could be declared to be right or justified before God in the first four chapters, he proceeded to show a number of benefits that had come from this divine act of justification: peace with God, the reversal of the effects of Adam's fall, and the work of the Holy Spirit in our mortal bodies.

That led to the troubling question in the promise-plan of God: "Did God reject his people?" (Rom. 11:1). Paul would have no part of the implications of that question: "Absolutely not!" The promises of God are "irrevocable"

---

9. E. P. Sanders, *Paul and Palestinian Judaism* (Philadelphia: Fortress, 1977), claimed this was not the point of tension between the Jewish people and Paul; it was only that Christians accepted Jesus as the Messiah and the Jews did not. In "covenantal nomism," Jews were saved not by merit but by being a member of the covenant community. For partial refutations, see Robert H. Gundry, "Grace, Works, and Staying Saved in Paul," *Biblica* 66 (1985): 1–38; and Frank Thielman, *From Plight to Solution: A Jewish Framework for Understanding Paul's View of the Law in Galatians and Romans.* Supplementum, Novum Testamentum 61 (Leiden: Brill, 1989).

(Rom. 11:29). The Roman letter ends with some practical out-workings of the gospel itself.

The times of the Prison Epistles in the promise-plan of God. Four of Paul's letters were written in the early AD 60s while he was in prison, probably at Rome: Colossians, Philemon, Ephesians, and Philippians. The emphases of the four letters are as follows: Colossians—the primacy of Christ and one's new life in Christ; Philemon—the fellowship found in the gospel; Ephesians—the "mystery" of God; and Philippians—the imitation of Christ. All were written to edify the body of Christ.

The times of the kingdom of God and the promise-plan. The gospels of Matthew and Mark were written about AD 63–65. Mark clearly focused on Jesus as the one who was given as a ransom for many (Mark 10:45). The kingdom was very different from what persons living under the Roman Empire had experienced. Instead of a demonstration of power similar to Rome's mighty show of force, God's kingdom was a "secret" (Mark 4:11) explained more fully in the parable of the sower and the four places the seeds fell.

Matthew's gospel was a straightforward unfolding of this kingdom of God in its ethics (Matt. 5–7), its authority (Matt. 8:1–11:1), its program (Matt. 11:2–13:53), its reaction to opposition (Matt. 13:54–19:2), and its future (Matt. 19:3–26). The Messiah was from David's line, and he fulfilled what the Psalms and the prophets had said about him. Matthew also was the only gospel that mentioned the church as part of the promise-plan of God.

The times of the promise of the Holy Spirit. Luke wrote his two-volume history, Luke-Acts, in the mid-60s of the first Christian century. His two books take up some 27 percent of the total New Testament. Probably he was a Gentile Christian, a doctor by profession, and a constant companion of the apostle Paul.

His desire was to give an "orderly account" of "everything from the beginning" (Luke 1:3). Luke stressed that there was a divine necessity to the plan of God, for out of the 101 times the Greek particle *dei*, "it is necessary," is used in the New Testament, Luke used it 40 of those times in his two-volume history.[10]

Luke also concentrated on the promise of the Holy Spirit, mentioning him 36 times in his gospel and 70 times in Acts. He was also the theologian

10. Darrell Bock, "Luke," in *The New Dictionary of Biblical Theology* (Downers Grove, Ill.: InterVarsity, 2000), 274.

of repentance, for in Luke 5:32, Jesus summarized his mission as "I have come not to call the righteous, but sinners to repentance," and in Luke 19:10, "For the Son of Man came to seek and to save what was lost." Real repentance was followed by a theology of discipleship and a concern for women, the poor, and the disreputable.

The times for purity of life and doctrine in the promise. The books of 1 and 2 Peter and Jude were written about AD 64–65. First Peter spoke of the suffering of believers along with a call to holiness of life and a call to purity. Second Peter and Jude concentrated on condemning false teachers and false doctrine. In this battle for the truth, the role of Scripture remained the heart of the matter.

The times of letters to pastors in the promise. Paul is usually credited with writing the Pastoral Epistles of 1 and 2 Timothy and Titus sometime around AD 62–67. Paul's concern, according to 1 Timothy, was for how one should behave in the household of God. Second Timothy 1:6–7 says, "I remind you to fan into flame the gift of God, which is in you through the laying on of my hands. For God did not give us a spirit of timidity, but a spirit of power, of love and of self-discipline." Timothy tended, apparently, to be rather shy, but this would not do for the godlessness of the last days Paul was concerned about.

Titus sets forth the grace of God in all of its splendor. The field of Crete may have been a hard place to minister the gospel, but Paul found the grace of God greater than all the obstacles Titus or his congregation could think up.

The times for announcing the supremacy of Jesus. The book of Hebrews, written sometime around AD 65, came to us without its author being declared. But whoever wrote this book saw a need to be pastoral for some who were tempted to desert the faith and a need to teach the supremacy and finality of Jesus Christ. It seems to be written to second-generation Jewish-Christian believers who were tempted to lapse back into the rituals and sacrifices given by Moses even after they had tasted of the good things from the Messiah. In every way, Jesus and the new way outlined in the ancient promise were superior. Not Moses, Melchizedek, Joshua, or anyone else could compare to Jesus the Messiah. Jesus' sacrifice of himself on the cross obviated all other sacrifices in its perfection, completeness, and finality. The new covenant was to be preferred over the old covenant of Moses.

The times of the gospel of the kingdom. The gospel of John, his three epistles of 1, 2, and 3 John, and the book of Revelation close out the biblical canon as they were written by John about AD 85–95.

John's gospel was written that we might believe that Jesus was the Messiah and that through believing we might have life in his name (John 20:31). This disciple of the Lord chose seven of Jesus' miracles as "signs" to point all who read and heard them to Jesus as the anticipated Messiah. He balanced these seven signs out with seven "I am" statements, most of which went along with the narratives that described the seven miracles.

In the second half of John's gospel (chaps. 13–17), Jesus gave his farewell address to his disciples in the upper room. This section was followed by the passion narrative in which our Lord is presented as an atonement for our sin.

John used "the Lamb of God" twice in his gospel (1:29, 36) to describe Jesus, but in Revelation he used it twenty-seven times of our Lord. This, too, had a redemptive connotation to it as recalled from the Old Testament. In John's very distinctive vocabulary, the word *witness* appears some nineteen times. The center of that witness was Jesus.

The three epistles John wrote all stress a need for love of the brethren as a sign that one loves God. False teachers are to be exhorted and challenged but treated gently.

The book of Revelation is saturated with almost four hundred allusions to the Old Testament yet without one direct quotation. Especially significant usages can be found from the books of Daniel, Ezekiel, Isaiah, Jeremiah, and Joel. The purpose of this book was to be a "testimony of Jesus," who is "the spirit of prophecy" (1:1–3; 19:10).

God is sovereign over all other powers and dominions, so that in the end "the kingdom of the world has become the kingdom of our Lord and of his Christ, and he will reign for ever and ever" (Rev. 11:15). All forces and shapes of evil are finally vanquished as the great dragon is hurled down. That ancient serpent, the devil, along with the beast and his sidekick who emerge from the sea with all the unclean spirits and demons, will be destroyed (12:9; 13:1, 11; 16:13; 18:2).

The book of Revelation, finally, is a book of worship as well, for the verb "to worship" (Gk., *proskyneo*) appears twenty-four times out of a total of fifty-four usages in the whole New Testament.

John is one of the most graphic writers of the New Testament, but he is also the one, more than most others, who stressed the need to confess and believe that Jesus has indeed appeared in the flesh and that he is the Son of God as well as the Son of Man.[11]

Conclusion

The promise-plan of God offers one of the finest ways to view the interconnectedness of the Bible. This offering comes from the New Testament itself as it reflects on the mind and purpose of God over the centuries of his revelatory disclosures in Scripture.

The promise-plan of God also simultaneously incorporates the large number of subthemes that form the wide diversity of the Bible's continuous narrative and the goal that leads to the cross of Christ and to his resurrection. While it celebrates the awesome unity of the text of Scripture, it is broad and wide enough to embrace the numerous strands of topics that flesh out its plurality in unity.

---

11. For a more definitive discussion of the topics in this chapter, see Walter C. Kaiser Jr., *The Promise-Plan of God: A Biblical Theology of the Old and New Testaments* (Grand Rapids: Zondervan, 2008).

The Unity *of the* Bible
and the Law *of* God

> Israel does not *become* God's people by obeying his commandments, but through obedience they show the reality of *being* the people of God.
>
> — Hetty Lalleman[1]

"The classic theme of all truly evangelical theology is the relationship of Law to Gospel. In fact, so critical is a proper statement of this relationship that depicts both a believer's standing in Christ and his or her acting and living, that it can become one of the best ways to test both the greatness and the effectiveness of a truly biblical and evangelical theology."[2]

However, the contrasts between the law (which all too many insist on attributing solely to "Moses" rather than first of all to "God"; see Ex. 34:6) and the gospel of "grace and truth" (John 1:17), which is sometimes unfairly limited to the New Testament, seem to be legion in number. Some describe the relationship between law and gospel as one that is dead,

---

1. Hetty Lalleman, *Celebrating the Law? Rethinking Old Testament Ethics* (London: Paternoster, 2004), 121.
2. These are essentially the same words I used to begin my chapter titled "The Law as God's Gracious Guidance for the Promotion of Holiness," in *Five Views on Law and Gospel*, ed. Stanley N. Gundry (Grand Rapids: Zondervan, 1996), 177. Other aspects of this argument I have traced out in my articles "The Place of Law and Good Works in Evangelical Christianity," in *A Time to Speak: The Evangelical-Jewish Encounter*, ed. James Rudin and Marvin R. Wilson (Grand Rapids: Eerdmans, 1987), 12–33; "Images for Today: The Torah Speaks Today," in *Studies in Old Testament Theology*, ed. Robert L. Hubbard Jr., Robert K. Johnston, and Robert P Meye (Dallas: Word, 1992), 117–32; and "James' View of the Law," *Miskan* 8, no. 9 (1988): 9–12.

wherein the law is no longer obligatory or functioning (2 Cor. 3:11; Eph. 2:15; Col. 2:14). Now that the promise has come to fulfillment, some carelessly reason, based on Romans 7:6; Galatians 3:19–25; and 4:1–5, that we are freed from the law's dominion (Rom. 6:14; 7:4) because Christ has fulfilled the righteousness of the law in us (Rom. 8:3–4; 10:4). For some, these statements are so definitive that there is no need for any further investigation of the issue. We are dead to the law and the law is dead to us now that Christ has come.

Typical though it may be for all too many contemporary believers, such a presentation of the law's relationship to the gospel of grace is all too absolute, antithetical, and one-sided to encompass a great number of Pauline passages, let alone the rest of the Bible. For example, Paul asks our question and answers it straightaway in Romans 3:31: "Do we, then, nullify the law by this faith? Not at all! Rather, we uphold the law."

Grace did not annul the law; instead, it "upheld" it. What did "fade away," or "was rendered obsolete" (Gk., *katargoymenen*), however, was the "ministry" (Gk., *diakonia*) that Moses and Aaron introduced (2 Cor. 3:8, 11). What also needed to be "removed" (Gk., *anakaluptomenon*) was the "veil (Gk., *kalumma*) [that] covers [Israel's] hearts" "when Moses [the old covenant] is read" (2 Cor. 3:14–15). "Only in Christ is [the veil] taken away" (Gk., *katargeitai*). Once more the apostle Paul asked the same question in Galatians 3:21: "Is the law, therefore, opposed to the promises of God? Absolutely not!"

Consequently, any solution to the question of the unity of the law and the gospel that quickly does away with the law for the believer today cannot look to the Scriptures for support. One cannot say that believers have nothing to do with the law anymore, for in that case they will stand opposed to the plain teaching of the Scriptures.

All too frequently people take an atomistic approach to this relationship and select an array of biblical phrases or verses from here and there in the Bible to prove their freedom from the law. Typical of such preferential treatment, in lieu of fully developed teaching or chair passages, is the use of Romans 3:21, "But now a righteousness from God, apart from law, has been made known"; Romans 7:4, "So, my brothers, you also died to the law"; Romans 7:6, "we serve ... not in the old way of the written code"; and Romans 7:9, "Once I was alive apart from law; but when the commandment came, sin sprang to life and I died."

But such partial selectivity only unnecessarily adds to the alleged wall of separation between law and gospel. When Paul flatly denied that the promise of God had annulled the law, he went on in Romans 3:21 to teach

*A*ny solution to the question of the unity of the law and the gospel that quickly does away with the law for the believer today cannot look to the Scriptures for support.

that the very righteousness he was announcing was witnessed to by "the Law and the Prophets." And when Paul used "apart from law" in Romans 3:21, he amplified that phrase in Romans 3:28 as "apart from *works of* the Law" (NASB, emphasis added).

John Wesley could observe in his day that "Perhaps there were few subjects within the whole compass of religion so little understood as [the law]."[3] C. E. B. Cranfield came to the same conclusion:

> The need ... exists today for a thorough re-examination of the place and sig-
> nificance of law in the Bible.... The possibility that ... recent writings reflect
> a serious degree of muddled thinking and unexamined assumptions with
> regard to the attitudes of Jesus and St. Paul to the law ought to be reckoned
> with—and even the further possibility that, behind them, there may be some
> muddled thinking or, at the least, careless and imprecise statements in this
> connection, which have helped to mould the opinions of the present generation
> of ministers and teachers.[4]

Nevertheless, James Dunn has used the "letter/Spirit" contrast in 2 Corinthians 3:6 to infer that the rules of the law encourage legalism and sin, whereas righteousness comes from the new impetus given to us by the Holy Spirit.[5] But the problem with that way of understanding the contrast between the "letter" and the "Spirit" is that it does not agree with the two Pauline passages in Romans 2:27–29 and 7:6 where the separation is not between the nature of the law and the Spirit, but instead is between a person having a desire to obey the law and simply wanting to display an outward observance of and compliance with the law. Romans 2:29 declares that "a man is a Jew if he is one inwardly; and circumcision is circumcision of the heart, by the Spirit, not by the written code. Such a man's praise is not from men, but from God." Thomas Provence argued that it was in this way that believers were released from the law to serve the law in the new way by the Spirit:

> [Paul] immediately launches into a defense of the law which he characterizes
> as "holy, just and good" (vii 12) and even "spiritual" (vii 14). Since it is impos-
> sible to give the law any higher commendation than this, the law of [Rom 7:]12
> and 14 cannot be the same as the "letter" of [2 Cor 3:6]. The Law, or "letter"

---

3. John Wesley, "A Series of Three Sermons on the Original [*sic*], Nature, Property, and Use of the Law," in *Sermons: On Several Occasions*, 1st ser. (London: Epworth, 1964), 381–415.
4. C. E. B. Cranfield, "St. Paul and the Law," *Scottish Journal of Theology* 17 (1964): 43–44.
5. James D. G. Dunn, "2 Corinthians III.17—'The Lord Is the Spirit,'" *Journal of Theological Studies*, n.s., 21, no. 2 (1970): 310n2.

from which we are being released [Rom 7:6] is the one without the Spirit ... thus [it is] the very opposite of the "spiritual" law of v. 14.[6]

C. E. B. Cranfield concluded the same:

[Here Paul] does not use "letter" as a simple equivalent of "the law." "Letter" is rather what the legalist is left with as a result of his misunderstanding and misuse of the law. It is the letter of the law in separation from the Spirit. But since "the law is spiritual" (v 14), the letter of the law in isolation from the Spirit is not the law in its true character, but the law as it was denatured. It is this which is opposed to the Spirit whose presence is the true establishment of the law.[7]

Therefore, rather than belittling or nullifying the law by demeaning it to the level and status of being only a "letter," Paul attributed the Law's weakness to the sinful nature of its users (Rom 8:3), who lacked the power of the Holy Spirit.

Even when the new covenant is given, the change that the new covenant envisages is in the heart of those regenerated by the Holy Spirit. The same Torah remains according to Jeremiah 31:31–34, Ezekiel 11:19–20; 36:26–27.

Some may object, however, that no one in the days of the older covenants got the relation of grace and law straight. They all took the law legalistically, it is claimed. But that would not be true, for God had to alert the prophet Elijah to the fact that he had a believing remnant of seven thousand that were not in that class of letter-bound legalists at all (1 Kings 19:18).

Where, then, can we go to find a large teaching passage (*sedes doctrinae*) on the proper use of the law? Romans 9:30–10:13 is just such a text.

A Chair Teaching Text on the Law: Romans 9:30–10:13

At the heart of Paul's most systematic statement of his doctrine of salvation in the book of Romans, he put this discussion of the law (Gk., *nomos*). As usual, Paul signaled the next stage in his argument, in Romans 9:30, with the introductory question, "What then shall we say?" (Gk., *ti oun*). The

---

6. Thomas E. Provence, " 'Who Is Sufficient for These Things?' An Exegesis of 2 Corinthians ii.15–iii.18," *Novum Testamentum* 24, no. 1 (1982): 64–65, as quoted by Daniel P. Fuller, *The Unity of the Bible: Unfolding God's Plan for Humanity* (Grand Rapids: Zondervan, 1992), 347.
7. C. E. B. Cranfield, *A Critical and Exegetical Commentary on the Epistle to the Romans*, 2 vols., International Critical Commentary (Edinburgh: T. & T. Clark, 1975–79), 1:339–40, as cited by Fuller, *Unity of the Bible*, 348.

problem he chose to deal with was this: How did it happen that the Gentiles attained "righteousness ... by faith" (Gk., *ek pisteos*), while the Jewish people failed to obtain that same righteousness, even though they pursued it "by works" (Gk., *ek ergon*)?

Paul did not mince any words here. He traced Israel's failure to five specific charges:

1. Instead of receiving God's righteousness by faith, Israel "[made] a law [out] of righteousness" (Gk., *nomon dikaiosunes*; 9:31; note the word order).
2. They pursued righteousness not by faith, "but as if it were by works" (9:32). Obviously, Paul did not think it could be done that way!
3. In contrast to many Gentiles, they refused to believe in the "*stone* that causes men to stumble and a *rock* that makes them fall" (9:33; quoted from Isa. 8:14 and 28:16, emphasis added). That "stone" and "rock" was certainly the Messiah!
4. Even though Paul's fellow Jews were extremely zealous for God, "their zeal [was] not based on knowledge" (10:2)—at least not divine knowledge!
5. Finally, in place of the righteousness that came from God, all too many Jews had decided "to establish *their own*" righteousness (10:3, emphasis added).

This context clearly distinguishes two different ways of obtaining righteousness: one is God's way, which is to receive it by faith in the Messiah; the other way is to externalize it and make one's own homemade righteousness by attempting to be worthy of God's righteousness by doing works.

Over against this confusion of correct approaches to the law, Paul went back to Moses to establish the true path to God's righteousness as found in the law of Moses (Rom. 10:5). This path was laid out in Leviticus 18:5 and Deuteronomy 30:10–14. Instead of these texts laying out two contrasting ways to get to righteousness from Moses, the Greek *gar ... de* should be translated "for ... and," as it is rendered in Romans 7:8–9; 10:10; 11:15–16, not "for ... *but*."

The expression in Romans 10:5 from Leviticus 18:5, "The man who does these things will live *by them*" (emphasis added) should not be rendered in the instrumental mode, "by [means of] them," but rather in a locative mode, "[in the sphere of] them."[8] Likewise, the context in Leviticus

8. See J. Oliver Buswell, *A Theology of the Christian Religion*, 2 vols. (Grand Rapids: Zondervan, 1963), 1:313.

18 begins and ends with the affirmation, "I am the LORD your God." Thus the quotation does not explain how one might earn one's salvation; rather, it deals with Israel's sanctification: they are not to do as the Canaanites and Egyptians do in the worship of other deities, because the Lord is their God.[9] Only the people who are the Lord's people will be able to both do and live in the context of obeying the law of God, for they first believed in order that they might go on in obedience.

Christ, then, was a "goal" (Gk., *telos*), not the "end" or the conclusion to the law (Rom. 10:4). Thus Christ is the *telos*, goal or purpose of the law (for righteousness), "for everyone who believes" (Gk., *eis dikaiosynen panti to pisteuonti*).

There are some who want to say that it was still hypothetically possible to be saved in the olden days of the first testament if one perfectly kept the whole law of God. But Paul, under the inspiration of the Holy Spirit, did not think that was at all possible, for he asserted in Galatians 3:21, "If a law had been given that could impart life, then righteousness would certainly have come by the law," thus Paul denied that such a rule existed or was possible even hypothetically.

A Threefold Division of the Law

But even if faith and a heart made sensitive by the Holy Spirit are used to obey the law, how much of the law should be the basis for living faithfully? Interpreters, as a matter of convenience, speak of the Ten Commandments, the holiness law of Leviticus 18–20, and parts of Deuteronomy as the "moral law"; the covenant code of Exodus 21–23 as the "civil law"; and the legislation from Exodus 25–40, all of Leviticus, and Numbers 1–10 as containing mainly the "ceremonial law." These terms are not indigenous to the Scriptures themselves any more than the term *trinity* is, but they do function to point to the way the text handles the various materials.

Moral law abides and is of permanent value because it is based on the character of God, which remains the same. He does not change; therefore his moral laws are not temporally conditioned. On the other hand, Exodus 25:9, 40; 26:30; and 27:8 show that the laws concerning the tabernacle, its furniture, the offerings, the priesthood, and the like were to be made according to the "pattern," or "copy" (Heb., *tabnit*), in heaven. Of course,

---

9. For further arguments, see Walter C. Kaiser Jr., "Leviticus 18:5 and Paul: 'Do This and You Shall Live' (Eternally?)," *Journal of the Evangelical Theological Society* 14 (1971): 19–28.

when the real (Christ) came, to which these patterns and copies pointed, then there would no longer be any need for the symbolic except to exhibit the principles involved. Therefore, the ceremonial laws had a built-in obsolescence to them, meaning they were valid as models for only as long as God would say so. Likewise, the civil laws were but illustrations of the moral laws.

Those who do not think there were any distinctions between what we have termed the "moral law," the "judicial or civil law," and the "ceremonial law," should note that our Lord, in Matthew 23:23, did as a matter of fact distinguish between the laws, saying some were "weightier" than the others: "Woe to you, teachers of the law and Pharisees, you hypocrites! You give a tenth of your spices—mint, dill and cumin. But you have neglected the more important matters of the law—justice, mercy and faithfulness."

All of this raises the further issue of a theological framework from which we can form principles to support a biblical ethic. Most would correctly turn down going through the Bible in a "proof-texting" method to support various ethical and moral standards as being too selective and too tendentious. So how can we proceed in a proper use of the law while still observing the divisions and relevancy tests we have listed above?

A Theological Framework for Ethics of the Bible

Various methods for applying the Bible to current ethical questions have been suggested. For example, Waldemar Janzen urged that every aspect of life in the Bible should be appealed to for ethical instruction; therefore the narrative materials are just as significant as the laws were. Janzen would distance himself from systematizing the laws of the Decalogue or other passages, such as Leviticus 19:1–18 and the teaching of Deuteronomy, by making them into principles or propositional teachings on ethics. Instead, he would look for the "paradigmatic functions" of the laws, decrees, and narrative materials that supply us with case studies and examples from the familial, priestly, wisdom, royal, and prophetic paradigms. These paradigms, claimed Janzen, dealt with life, land, and hospitality.[10]

Chris Wright sharpened the concept of *paradigm* by claiming that a paradigm is a model or example for other situations, but one that also has a basic "principle" that remains unchanged, even though it differs in details.

---

10. Waldemar Janzen, *Old Testament Ethics: A Paradigmatic Approach* (Louisville: Westminster John Knox, 1994), 90.

The paradigm, then, is not for imitation, but for *application*. The concept of a paradigm comes, for example, from the area of language study in which one example of a verb form in its entire conjugation is given as the basis for applying that paradigm to other regular or irregular verbs. Accordingly, we look in the Old and New Testaments for commands, decrees, and narratives for which we can state the paradigm that is behind them and then move from that example to a new application of the principle found in that paradigm according to Wright's use of the term.[11]

Wright, in contradistinction from Janzen, did not attribute the paradigm to human insight as the guiding hand that developed Israel's rules; he believed that God himself revealed these laws, commands, and narratives to the writers. Wright was not frightened by propositional revelation as much as Janzen. But Wright preferred to develop his ethical directions by using biblical paradigms from all types of biblical genre, especially narratives, rather than depending on the Decalogue or the like as the primary source of ethical instruction.

I agree that moving from the paradigm to the principle is what the application process is all about. Some would like to limit the first part of this process to the exegetical task and then go on to claim that it is a very private and subjective matter to see personal or communal applications in the paradigms—apart from the preceding interpretive process. But that suggestion leaves behind the needed *authority* status of the ethical teaching and tends to demean the *sufficiency* of Scripture.

I have long held that principlizing is one of the primary goals of interpretation. "To 'principlize' is to restate the author's propositions, arguments, narrations, and illustrations in timeless abiding truths with special focus on the application of those truths to the current needs of the Church or the individual."[12]

Too many Old Testament scholars give up and claim that all attempts to find a unifying theme in the Bible are pointless and a waste of time. For example, Cyril Rodd warns that it is impossible to say that this or that is what the Bible says on this ethical or that moral position.[13] Rodd argues that "the first requirement is to abandon the propositional view of revelation, and with it the belief in the Bible as an external authority."[14] Rodd

---

11. C. J. H. Wright, *Living as the People of God: The Relevance of Old Testament Ethics* (Leicester, UK: Inter-Varsity, 1983), 43; also C. J. H. Wright, *Walking in the Ways of the Lord: The Ethical Authority of the Old Testament* (Leicester, UK: Apollos, 1995), 60, 63.
12. Walter C. Kaiser, Jr. *Toward an Exegetical Theology: Biblical Exegesis for Preaching and Teaching* (Grand Rapids: Baker, 1981), 152.
13. Cyril Rodd, *Glimpses of a Strange Land* (Edinburgh: T. & T. Clark, 2001), 313, 322, as cited by Lalleman, *Celebrating the Law?* 54–55.
14. Ibid., 327, as noted by Lalleman, *Celebrating the Law?* 54.

represents a certain type of Bible reader and set of scholars who are opposed to a canonical or a synchronic reading of the Old Testament. In its place he and they would see a variety of historical and theological contexts in its different parts. This eliminates, of course, any objectivity in the search for an Old Testament ethic. There is no authority in Scripture according to this view, for it says many different things at the same time, which ultimately, of course, must end up saying nothing.

But even if the Old Testament does have a unified ethical system with a divine authority, how are we to compensate for the historical distance between the times in which it was written and contemporary times and issues? Would this distance not imply that we can use the Bible only descriptively and not prescriptively? Would we not need to overlook the complexity found in the Mosaic laws as well as the complexity of modernity?

My proposal for bridging this gap between the text's ancient "then" and the contemporary "now" is, in keeping with the new so-called "ethnohermeneutics," to include the three horizons of the text in this delicate cross-cultural interpretation: (1) the culture/horizon of the Bible, (2) the culture of the interpreter, and (3) the culture of the receptor. The early church fathers discussed these topics under the terms of *condescension, accommodation,* and *acculturation.* Some also referred to the *particularismus,* that is, the historical and cultural specificity of the Scriptures, meaning the wording and setting were much more at home in another day than in our times.

But the specificity or particularity of those references in the Bible was not meant to obscure or to detract us from making them instructional for all later generations and cultures; instead, it was meant to show us how to apply that word so that it could be used in later times in similar, even if not exactly the same ways. For example, in the New Testament there is a culturally specific reference to "I plead with Euodia and I plead with Syntyche to agree with each other in the Lord" (Phil. 4:2). The particularity of the names and unspoken altercation between these two women was not a "situation specific moment" only, with no relevance to later readers who were not part of that fellowship at Philippi. On the contrary, we usually do not skip over that verse when we are reading or teaching the book of Philippians; instead, we urge in light of Ephesians 4:32 that these two women and we also should "be kind and compassionate to one another, forgiving each other, just as in Christ God forgave [us]." If that is a legitimate way to handle particularisms in the New Testament (and it is), then should not that same approach be used in other times and places and with other issues and people in the Old Testament as well?

In recent years I have used the "Ladder of Abstraction"[15] to show how principlization functions. This Ladder of Abstraction may be defined as a continuous sequence of categorizations from a low level of specificity on the ladder to a high point of generality in a *principle* and then down again on the other ladder leaning up against the first one to a specific application in the contemporary culture.

A good example of this is the way most secular courts use case law. They appeal to the *reason* behind the case law (*ratio decidendi*), which on the surface (prima facie) appears to be no more than a local prohibition. But it provides a principle from which to draw other situations in which the same reasons operated.

A good biblical example comes from Deuteronomy 25:4, "Do not muzzle an ox while it is treading out the grain." Since most readers of the Bible do not own oxen today (or even if they did, they would not use the oxen in place of a combine for threshing their grain to separate the husk from the grain), the question is, does this text have any contemporary relevancy for us today?

The apostle Paul thought that it did have relevancy, for he used it twice (1 Cor. 9:11–12 and 1 Tim. 5:18) to teach that persons who had had the word of God ministered to them should be no stingier than farmers should be as they remove the muzzles from their oxen as they are going round and round trampling out the grain. It would not be fair for the oxen to see all that grain while longing to take a mouthful of that food for themselves. But, many ask, "How did Paul get from allowing an unmuzzled ox to take a swipe of grain to exhorting people to pay their pastors when they had labored in preaching the word of God? Paul could just as well have gone to Deuteronomy 24:14–15, "Do not take advantage of a hired man.... Pay him his wages." But Paul appealed instead to the text about oxen and then declared that it was written "for us"! What was his point?

It is not as all too many scholars have incorrectly argued: Paul was interpreting the text allegorically. In that scenario, Paul would have been bypassing the original meaning and fixing on the text a secondary or an arbitrary meaning instead. Others decided that Paul was using a rabbinical form of exegesis. But no, Paul's argument was a well-grounded a fortiori type of logic (from the lesser to the greater) that went from generosity on a lower level of relations (from the oxen and the owners of those same oxen) to

---

15. I am indebted to Michael Schuter and Roy Clements for this concept of the "Ladder of Abstraction," which first appeared in my book *Toward Rediscovering the Old Testament* (Grand Rapids: Zondervan, 1987), 164–66.

generosity on a higher level of relations (of those who were being served by the oxen and all who were similarly being ministered to by God's servants) as well. Paul was not interested solely in seeing that oxen were fed or that pastors were paid (or even paid well). No, he was interested in the attitudes of kindness and graciousness being inculcated in farmers who owned oxen and in congregations that had pastors serving them.

Thus the Ladder of Abstraction moves from the specific situation (an ox who treads out grain for a farmer) up the ladder to the institutional and personal norms (animals are God's gifts to humanity and should be husbanded kindly) to the top, which gives us the general principle (giving engenders gentleness and graciousness in those mortals who care for and are ministered to by these servants, whether they be animals or otherwise). Then we descend on the second ladder to a similar specific situation where other recipients are being served and ministered to, namely, by pastors. The specific leads to the general principle behind it and moves down again to a corresponding specific in contemporary time.

Do Modern Ethical Questions Take Us "beyond the Bible" to Get Answers?

In recent years there has been talk about going "beyond the Bible"[16] or "beyond the concrete specificity of the Bible."[17] In its best forms, it warns against omitting reading a text first of all in light of its cultural and ancient Near Eastern, Greco-Roman, or Second Temple Judaism contexts as one attempts to move from that day into the contemporary applications in our day. In its poorest moments of explanation, it argues for trajectories that take off from the scriptural text, which is sometimes demeaned by the calling of its words "static" and "isolated," so that answers can be found "beyond the Bible."

At this moment in time, those who want to go beyond the Bible want to do so in a biblical way that gets most of its contemporary trajectory from the import of what the Bible is saying. But this apparently does not mean that there is only one meaning or a single propositional principle behind the trajectory. Rather, it is claimed that there are a number of ways in which one can go "beyond the text" to find modern answers. First, a theologian

16. I. Howard Marshall, *Beyond the Bible: Moving from Scripture to Theology* (Grand Rapids: Baker, 2004).
17. William J. Webb, *Slaves, Women and Homosexuals: Exploring the Hermeneutics of Cultural Analysis* (Downers Grove, Ill.: InterVarsity, 2001).

may use formulations such as the trinity or substitutionary atonement to bring out concepts that are latent within Scripture but which Scripture does not speak of in those precise terms.

Second, we can go "beyond the Bible" when we seek answers the Bible never asks directly or in their current modern formulation. We may use the prohibition on stealing to refer not to stealing a man's donkey or sheep, but in our world to stealing intellectual or digital properties and the like. That would illustrate a modern application of the same ancient principle.

But there is a third way some wish to go "beyond the Bible." We may decide that the descriptions of hell or of everlasting punishment in the Bible are unacceptable for modern ears and eyes and therefore may either ignore these concepts or interpret them in such a way that they do not communicate the same thing the original writers intended. This, of course, is to declare that the Bible is wrong and that we have a better idea of what should have been said or left unsaid on this topic, especially for it to function well in our day. That, of course, would be unacceptable from an evangelical or biblical stance.

Conclusion

God's law is a gift from heaven that is grounded in his grace of redemption. When we live as God intends, we respond in gratitude and joyful thanksgiving to God for his marking out the way we ought to go. God's law is not only for individuals; it is also for the community. In fact, communities and individuals are so interrelated that the concept of "corporate solidarity" is constantly present in the older testament. It expresses the relationship between the "one" and the "many" in such a way that the one often stood for the many and the many were best represented in the one.

Finally, Old Testament ethics focused on such important words as *hesed*, God's "loyal fidelity" and *tsedaqah*, God's "justice" and "righteousness." God has not left us with nowhere to go and without knowing what we are to do or how we are to live. His directions are excellent and perfect.

The Unity *of the* Bible *and* *the* Doctrine *of* Salvation *in* Both Testaments

> "Salvation is found in no one else, for there is no other name under heaven given to men by which we must be saved."
>
> —Acts 4:12

Some Christians incorrectly assume (or at times even boldly announce) that the method by which individuals were converted and received salvation in the Old Testament was different from what was later proclaimed in the New Testament.[1] Perhaps the most progra mmatic statement of this challenge (which was to emerge from such declamations and later to impinge on areas such as missiology and apologetics) came from Charles Ryrie's pen in 1965. He taught: "The *basis* of salvation in every age is the death of Christ; the *requirement* of salvation in every age is faith; the *object* of faith in every age is God; the *content* of faith changes in the various dispensations.[2]

Ryrie is right about the first two points. The problem comes with the third point, for Ryrie implies that the object of faith was not Christ in any of the scores of names used to refer to the Messiah throughout the Old Testament, but only "God." This could easily mean for an Old Testament person or for a tribal person among the hidden peoples of the world, that he or she

---

1. I repeat in this chapter in a reformulated way much of what I said in my article "Salvation in the Old Testament: With Special Emphasis on the Object and Content of Personal Belief," *Jian Dao: A Journal of Bible and Theology* 2 (1994): 1–18.
2. Charles Ryrie, *Dispensationalism Today* (Chicago: Moody, 1965), 23 (italics in original).

could become a theist in general but not a believer in that Man of Promise who was to come, and this would in these unusual circumstances be sufficient for the person's eternal salvation. But does this position accord with the biblical evidence?

This question is all the more important in a day when the argument is made for a general inclusivism for those, who through no fault of their own, as the argument goes, have never heard the name of Jesus as their redeemer. If Abraham merely went outside, looked up at the stars, and concluded that there must be a God, and God therefore approved and accepted Abraham as redeemed, then the object and content of Abraham's faith are separate from ours and changeable—and presumably able to be offered at a discounted rate in similar modern situations as well. But Scripture raises a strong protest against that type of exegesis. Inclusivists and universalists often argue that there are those they call "holy pagans" described in the Bible who have come to faith in the past (as some still do today, they urge) with a minimal understanding about God, never mind about the gospel or about Jesus Christ.[3] Thus those who were what some call "informationally BC" but "chronologically AD,"[4] are given a special, or an exceptional, easy pass to salvation in God.[5]

Of course, all parties do agree, there is progress in the divine revelation in Scripture, for certainly more detail is given in the New Testament than was available in the Old. However, in my view, the process of conversion in both testaments shares more similarities than most students of the Word apparently have thought possible heretofore. Nowhere is this aspect of the case for diversity more apparent than in the identification of what is the *object* of faith. Thus the arguments made today in the name of God's mercy and grace for those who have never heard of the name of Jesus are wide of the mark set for salvation in both testaments. They are based on a false premise that the Old Testament had a different object with different content as the grounds for one's salvation. Not only is the case for the unity of the Bible's view of salvation broken by such a doctrinal conclusion, but it does not fit the case that the Old Testament itself makes in its books.

3. I have argued against such stands in my chapter called "Holy Pagans: Reality or Myth?" in *Faith Comes by Hearing: A Response to Inclusivism*, ed. Christopher W. Morgan and Robert A. Peterson (Downers Grove, Ill.: InterVarsity, 2008), 123–41.
4. This term comes from Charles H. Kraft, *Christianity in Culture* (Maryknoll, N.Y.: Orbis, 1979), 254.
5. Two of the most widely read books claiming this thesis, or variations on the same, are Clark H. Pinnock, *A Wideness in God's Mercy: The Finality of Jesus Christ in a World of Religions* (Grand Rapids: Zondervan, 1992); and John Sanders, *No Other Name: An Investigation into the Destiny of the Unevangelized* (Grand Rapids: Eerdmans, 1992).

Salvation in the Old Testament may be rightly summarized as follows: it was (1) by means of grace, (2) through the regenerating work of the Holy Spirit, (3) by putting one's trust in the coming Man of Promise, who was the "Seed" of Eve, Abraham, Isaac, Jacob, and David. (4) Forgiveness and cleansing from sin were provided by the ultimate sacrifice of a substitute who was yet to come, and resulted in (5) a justification by faith, and (6) a sanctification to a life of holiness, with (7) a hope of the resurrection from the dead. Each of these elements in the Old Testament salvation process is worthy of a fuller demonstration and exposition from the text of the Old Testament itself.[6]

Salvation by Means of Grace (Ex. 34)

Despite the expectations of some that the Old Testament would envelop its message of salvation in a system of works, we can find therein, on the contrary, some of the profoundest and tenderest expressions of God's love. Rather than using abstract terms as the Greek language usually prefers, Hebrew uses concrete expressions for the love of God.

The classic text on the love of God in this earlier testament is found in Deuteronomy 7:7: "The LORD did not set his love on you and choose you because you were more numerous than other peoples, for you were the fewest of all peoples. But it was because the LORD loved you and kept the oath he swore to your forefathers that he brought you out with a mighty hand and redeemed you from the land of slavery, from the power of Pharaoh king of Egypt."

The Hebrew word *'aheb*, "to love," is fairly frequent in the earlier testament, whereas it is not so frequent in cognate Semitic languages of the ancient Near East. God dealt with Israel on the basis of his gracious love. Nothing attracted that love from a human point of view; it was simply a matter of God's matchless grace and nothing else. But this grace had to be appropriated by the individual's faith.

Closely related to the Hebrew word for love is the word *hanan*, "to be favorable to," or "to be gracious to." Related to this verb is the noun *hen*, "unmerited favor," or "grace." And the best word of all, appearing some 248 times in the Old Testament, is *hesed*, a word that is almost impossible to put

---

6. See my chapter "The Old Testament as the Plan of Salvation" in Walter C. Kaiser Jr., *Toward Rediscovering the Old Testament* (Grand Rapids: Zondervan, 1987), 121–44. Much of this chapter is an expansion and revision to my "Salvation in the Old Testament," 1–18.

into one, two, or more English words. It is rendered, "covenantal love," "loyal fidelity," or perhaps best of all as just plain "grace." God granted his favor and love because he wanted to do it, not because anyone naturally deserved it or attracted it by his or her own volition.

God announced in the Mosaic covenant, which was first to be fully operative in Israel, that it was full of "grace and truth" (that is, it was full of *hesed* and *'emet*, Ex. 34:6), just as John 1:17 also alluded to it: "For the law through Moses was given; *grace and truth* in Jesus Christ happened" (my translation, to bring out the fact that Moses was merely the transmitter of God's law, while actual grace and truth took on flesh and blood in the person of Jesus Christ). It is the same grace that had come in the Abrahamic covenant and would reappear in the Davidic new covenant promise-plan of God.

Some think that there is too much dissimilarity between the grace of God as found in the Old Testament with that announced in the New Testament. Usually at this point appeal is made to the story of the rich young ruler in Matthew 19:16 – 26. One commentator sharply drew the contrasts between the Old and the New Testaments by using this story.

> True to the Jewish dispensation [the Old Testament], [Jesus] said with reference to the law of Moses: "This do and thou shalt live"; but when contemplating the cross and Himself as the bread [which had] come down from heaven to give life for the world, He said, "This is the work of God, that ye believe on him whom he hath sent" (John 6:29). These opposing principles are not to be reconciled. They indicate the fundamental distinction which must exist between those principles that obtain in an age of law, on the one hand, and age of grace, on the other hand.[7]

As a further complication of the issue, this same author distinguished between the presentation of the gospel in the Synoptic Gospels and the presentation of the gospel given in John's gospel. The Synoptics offered life as a future blessing on the basis of "faithful law-keeping works: the other [in John's gospel] is gained only through the grace which is in Jesus Christ our Lord."[8]

But that picture does not fit the one the apostle Paul depicted in Romans 4, where both Abraham and David were justified on the basis of faith by grace and not on the basis of "law-keeping works." Moreover, Paul would block any such thoughts of a works kind of righteousness by declaring in Galatians

7. Louis Sperry Chafer, *Grace* (Chicago: Moody, 1947), 92.
8. Ibid.

2:21, "If righteousness could be gained through the law, Christ died for nothing!" No one in either testament or in any age was saved either really or even hypothetically by working for their salvation. No such offer of the gospel ever existed—in fact or even as an outside hypothetical possibility.

Similar to the case of the rich young ruler was the lawyer's question to Jesus, which also had as its working assumption the Pharisaic doctrine of self-justification by means of works. This lawyer wanted to reduce everything to "What [one thing] must I *do*?" (Luke 10:25–37, emphasis added). He thought it was possible to earn his salvation by doing something. Jesus apparently decided to meet this lawyer on his own grounds rather than by challenging his false assumption. In this way Jesus showed that the lawyer, too, stood condemned on those very grounds—his own works, much less on the biblical grounds.

For the rich young ruler, Jesus designed a special test for a particular case in order to show the absurdity of anyone even thinking that someone could earn the favor of God and eternal life. Thus the Bible *reports* what the rich young man said, but it *does not teach* what he said or implied; salvation is and always has been by grace alone and not by "law-keeping works."

Salvation through the Regenerating Work of the Holy Spirit

The work of the Holy Spirit in regeneration and sanctification in the Old Testament is not set forth as clearly as it is taught later on in the Bible. But there can be no question that every new birth before the advent of the cross of Christ was effected only through the work of the Holy Spirit.[9] Self-help could not avail for so significant a new birth.

The best entry point into the discussion of the role and ministry of the Holy Spirit in the salvation process of people in the Old Testament is to go to the conversation our Lord had with Nicodemus in John 3—a precross episode. Nicodemus was "a member of the Jewish ruling council" (v. 1). His nocturnal visit to Jesus, despite his extremely generous estimate that Jesus must have been a "teacher who has come from God," based on the miraculous signs Jesus was exhibiting, led immediately into the discussion of whether a person could get into the kingdom of God without being "born again" and having the work of the Holy Spirit (vv. 3, 5, 8).

---

9. See Geoffrey W. Grogan, "The Experience of Salvation in the Old and New Testaments," *Vox Evangelica* 5 (1967): 12–17. Also see J. C. J. Waite, *The Activity of the Holy Spirit within the Old Testament Period* (London: London Bible College Annual Lecture, 1961).

Nicodemus was rather shocked to be led into this turn of thinking, for these concepts were utterly foreign to him. Then it was Jesus' turn to be amazed, for our Lord wondered where Nicodemus had gone to Yeshiva or seminary. How could it be that he was a teacher of the Jews yet these truths were altogether new to him?

If it is asked, "But where could Nicodemus have turned in the TaNaK [see chap. 4] to learn about the new birth and about the Holy Spirit?" the answer is Ezekiel 36:25–32 where the "new heart" and the "new Spirit" were taught. Even more remarkable is the fact that this was still during the time before the cross, thereby reflecting the days of the Old Testament and the Synoptic Gospels, even though we are now in John's gospel.

The work of the Holy Spirit could also be seen in Psalm 51:11–12, where David prayed, "Do not cast me from your presence or take your Holy Spirit from me. Restore to me the joy of your salvation." David was not concerned about losing the Spirit's guidance in his gift of governing, which had already come upon him when he was anointed by the Holy Spirit (1 Sam. 16:13–14), but was concerned about his soul. He had just prayed in Psalm 51:10, "Create in me a pure heart, O God, and renew a steadfast [KJV, 'right'] spirit within me." Thus, as A. B. Simpson commented, David's mention of the Holy Spirit in this text referred to the Holy Spirit who "will come into the heart that has been made right, and dwell within [him] in His power and holiness."[10]

The New Testament passages about the coming of the Holy Spirit fall into three main groups. The first group deals with the promise of the Holy Spirit who would assist those who would later compose the New Testament, that is, the apostles. The Holy Spirit would remind them of everything: (1) that had happened in the life and ministry of Jesus (John 14:26, "The Holy Spirit ... will teach you all things and will remind you of everything I have said to you"); (2) having to do with the works of Jesus (John 15:26–27, "You also must testify, for you have been with me from the beginning"); and (3) having to do with the doctrine that belonged to the Father (John 16:12–15; "I have much more to say to you, more than you can now bear. But when he, the Spirit of truth, comes, he will guide you into all truth ... [and take] what is mine and [make] it known to you"). These texts should not be confused with the work of the Holy Spirit in other individuals' lives, as so many are tempted to understand them, for these promises were directed to those apostles who would give us the New Testament canon.

10. A. B. Simpson, *The Holy Spirit*, 2 vols. (Harrisburg: Christian Publications, n.d.), 1:137.

The second group of texts focuses on the coming of the Holy Spirit in a new and distinctive way. Thus the new work to which these texts pointed came somewhere between the two terminal points set by the Gospels and Paul's rendering of the significance of this coming in 1 Corinthians 12:13 where he said: "For we were all baptized by one Spirit into one body...." In Acts 1:5 this baptism was "in a few days"; therefore the promised baptism of the Holy Spirit most naturally would be understood to refer to the Jewish Pentecost in Acts 2, the Samaritan visitation of the Spirit in Acts 8, and the Gentile inclusion in the body of believers in Acts 10. That baptism was the work of God whereby the Holy Spirit visibly incorporated for the first time all who believed and then included all who subsequently believed into one body of Christ, his universal church, as taught in 1 Corinthians 12:12–13. That is the baptism of the Holy Spirit.

But there is also a third group of texts dealing with the Holy Spirit in the New Testament. For example, in John 14:16–17, just prior to our Lord's crucifixion, Jesus announced in the upper room discourse: "I will ask the Father, and he will give you another Counselor to be with you forever—the Spirit of truth. The world cannot accept him, because it neither sees him nor knows him. But you know him, for he lives *with* [Gk., *para*] you and *is* [Gr., *estin*] or *will be* [Gr., *estai*] in you" (emphasis added).

The resolution of the tense of the verb "to be" is crucial here. Is it "is" (present tense *estin*) or the future tense (*estai*)? On this distinction hangs the question as to whether the Holy Spirit indwelt the Old Testament believer or whether this was the new work of the Holy Spirit after the resurrection of Christ to indwell all believers for the first time from there on out.

If one chooses the more difficult reading (as the normal practice goes in such textual difficulties), then the present tense is to be preferred. Moreover, the use of the Greek preposition (*para*) translated "with" does not point to a fluctuating relationship, but to one of permanence. The present tense also goes better with the context that says "He lives/remains with you," and then adds "and is in you."

An even more difficult text to explain on the grounds just adopted in the previous paragraph is the text in John 7:38–39. " 'Whoever believes in me, as the Scripture has said, streams of living water will flow from within him.' By this he meant the Spirit, whom those who believed in him were later to receive. Up to that time the Spirit had not been given, since Jesus had not yet been glorified."

So how could it be true at one and the same time that the Holy Spirit was in the Old Testament believer and yet the Spirit had not yet been given? The answer is probably along the lines that Thomas Goodwin indicated when he saw the difference between the internal and quiet coming of the Holy Spirit in individual Old Testament believers prior to Christ's resurrection and the coming of the Holy Spirit "in state, in solemn and visible manner, accompanied with visible effects [just] as [the coming of] Christ [was accompanied with visible effects] …, and whereof all the Jews should be, and were, witnesses."[11] Goodwin's argument, which seems to me to be correct, is that just as it was necessary to have Christ's visible act of dying on Calvary, even though all the Old Testament saints were saved proleptically by believing in this coming work of the Savior, it was also necessary to have the visible work at Pentecost when the Holy Spirit came as it were in state, validating all of the experiences of those who had benefited from his work in regeneration and indwelling during Old Testament times.

Salvation in the Old Testament was Grounded in the Man of Promise (Gen. 15)

Genesis 15:1–6 makes the strongest case possible for the fact that the object of faith for one's salvation is no one less than that "Seed" that was to come from the line of Abraham. Since Acts 4:12 claims that there is salvation in no other name under heaven, the arguments for a reduced plan that would admit persons with a lesser object needs to be reexamined.

The central text in this debate is Genesis 15:6, "[And] Abram believed the LORD, and he credited it [Abram's trust/belief in God's promised 'Seed'] to him as righteousness." What is the context and connection of the "And" as verse 6 begins (left untranslated in the NIV) and the action of Abraham in that verse? It must be Abraham's belief in God's promise of the Seed that would come out of his own body.

T. V. Farris disagreed. "Verse 6, following immediately [vv. 2–5], would suggest that Abraham's faith was in response to the preceding promise [about God's provision of a 'Seed']. The syntactical form of the verb "believed," however, *precludes* that interpretation. The precise nuance of the syntax formula used in this instance, the conjunction *vav* plus a perfect form of the verb, is a matter of dispute among Hebrew grammarians."[12]

---

11. Quoted by George Smeaton, *The Doctrine of the Holy Spirit* (London, 1958), 49, from Thomas Goodwin, *Works,* 12 vols. (Edinburgh, 1861), 6:8.
12. T. V. Farris, *Mighty to Save: A Study in Old Testament Soteriology* (Nashville: Broadman, 1993), 76–77 (emphasis added).

Allen P. Ross likewise wished to separate verse 6 from its context in Genesis 15:2–5 by observing that the NIV left the conjunction untranslated "to avoid the implication that verse 6 resulted from or followed chronologically verse 5." Ross added:

> If the writer had wished to show that this verse followed the preceding in sequence, he would have used the normal structure for narrative sequence (*wa'amin*), "and [then] he believed"—as he did within the sentence to show that the reckoning followed the belief.... "and [so then] he reckoned it." We must conclude that the narrator *did not wish to show sequence* between verses 5 and 6; rather, he wished to make a break with the narrative in order to supply this information about the faith of Abraham.[13]

But both of these analyses leave the context dangling in the air, omitting the conjunction *and*, not to mention the fact that the Hebrew grammarians are not at all agreed about the meaning of the suffixial or the perfect conjugation in this type of construction. By omitting the conjunction lest they connect verses 1–5 with verse 6, they create another problem in order to solve the first one! My conclusion is that verse 6 must be connected with verses 1–5.

Abraham had obeyed God some twenty-five years earlier, when he left Ur of the Chaldeans at age seventy-five. But nowhere in Genesis 12, 13, or 14, which cover the intervening twenty-five years, is there a discussion of his faith. Instead, those chapters focus on the land promised to him. But when Abraham turned one hundred and Sarah ninety, Abraham offered to help God fulfill his own promise by legally adopting his servant from Damascus, Eliezer, to hasten the delayed promise of a "seed." God, however, rejected Abraham's proposal outright and promised instead that a "seed" would come from his own loins; Sarah would conceive, old as she was!

This promise—and person—was the object of Abraham's faith. He simply trusted what God had said, and thereby God counted it as being righteous. That coming one from Abraham's own loins was the object of his faith, and that one was no one less than the Messiah to come.

Salvation Provided by the Blood of a Substitute (Ex. 12; Lev. 16)

Israel had graphically been taught while still in Egypt that the redemption of their firstborn sons was possible by the substitution of the blood of a lamb

---

13. Allen P. Ross, "The Biblical Method of Salvation: A Case for Discontinuity," in *Continuity and Discontinuity*, ed. John Feinberg (Westchester, Ill.: Crossway, 1988), 168 (emphasis added).

smeared on the lintels of the door of every Israelite household as the death angel "passed over" the houses under the blood (Ex. 12:7, 12). In contra-distinction death came to every firstborn human or animal that belonged to the unbelieving Egyptians. Annually thereafter at the Feast of the Passover and the Feast of Unleavened Bread, provision was made for a sin offering to make atonement for the sins of the people (Num. 28:22). One day the real Lamb of God, the Messiah, would come, and the final sin offering would be offered, for what was then only in picture form would come to take on living reality in Christ.

The Hebrew word for "atonement" (*kipper*) did not mean "to cover" the sins of the Old Testament saints until Christ came. Rather, this Hebrew root *kpr* meant "to ransom, or to deliver by means of a substitute." Nowhere is this more graphically taught and illustrated than in the Day of Atonement described in Leviticus 16. After the high priest had divested himself of his splendid robes (as Jesus would do in a similar way, but with a different act, and in the words of Philippians 2:8, "he humbled himself"), not being himself sinless, he first had to offer a sin offering for his own sin.

That completed, the high priest would then choose two goats for the one sin offering for all the people who were truly repentant. One goat was slain "to make atonement ... for ... the whole community of Israel" (Lev. 16:17). The blood of that slain goat was taken into the Holy of Holies this one time each year and placed on top of the mercy seat over the ark of the covenant. It was for all the sin of all Israel—that is, of all who had afflicted their own souls in true repentance.

The second goat, also selected by lot, had all the sins of all the people likewise confessed over its head, and it was led into the wilderness to be lost forever. Thus sins were *forgiven* on the basis of a substitute, and sins were *forgotten* and removed as far as the east is from the west to be remembered against them no more (Ps. 103:12).

One must not infer that the blood of bulls and goats could or did remove sins, for nowhere does the Old Testament claim such (Heb. 10:1–4). But the Israelites did experience *subjective efficacy* for their sins even though they had to wait for *objective efficacy* until Christ's death on the cross. Therefore the sacrifices in the Old Testament were only pictures of the real that was to come. They were models or patterns, with a built-in obsolescence with regard to the ritual, while waiting for the real to come from heaven (Ex. 25:9, 40).

One day the real Lamb of God, the Messiah, would come, and the final sin offering would be offered, for what was then only in picture form would come to take on living reality in Christ.

Salvation Resulted in Justification by Faith (Hab. 2)

So central was Habakkuk 2:4 in the history of the Reformation that it became one of the main cries of that day: "The just shall live by faith." The Greek translators of the Septuagint modified the Hebrew text behind Habakkuk 2:3 from: "Though it [the vision] linger, wait for it" into "If *he* tarry, wait for *him*." In fact, the Hebrew text may be read both ways. No doubt the writer of Hebrews, in 10:37, followed the Greek rendering when he affirmed that those who were righteous must wait for "he who is coming."

The principle that "the righteous shall live by [their] faith" sets forth the doctrine of justification. In this text, the "righteous" are the opposite of the "puffed-up" ones in Habakkuk 2:4. Those who are conceited and who rely on their own wits and resources to bail them out of their difficulties do not need the grace of God. Not so with the righteous: their hope is in the God who had given his word of promise. No greater disparity could be imagined between two such groups.

What, then, is "faith"? Is it the "faithfulness" of the righteous, as most commentators favor today? No, the Hebrew word *'emunah* is more accurately translated here as "faith," or "trust," especially since this text seems to be quoting and building on Genesis 15:6 — "[And] Abram believed the LORD, and he credited it to him as righteousness." Since there is no antecedent for the feminine "it" in Genesis 15:6, "it" must refer back to the verb "believed," and to the corresponding feminine noun for the verb, "to believe." That noun would be *'emunah*, "belief." That is the precise noun that Habakkuk chose to use in 2:4 to describe the justified person vis à vis the life of the arrogant, proud, and puffed-up person. Steadfast trust in God's promised Seed is the only way to receive God's gracious gift of life. In fact, faithfulness cannot even be conceived apart from trust and reliance on the one who was to come and the God who sent him.

How would anyone become "righteous"? Righteousness in this context was not an ethical term, but a religious one. It has a forensic or legal aspect in that it was a judge's term, whereby he pronounced a person to be innocent of all charges against him. This usage can be seen in Exodus 23:7, "[God] will not acquit the guilty," and in 2 Kings 10:9, where Jehu exonerated the people of any bloodguilt of the sons of Ahab he had just murdered, by saying, "You are innocent [righteous]" (cf. also Job 13:18; Isa. 5:23).

Therefore, the righteous person is the one whom God has declared innocent, not the one who has worked for a certain ethical status or shown his or her faithfulness to a certain standard. When an Old Testament person put his or her trust in the Man of Promise/Seed who was to come, God acted as the Judge and pronounced that person already in Old Testament times "justified" and free of any further guilt as a result of the sin that had been committed.

A Call to a Life of Holiness (Lev. 19)

Belief in this coming Man of Promise was not the end of the matter, for repeatedly the law of Moses and the Prophets kept calling God's people back to the one and only standard set by God. It was this: "Be holy because I, the LORD your God, am holy" (Lev. 19:2 et al.). Thus, just as God was distinct and set apart to himself, so all who were called by his name likewise were set apart from all that did not fit the mark or the goal of matching what he was in his person and character.

No higher definition of holiness or sanctification could be given than the one that used the very character and nature of God as its mark of their high calling in God their Lord. The mark of excellence, then, was the person of the living God; the Law served only as a guide for promoting that type of holiness.

The Resurrection from the Dead (Isa. 26)

The Lord identified himself as being not the God of the dead, but of the living: the God of Abraham, Isaac, and Jacob (Ex. 6:3; cf. Luke 20:37–38). The prospect of life after death is not as fully developed in the Old Testament as in the New,[14] yet there can be no doubt that the saints of the older testament believed they would see God after their death and enjoy his presence.

As early as the days of Enoch (the seventh from Adam) in Genesis 5:24, there was confidence that mortals could go into the very presence of God in heaven, for that is what Enoch did. Enoch "was taken" to be with God without going through the painful process of dying. That ought to have

The righteous person is the one whom God has declared innocent, not the one who has worked for a certain ethical status or shown his or her faithfulness to a certain standard.

---

14. George Mark Elliott, "Future Life in the Old Testament," *Seminary Review* 3 (1957): 41–49; S. Zandstra, "Sheol and Pit in the Old Testament," *Princeton Theological Review* 5 (1907): 631–41; Walter C. Kaiser Jr., "What Hope Did OT Believers Have of Life beyond the Grave?" in *Toward Rediscovering the Old Testament*, 141–44; and Harris Birkeland, "The Belief in the Resurrection of the Dead in the Old Testament," *Studia Theologica* 3 (1950): 77.

settled the question both in theory and in fact as to whether mortals can live with God after death.

Interestingly enough, several ancient cultures, such as Egypt, built the whole economy of their state around the concept of life after death, as evidenced by their massive pyramids and wall paintings depicting their concepts of life after death. So the topic of life after death was not an unthinkable topic for that culture or for those times. These men and women lived close to life and death every day, for they heard the wail of newborn babies as they walked down the streets and the death rattle of those passing from this life. Such things were almost daily occurrences, not ones isolated from the rest of humanity in sanitized hospitals or senior living facilities as they are today.

Abraham is a witness to a concept of life after death, for he must have believed that God was able to raise his slain son back from the dead (Gen. 22:5). He told his servants to wait at the foot of the mountain until he and his son returned from worshiping God! Likewise, David was certain of his own immortality as he explained in Psalm 16. If God was going to resurrect his "Holy One" (Heb., *hasid*) from the grave, David, too, was resurrectible on the same basis.

Almost all interpreters concede the point that Isaiah 26:19 and Daniel 12:2 promise life after death as well. The only quibble is over the dating of these passages. Other texts could be brought to bear here as well: Job 14:14; 19:25–27; Pss. 49; 73:17; Eccl. 2:14–16; 3:19–21; 9:1–3. These passages and more make a mighty case for the fact that there was real hope for all who believed on the one who was to come, the Messiah himself.

Conclusion

The offer of salvation in the Old Testament carried in its seminal form an organic connection with the continuation of the same doctrine in the New Testament. But no less important was the fact that its *object* of hope was the coming Son of God that New Testament believers have also been taught to expect and to put their trust in. Indeed, salvation in the Old Testament was part and parcel of the "so great salvation" that stretched across two testaments in a single unified approach as to how men and women would inherit eternal life.

The Unity *of the* Mission *in the* Old Testament

When we call the message of the Old Testament "universal," we mean that it has the whole world in view and that it has validity for the whole world. This universality is the basis for the missionary message of the Old Testament.

—Johannes Blaw[1]

Almost all modern readers of Scripture will grant that there is clear evidence for asserting that the New Testament has a strong mission emphasis (especially in the so-called Great Commission and in the book of Acts), but few will grant that the Old Testament has anything even approaching such a missiological emphasis. In fact, many Old Testament scholars conclude that in the older testament God's purpose was concerned solely with the election of Israel and their calling; there was no plan for the salvation of foreign nations!

Is that estimate correct? Can the term *missions* or *missionary* be employed in relation to God's program prior to our Lord's commissioning his disciples shortly before his ascension? And did either term have any part in the ongoing cohesive purpose and plan of God? As always, part of the answer depends on how the terms are used. However, an even larger part of the case will hang on how the Old Testament texts and contexts are understood and how they are applied to the whole purpose of God as announced in the older testament.

---

1. Johannes Blaw, *The Missionary Nature of the Church: A Survey of the Biblical Theology of Mission* (London: Lutterworth, 1962), 17.

A case for missions forming a central role in the plan of God in the Old Testament can indeed be successfully argued, for an international invitation of the gospel to all nations is explicitly set forth in the Old Testament, and it forms one of the great unifying threads of meaning in the purpose-plan of God. This invitation focuses on the Man of Promise who was to come in the line of Eve, Shem, Abraham, Isaac, Jacob, and David. And its most programmatic statement can be found in Genesis 12:3: "All peoples on earth will be blessed through you" — a thesis that Paul declared in Galatians 3:8 was nothing less than the gospel itself!

But even prior to that formal announcement, the scope of the message and mission of Genesis 1–11 was nothing short of being universal, embracing all peoples and all nations of the earth. Only in Genesis 12:3 was the mission channeled through that one man, family, and nation as the medium by which God would bless all nations on the earth. It is this line of revelation that I propose to trace here.

The Case for Missions in the Torah

Even before God began to call any of the patriarchs or even the nation Israel, the bent of revelation during the first eleven chapters of the Bible (that must cover at least as much time in history as the rest of the entire Old Testament), was aimed at all the nations of the world. It was universal in its scope.

The principal person through whom God made his address known to the seventy nations of that time was Noah. He, for all his faults, was declared to be "a righteous man, blameless among the people of his time" and one who "walked with God" (Gen. 6:9). During the many years that construction on the ark ensued (were they the 120 years mentioned in Gen. 6:3?), Noah surely preached the gospel to the people who came to see this bizarre anomaly of building a huge vessel high and dry on land! Nevertheless, does not 2 Peter 2:5 represent Noah as "a preacher of righteousness"? And does not 1 Peter 3:18–20 affirm that Christ himself "went" "by the Spirit" and preached to those who had been held captive by their own sins and disobedience, through the preaching of Noah "while the ark was being built"? If the argument of Peter is correct, and it surely is, then the mission to the nations had an early start indeed! Noah may well have been the first missionary as he was sent to warn all people on earth at that time of the impending disaster and God's provision for deliverance if it would be accepted.

The torch passed from Noah to the line of Noah's son Shem, later to be known as the Semites. But it was one Semite in particular, Abraham, whom God would call to be the instrument through whom all people in all the nations of the earth could be blessed (Gen. 12:3). It is especially important that the verb meaning "be blessed" be translated as a passive[2] and not as a reflexive as many moderns have persisted in translating it. That is the way the third-century BC Greek Septuagint translation rendered it, as did the intertestamental and apocryphal work Ecclesiasticus (44:21). Likewise, the apostle Paul rendered it as a passive in Romans 4:13 and Galatians 3:8.

Certainly if the passive form is correct, as I have argued here, God surely intended to use Abraham as a means of blessing all the nations of the world. This would be God's answer to the most recent curse imposed on the earth at the dispersion of the human race at the Tower of Babel (Gen. 11:7–8). But does all this add up, you may ask, to being a missionary text? If Abraham is to be no more than an intermediary of the divine blessing, where is the initiative that is usually associated with actively taking the message to the nations? Surely Abraham was more than a foil for the gospel. By the very nature of his status as the current officeholder of the promise line, and by virtue of his wealth and wide contacts with the likes of Pharaoh of Egypt and Abimelech of the Philistines, he was called upon to bear witness constantly before a watching world about the Man of Promise who would come from his offspring. Furthermore, since whole nations came from his immediate lineage, what he said, practiced, and proclaimed would be remembered for years to come.

The promise of a universal blessing in Genesis 12:3 for all the "families" of the earth is essentially repeated in Genesis 18:18; 22:18; 26:4; and 28:14. The fact is that the Hebrew word in Genesis 12:3 and 28:14 is *mishpahah*, which regularly denotes a fairly small group of people, usually less than a tribe. The Greek Septuagintal translation of the other three passages from Genesis has the familiar *panta ta ethne*, a phrase that has the ring of people groups rather than Gentile individuals. In fact,

Noah may well have been the first missionary as he was sent to warn all people on earth at that time of the impending disaster and God's provision for deliverance if it would be accepted.

2. The Hebrew grammar is no less decisive here, for the niphal is the passive form of the Hebrew verb *brk*. The most definitive article ever written on this point of grammar, which also has never been answered by any who insist on translating this verbal form as reflexive, is O. T. Allis, "The Blessing of Abraham," *Princeton Theological Review* 25 (1927): 263–98. Genesis 12:3; 18:18; and 28:14 all use the niphal form of the verb, while Genesis 22:18 and 26:4 use the hithpael form, presumably translated as "bless oneself." Yet it must be noticed that all *five* passages listed above are treated in the Samaritan Version and the Babylonian (Onkelos) and Jerusalem (Pseudo-Jonathan) Targums as passives. Moreover, Allis listed eighteen hithpael forms of the Hebrew verb that also had a possible passive meaning.

the Greek phrase in Acts 3:25 for "all the families" is *pasai hai patriai*. This is an independent translation of Genesis 12:3, different from both the Greek Old Testament (*pasai hai phulai*) and the way Paul translates it in Galatians 3:8 (*panta ta ethne*). But by choosing another word that refers to people groups (*patriai*), the writer confirms that the promise was understood in the early church in terms of people groups, not only in terms of Gentile individuals.[3]

Thus the desire is that not just "all the nations" (*panta to ethne*) would respond to the truth and worship God, but even the smaller groupings of peoples would hear and believe.

Besides Noah, Abraham, and the other patriarchs who shared Abraham's identical call, the mission of what was by now a young nation became even clearer: Israel was being called to be "a kingdom of priests and a holy nation" according to the famous "eagles' wings speech" of Yahweh in Exodus 19 (see v. 6). From this same text, centuries later would emerge the famous declaration of the priesthood of all believers as the text was repeated in 1 Peter 2:5 and Revelation 1:6.

God's intention had been that every Israelite would serve as a priest. And if it be asked for whom they were to serve as priests, the answer was readily available: for all the nations of the earth. Only after the nation's refusal to confront so awesome an experience as directly hearing the voice of God from heaven did God appoint the tribe of Levi to minister on their behalf (Ex. 32:29). But there could be no doubt about God's original plan: every Israelite was to be a ministering priest.[4]

Did the call of the Levites change the missionary imperative for the whole nation? No! All that was changed was the individual's direct access to hearing from God: now the Levitical priests would represent the people before God. Meanwhile, the election of God was never meant to be an election for privilege or position; instead, it was to be an election *for service*. And that service was taking the gospel to all the people groups of the world (Gal. 3:8).

The Case for Missions in the Earlier Prophets

The books of Joshua, Judges, Samuel, and Kings would not appear on the surface to offer any missionary imperatives. But surprisingly, they contain

The election of God was never meant to be an election for privilege or position; instead, it was to be an election for service. And that service was taking the gospel to all the people groups of the world.

---

3. John Piper, *Let The Nations Be Glad! The Supremacy of God in Missions* (Grand Rapids: Baker, 1993), 182.
4. Blaw, *Missionary Nature of the Church*, 24, explained, "She [Israel] represents God in the world of nations. What priests are for a people, Israel as a people is for the world."

one of the great pivotal points in the history of missions in the Old Testament. It came in King David's response to Nathan's prediction that God would bless David by giving to him a throne, a dynasty, and a kingdom that would last forever (2 Sam. 7:16).

David was so overwhelmed by such a strong affirmation from God in return for his measly, and premature, offer to build a house for God similar to his own recently constructed palace, that he blurted out in 2 Samuel 7:18–19, "Who am I, O Sovereign LORD, and what is my family, that you have brought me this far? And if this is not enough in your sight, O Sovereign LORD, you have also spoken about the future of the house of your servant. Is this your usual way of dealing with man, O Sovereign LORD?" My rendering of the last line is, "And this is [(or) will be] the *charter for [all] humanity!*"[5]

David instinctively knew that what was being offered to him in this new divine blessing was essentially a repetition and expansion of the blessing already given to Abraham, Isaac, and Jacob. Not only were some of the key phrases from those earlier promises repeated in David's prayer in verses 20–29,[6] but even the peculiarly distinctive way of addressing God as "Adonai Yahweh" (NIV's "Sovereign LORD") is never found in the rest of the books of Samuel and Kings. It is, however, precisely the form of address used in Genesis 15:2, 8 where God promised Abraham a "seed." Therefore, with the realization that David had just been granted an everlasting dynasty, dominion, and kingdom, David exploded with uncontainable joy: "And this is the charter for all mankind, O Lord Yahweh!" Thus the ancient plan of God would continue. Only now it would involve a king and a kingdom, but that blessing would also involve the future of all humanity.

Earlier in David's life, when the ark of Yahweh had been returned to Jerusalem, David appointed for the first time a choir to sing praises to the Lord. But it is not the uniqueness of the appointment that commands our attention; it is the theology of the songs. One such song, 1 Chronicles 16:23–33, was the basis for one of the greatest missionary psalms in the psalter, Psalm 96. There the anonymous psalmist ordered "all the earth" (vv. 1, 9) and "families of nations" (v. 7) to "proclaim (*bisser*, v. 6) his salvation day after day" (v. 2), to "declare (*sipper*) his glory among the nations" (v. 3), and to "say (*'amar*) among the nations, 'The LORD reigns'" (v. 10).

5. For a further expansion and explanation of this phrase, see Walter C. Kaiser Jr., "The Blessing of David: The Charter for Humanity," in *The Law and the Prophets* (Oswald T. Allis Festschrift), ed. J. Skilton (Philadelphia: Presbyterian and Reformed, 1974), 298–318.
6. See the list of parallels in Walter C. Kaiser Jr., "A Charter for Humanity," in *Toward an Old Testament Theology* (Grand Rapids: Zondervan, 1978), 152–55.

This psalm is not completely eschatological; it is also a *present* expectation of the psalmist, for the missionary motivation is built on the pivotal verse 5, which asserts that only Yahweh is the true God, while the gods of all the nations are but idols.

Despite the transparent universal call to all the peoples in Psalm 96, most scholars have failed to notice this psalm and the role it played in Israel's summons to carry out the work of missions. The opening three verses of the psalm are a clear call to active, evangelistic mission, while verses 4–6 contrast Yahweh's greatness with the emptiness of the gods and idols of the Gentiles. An urgent call to the nations to worship Yahweh follows in the psalm, with a promise of the joyous results of such a conversion in verses 11–12.

Even though the psalm does not offer a title or any internal evidence that would help to date it, its utilization in 1 Chronicles 16:23–33 during the early years of David should be enough to establish it as being monarchical in origin, if not Davidic.[7] Nevertheless, Psalm 96 is perhaps the most striking missionary passage in the book of Psalms. Given the fact that the nation had just come through such a spiritual low and an ebb of emotion during the days of the Judges, it is remarkable that such a statement of mission would emerge after centuries of neglect of the universal call of the gospel and a commission to mission work among the Gentiles and nations at large.

The other great moment for missions and universal outreach during this period was the dedicatory prayer of Solomon in 1 Kings 8:41–43. He specifically provided for the eventuality that the "foreigner who [did] not belong to your people Israel" would come from a distant land to pray to the Lord in the temple in Jerusalem. Solomon's request was that God would hear whatever this foreigner asked of him "so that all the peoples of the earth may know your name and fear you, as do your own people Israel" (v. 43). It is clear that what God had given to Israel was a treasure that should be shared with all the nations of the earth.

It is clear that what God had given to Israel was a treasure that should be shared with all the nations of the earth.

The Case for Missions in the Psalms

George W. Peters found that there were "more than 175 references of a universalistic note relating to the nations of the world.... Indeed, the Psalter

---

7. Characteristically, Old Testament scholarship has denied the early date for Psalm 96. Charles Briggs, *The Book of Psalms*, 2 vols., International Critical Commentary (Edinburgh: T. & T. Clark, 1907), 2:300, claimed that Psalm 96 was a late insertion into Chronicles and that the cause of joy in the psalm was the overthrow of the Persian Empire by Alexander the Great (p. 303). Others seemed to date it to the postexilic period, even if for different reasons.

is one of the *greatest missionary books in the world*, though seldom seen from that point of view."[8] Few psalms can be classified as being explicit missionary psalms in total, but usually Psalms 2, 33, 67, 96, 98, 117, and 145 are categorized as such.

In addition to Psalm 96, which has been discussed already, Psalm 117 is one of the most universalistic in calling all nations to worship Yahweh. The grounds on which they are urged to join in this doxology to the Father are given in verse 2: Yahweh's grace and mercy to Israel. While it does not call Israel to tell the Gentiles of God's grace, it certainly expects that the nations *at that time* would be able to worship Yahweh and to acknowledge his "grace" (Heb., *hesed.* Thus what David vowed to do through song in Psalm 18:48–49 ("I will praise you among the nations") is now required of all the nations in Psalm 117—that is, to make Yahweh known to all mortals.

In this same category is Psalm 67. There the prayer in verse 1 is stated in terms of the famous Aaronic benediction where it is hoped that God would "be gracious to [Israel] and bless [them] and make his face shine upon [them]." But the reason for this request is given in verse 2: "that (Heb., *lada'at*) your ways may be known on earth, your salvation among all nations." In fact, "all nations" is placed in the emphatic position in the Hebrew text.

The strophe dividers for this psalm come in the repeated desire of verses 3 and 5: "May the peoples praise you, O God; may all the peoples praise you." The ultimate goal of the psalm is found in v. 7: "God will bless us, and all the ends of the earth will fear him." That is hardly a provincial or chauvinistic orientation, for the grace of God was to penetrate in that same period of time to the "ends of the earth"!

The Case for Missions in the Prophets

The most significant proponent of the concept of mission among the prophets is Isaiah. And at the center of this concept of the universal offer of the gospel and mission are the famous Servant Songs of Isaiah (Isa. 42:1–7; 49:1–7; 50:4–11; 52:13–53:12). One of the great themes in these Servant Songs is that Israel is to be Yahweh's witness to the nations. In fact, God will restore Israel once again "so that from the rising of the sun to the place of its setting men might know there is none else besides me" (Isa. 45:6).

---

8. George W. Peters, *A Biblical Theology of Missions* (Chicago: Moody, 1972), 115 (emphasis added).

In the very first servant song, it is promised that God would "put [his] Spirit on [his servant] and he [would] bring justice (Heb., *mishpat*) to the nations.... He [would] not falter or be discouraged until he establish[ed] justice on earth. In his law the islands [i.e., the distant countries around the Mediterranean Sea] [would] put their hope" (Isa. 42:1–4). Unfortunately, some scholars, reading "judgment" for the twice-repeated word "justice," interpreted the prophecy politically, as if the servant would exercise some kind of government over the nations during this present age. But that rendering does not match the conclusion the second parallel servant song reaches—namely, "I will also make you a light for the Gentiles, that you may bring my salvation to the ends of the earth" (Isa. 49:6).

The best rendering of *mishpat* in Isaiah 42:1 and 4 is something like "religion,"[9] since it is paralleled by *torah*, that is, "instruction in the right way." Thus a standard in revealed religion is indicated by *mishpat*. It is for this standard and this instruction that the nations "wait," a word that meant in the Hebrew piel "to wait expectantly" rather than to wait in dread of judgment as Snaith and others had wanted it to turn out. Moreover, since the Spirit was needed to accomplish this task of imparting to the nations this standard and instruction, it was an intensely spiritual task, not a judicial one as some scholars had assessed it.

Those who have balked at the missiological conclusions advocated here have resorted to holding with N. H. Snaith that the prophet is concerned only with the nation of Israel throughout this whole section of Isaiah. To maintain this view, Snaith must resort to translating the phrase "light to the nations" (Heb., *le'or goyim*; Isa. 42:6; 49:6 NASB) as "a light of the nations" in the sense of "a light throughout the Gentile lands," but reserved for Israel, "since this is the only salvation in which the prophet is interested."[10] But this is just as forced an exegesis on the part of Snaith as is his treatment of Isaiah 45:22, which reads: "Turn to me and be saved, all you ends of the earth; for I am God, and there is no other." Snaith interpreted this to mean that it referred "to all the scattered Israelites amongst the heathen everywhere."[11] That hardly suited the context or the meaning of the words in Isaiah 45:22.

What, then, does "light" imply? Is it literal light, that which illuminates and brings information? Or is the light to be understood metaphorically,

---

9. See A. Gelston, "The Missionary Message of Second Isaiah," *Scottish Journal of Theology* 18 (1965): 315, where he appealed to 2 Kings 17:26, with its rendering of "manner" and to Jeremiah 5:4; 8:7, where "ordinance" was the best way to translate *mishpat*.

10. N. H. Snaith, "The Servant of the Lord in Deutero-Isaiah," in *Studies in Old Testament Prophecy*, ed. H. H. Rowley (Edinburgh: T. & T. Clark, 1957), 191, 198.

11. Ibid., 197.

that is, of the "salvation" of the nations? While Isaiah 42:6 does not supply ample context to decide between these two options, Isaiah 49:6 does. In verse 6e the light was given in order that the servant might bring God's salvation to the ends of the earth.

One more hurdle must be crossed, for those resisting a missionary interpretation, having lost the exegetical argument on the issues of *mishpat* and *le'or goyim*, fall back to identifying the "covenant for the peoples" (*librit 'am*) in Isaiah 42:6d as a reference to Israel. At first the attempt is made to say that *'am* in the singular always stands for Israel while only the plural refers to the nations. But there are clear exceptions to this suggestion that the word must be plural if it is to refer to the other nations. Several of these so-called exceptions can be found right in this same context: Isaiah 40:7 and 42:5 have the singular *'am*, but it refers to people groups at large, as all sides agree. Furthermore, the fact that the "covenant" includes the nations is no more startling than the fact already discussed in 2 Samuel 7:19 that what David was promised was a "charter/law for all humanity." Neither is it more surprising than Amos 9:11–12 saying that all the nations that bore God's name (in that typical act of ownership) were therefore part of the "house of David." Though that "house" had been reduced at that time to a mere "hut," God would one day repair and fully restore it. Thus the "covenant for the people" would include the restoration of Israel (where the identical phrase of "covenant for the people" and the concept of the restoration of Israel occurs in Isa. 49:8) along with the mission to the people groups of the world.

The only other way to avoid the clear missiological implications of these two great servant songs in Isaiah 42 and 49 is to designate the "servant" exclusively as an individual and to project all the summons to proclaim God's name among the nations to an eschatological time. But that view cannot stand either, for the servant is specifically declared to be both "Israel" and a coming representative who will effect a work *on behalf of Israel*. Therefore, in the corporate solidarity of the figure of the servant who is both the whole nation and a coming individual, lies the real justification for speaking of a missionary calling of Israel to serve the nations.

Israel as a nation, then, was just as much "sent" as was the prophet Jonah to the ancient capital of Assyria, Nineveh. In that role of being sent, three principles became most important for those who were to participate in God's plan for the nations: (1) Israel had to conserve themselves for this task; therefore they were called to be "holy" to the Lord. All compromise dishonored God before the nations (Lev. 20:3; Ezek. 36:17ff.; et al.). (2)

In the corporate solidarity of the figure of the servant who is both the whole nation and a coming individual, lies the real justification for speaking of a missionary calling of Israel to serve the nations.

191

Israel had to be receptive to the principle of the universal nature of the call to all nations, for the "election" of God presumed an election for service and not an election for privilege or pride. (3) Israel's concern was to be not their own reputation, but the "Name" of God.[12]

It is impossible, of course, to survey all the data that the prophets supply on the call of God to Israel for their involvement in missions. But one concluding text from the last prophet will help to clinch the case for missions from the prophets. It is that startling text from Malachi 1:11. In the midst of a series of severe condemnations of the priesthood for lacking credibility and authenticity in (1) their professions of faith (1:6–7), (2) their gifts to God (1:8–9), (3) their service to God (1:10, 12), and (4) their time serving God (1:13–14), Malachi interjects verse 11, which shines like a ray of sunshine in an otherwise dark and gloomy litany of failures. God declared: " 'My name will be great among the nations, from the rising to the setting of the sun. In every place incense and pure offerings will be brought to my name, because my name will be great among the nations,' says the LORD Almighty." The geographic, political, and ethnic scope of this promise would be breathtaking, for God's reign would extend from one end of the world to the other. And no longer would kosher sacrifices be restricted to being offered only in Jerusalem at the temple, but in "every place" "pure" offerings would be offered. That must have blown away every category known to the audience of that day who first heard Malachi's disturbing words. God's name and reputation would also be great among the Gentiles. The nation that had been called to be "a kingdom of priests" (Ex. 19:5–6) and a "light for the Gentiles" (Isa. 42:6; 49:6), and the one through whom all the nations of the earth would be blessed (Gen. 12:3), was now being told that God would still succeed in his plan and purpose to invite all the nations of the earth to his salvation. He would indeed bless "all the ends of the earth" (Ps. 67:7) exactly as the Aaronic benediction had stated (Num. 6:24–26).

Conclusion

The Old Testament does provide a central place for missions in the whole plan and purpose of God. Israel was faulted not only for their idolatry and sins of the flesh, but also because they failed to carry out that central mission given to them to be the channel by which the nations of the world

---

12. These three points are adaptations of the argument made by John R. Peck, "The Missionary View of the Old Testament," *Theological Students Fellowship Bulletin* 54 (1969): 6–7.

would hear about the Promised One who was to come and redeem the world from their sins.[13] Any treatment of the Old Testament that neglects this theme of the universal call of God to all the nations and of Israel's call to be the means of announcing that blessing to all the people groups of the world falls far short of apprehending just what it was that God was about in the older testament.

When the total picture of the call for Israel's missionary activity is realized, it is not a long stretch at all to see how unified the two testaments are in encouraging the same kind of response from all of God's people in the mission of the gospel. Instead of presenting two divine plans as the mission of God, the cohesiveness of the single plan becomes all the more apparent as the progress of revelation enlarges and enhances that plan that grows from the seed sown prior to the patriarchs and is organically connected with the Great Commission and the great missionary journeys of the apostle Paul.

13. For greater detail in this argument, see Walter C. Kaiser Jr., *Mission in the Old Testament: Israel as a Light to the Nations* (Grand Rapids: Baker, 2000).

The Unity *of the* Bible *and* Hermeneutics

A fundamental principle in grammatico-historical exposition is that words and sentences can have but one signification in one and the same connection. The moment we neglect this principle we drift out upon a sea of uncertainty and conjecture.

— Milton Terry[1]

We affirm that the meaning expressed in each biblical text is single, definite and fixed. We deny that the recognition of this single meaning eliminates the variety of its application.

— International Council on Biblical Inerrancy[2]

General Hermeneutics

No definition of the process of interpreting the Bible can be more fundamental than this: to interpret we must in every case reproduce the sense the scriptural writer intended for his own words. The first object in the interpretive process must be to link those ideas with the author's language that he first connected with them.[3] Then we may proceed to express those same ideas understandably for our own day.

---

1. Milton S. Terry, *Biblical Hermeneutics: A Treatise on the Interpretation of the Old and New Testaments* (1885; repr., Grand Rapids: Zondervan, 1947), 205.
2. Article VII, "Articles of Affirmation and Denial," adopted by the International Council on Biblical Inerrancy, Chicago, November 10–13, 1982.
3. See Walter C. Kaiser Jr., "Legitimate Hermeneutics," in *Inerrancy*, ed. Norman Geisler (Grand Rapids: Zondervan, 1979), 117–47; reprinted in *A Guide to Contemporary Hermeneutics: Major Trends in Biblical Interpretation*, ed. Donald K. McKim (Grand Rapids: Eerdmans, 1986), 111–41.

To interpret we must in every case reproduce the sense the scriptural writer intended for his own words.

However, never has our postmodern society, including now a host of evangelical writers and preachers, resisted hermeneutical rules more strenuously than at the point of this definition. While the evangelical wing of interpreters would not knowingly concur with the postmodern approach that "all knowledge is relative,"[4] many evangelicals today want to violate the single-meaning hermeneutic by affirming variously such statements as these: (1) It is often possible to extend the authorial intention and world *beyond* the human author by means of the canonical context.[5] (2) The New Testament writers read new meanings into the Old Testament.[6] (3) "The meaning of the Bible is not static and locked up in the past, but is something living and active."[7] (4) "An author may intend to convey multiple meanings or levels of meaning."[8] Evaluations of the interpretive process such as these tend to introduce a whole new set of rules into the way biblical texts have been interpreted for centuries.

For example, recently I heard an evangelical scholar assert that there are an "infinite number of meanings to every passage in the Bible." Surely that would be enough to indicate that the author and his meaning were no longer needed or were not at all relevant for validating one meaning over against some of the many other meanings. The author's meaning was said to be only one of the many meanings now available in a whole potpourri of meanings.

However, many who have taken what we may here call an "antiauthorial intentional meaning" and applied it to understanding the Bible also want to claim that what an author meant is likely to be of *some* use in determining what the multiplicity of meanings could mean. While this of course is generous, it is inconsistent with the whole thesis of the antiauthorial intention school of interpretation. To say that the author's meaning may be useful but not determinative is merely to be paternalistic. And showing that this type of pluralism does not favor any one meaning to the exclusion of all the others, but out of deference to the way previous generations looked at the text, some are willing to concede that the author's meaning does play some

---

4. E. D. Hirsch, *Validity in Interpretation* (New Haven, Conn.: Yale University Press, 1967), 4.
5. E. R. Clendenen, "Postholes, Postmodernism, and the Prophets: Towards a Textlinguistic Paradigm," chap. 8 in *The Challenge of Postmodernism: An Evangelical Engagement*, ed. David Dockery (Wheaton: Victor, 1995).
6. Vern Poythress, "Divine Meaning of Scripture," *Westminster Theological Journal* 48 (1986): 253–58.
7. Clark Pinnock, "Biblical Texts: Past and Future Meanings," a paper read in November 1998 at the Evangelical Theological Society Hermeneutics Study Group, later printed in *Wesleyan Theological Journal* 34, no. 2 (1999): 136–51; citation from p. 140.
8. W. W. Klein, C. L. Blomberg, and R. L. Hubbard Jr., *Introduction to Biblical Interpretation* (Dallas: Word, 1993), 122 (emphasis in the original).

unspecified but nondeterminative role! This thesis has moved us a long ways off from where evangelicalism was not more than fifty years ago.

The Origins of the Modern Interpretive Movement

The modern interpretive movement started, it would appear, as two modern writers, William Wimsatt and Monroe Beardsley, writing in the *Swanee Review* in 1946, fired what may be regarded as the literary shot heard round the world. They maintained that the author's intention was not the determinative factor in what a literary work meant; in fact, the author's intention was probably irrelevant to what the work meant![9]

However, given the fact that the author's beliefs, feelings, and intentions are so closely connected with his or her use of words, which carry with them associations or connotations employed by that writer, the whole antiauthorial intentionality argument begins to break down. In our post-Kantian relativism, where "all knowledge is relative," we need to assure such "cognitive atheists" that there is a real possibility of learning and that knowledge is not to be reduced to the horizon of one's own prejudices and personal predilections. Such interpretive solipsism can be escaped by heeding the distinction made by E. D. Hirsch between "meaning" and "significance." His theses can be put into four propositions:

1. Verbal meaning is what a person (either the speaker or writer) has willed to convey by a set of words shared either verbally or by means of linguistic signs.
2. The speaker or author's truth-intention or assertions provide the only genuinely discriminating norm for ascertaining a valid or true interpretation from false or invalid ones.
3. The first task of the interpretive process is to make clear what the spoken or written words mean, not what their significance is. Meaning is represented by the spoken words selected or what the writer meant to say by the use of the linguistic signs chosen. Significance, by way of contrast, names a relationship between that meaning and a person, concept, situation, or any other possible number of things.

---

9. William K. Wimsatt and Monroe C. Beardsley, "The Intentional Fallacy," *The Swanee Review* 54 (1946); reprinted in Wimsatt and Beardsley, *The Verbal Icon: Studies in the Meaning of Poetry* (Lexington: University of Kentucky Press, 1954), 3–18.

4. The meaning of a speech or text cannot change once it is spoken or written, but its significance can and does change as it is viewed against different times, cultures, or situations. If meanings were not determinative, then there would be no fixed norm by which to judge whether a passage was being fairly interpreted or not.[10]

The argument here is countercultural to our times in that we argue that texts do have "meaning" in themselves, meaning that is objectively there. The denial implied here is that "meaning" is not created afresh every time a reader interacts with the text. Instead, there is a fixed meaning once the text has been written or spoken into a recorder. If that were not so, speakers and writers would not need to go through the embarrassing task of retracting or apologizing for what they said when they committed an error or spoke in an unfair way; they would merely need to reinterpret what had been said in a fresh way that went beyond what had been recorded or put on paper! The meaning that people had taken offense to would now be superseded by one or more newer meanings. But would this answer the problem?

A Literal Meaning versus a Deeper Meaning

Most interpreters agree that good interpretation must replicate the way the Bible interprets itself if we are to expect authority from our teaching or preaching. But for many, that is where the tension begins: "Most do not interpret the Bible the way that it appears to interpret itself."[11] James De Young and Sarah Hurty, who made that claim, went on to say: "It may come as a surprise to most Christians that the traditional view is that we cannot follow Jesus and His disciples in their method of interpreting Scripture. This is because they find meaning which we cannot or should not find by a literal interpretation."[12]

DeYoung and Hurty reduce our options for interpreting New Testament quotations of the Old Testament to three choices. The first choice argues that there is only one meaning, the literal meaning of a text, therefore the New Testament uses the Old Testament citations in this manner

10. These theses are a slightly reworked citation of the theses listed in Walter C. Kaiser Jr. and Moisés Silva, *Introduction to Biblical Hermeneutics: The Search for Meaning*, 2nd ed. (Grand Rapids: Zondervan, 2007), 32.
11. James DeYoung and Sarah Hurty. *Beyond the Obvious: Discover the Deeper Meaning of Scripture* (1995; repr., Eugene, Ore.: Wipf & Stock, 2004), 31.
12. Ibid., 42.

when it quotes the Old Testament for doctrinal or apologetical reasons. But DeYoung and Hurty do not think this was the view of the church throughout its history. They believe the church saw that Jesus used a more-than-literal method and that therefore the church followed our Lord's lead.

The second view is one in which the New Testament finds additional meanings beyond those the human writers of the Old Testament intended. But this view warns that we cannot practice what the apostles did, since they had a special revelatory and inspired stance as apostles, which we in our day do not have. This allows an exception for the writers of Scripture, but it does not grant the same privilege to readers of the Bible.

A third alternative, DeYoung and Hurty continued, was one in which we did find additional and deeper meanings of the Old Testament, and therefore we could claim normativity and divine authority for those meanings based on the assumed fact that the canon of Scripture was not closed and based on a second assumption that the Holy Spirit still leads us into new truth in an authoritative way! Alas, however, DeYoung and Hurty did realize that the canon of Scripture had indeed been closed, so both authors fell back on finding additional meanings in the text but insisted that there could be no claim to normativity for any of these interpretations, since postapostolic interpreters, such as themselves, are not inspired and the canon of Scripture is closed.[13] The theory of deeper meanings is saved, but at what price? What these postapostolic interpreters will now interpret and teach will not come with the authority of God or with any element of normativity—according to their own testimonies!

Among the examples DeYoung and Hurty raised is the one from Genesis 14 and its use in the book of Hebrews. Accordingly, they argued, "Literal interpretation is utterly incapable of discovering this meaning [i.e., that Melchizedek of Genesis 14 is himself prophetic of Jesus] ... that Messiah should be both King (v. 1) and Priest (v. 4)."[14] No literal or natural interpretation of Genesis 14 can yield these deeper meanings, according to these two authors. But DeYoung and Hurty missed the literal point made in Genesis: Melchizedek the priest preceded Aaron the high priest and blessed Abraham, thereby showing that someone greater than the Levitical line from which Aaron came was present. Indeed, what was "absent in Genesis" became the points in the progress of revelation that were added, but added by the writer of Hebrews precisely because they were absent from

13. Ibid., 43–44.
14. Ibid., 34.

Genesis—namely, that we know nothing about Melchizedek's genealogy, birth, or death. It was the fact that Genesis did not record any of that data that made Melchizedek a good type for the Messiah and his offices in each of these points that now supplemented what had been revealed previously.

Another problem passage, selected by DeYoung and Hurty is Matthew 2:15, which quotes Hosea 11:1. They ask, "How can Matthew take words spoken with reference to Israel and say they were fulfilled a thousand years after the exodus by Joseph and Mary?"[15]

The answer is this: Instead of focusing on "my son" in the quotation from Hosea 11:1, which in its corporate solidarity also refers to all Israel though it is represented preeminently by Jesus, who is the summation of what "my son" means, DeYoung and Hurty focused on "out of Egypt," thinking the comparison was between the exodus of Israel from Egypt and, in the same manner, the flight of Jesus from Egypt. But nothing in that analogy works, for the citation is given in Matthew 2:15, as Jesus and the family go *into* Egypt, and not in verse 22 when they leave Egypt, for in that case the emphasis would have fallen on the words "out of Egypt."

Again our two authors who insist on going "beyond the obvious" claim, "Finally, Paul says almost explicitly that earlier scripture has a deeper meaning beyond that known by the human author and now revealed in the gospel. He says in Galatians 3:8: '*The Scripture foresaw* that God would justify the Gentiles by faith, and *announced the gospel in advance* to Abraham: "All nations will be blessed through you." ' "[16] But, on the contrary, that is the real meaning of the earlier text, as the quotations explicitly claimed: the Old Testament "foresaw" this and "announced" the same gospel. There is no deeper meaning here or one that goes beyond the text: it is right there in the text—literally according to the writer's determined meaning! The word given to Abraham that "in his seed all the nations of the earth should be blessed" was precisely what the gospel consisted of for all those nations; it was the same object of faith: the Seed of Abraham, Jesus the Christ.

Often what is sought by those who claim that the text has a plurality of meanings is the desire to show how that text has relevancy for our day. This leads us to the topic of how we apply Scripture or show its significance for contemporary issues and questions.

The word given to Abraham that "in his seed all the nations of the earth should be blessed" was precisely what the gospel consisted of for all those nations; it was the same object of faith: the Seed of Abraham, Jesus the Christ.

15. Ibid., 35.
16. Ibid., 37.

The Application or Significance of Scripture

To become acquainted with this topic, let us turn to one who has contributed much to the evangelical movement, J. I. Packer. In a 1990 essay titled "Understanding the Bible: Evangelical Hermeneutics,"[17] he listed the following four principles to govern our interpretation of the Bible.

1. "Biblical passages must be taken to mean *what their human authors were consciously expressing*, for what the human authors say is what God says" (p. 153).
2. "The *coherence, harmony and veracity* of all biblical teaching must be taken as our working hypothesis in interpretation" (p. 155).
3. "Interpretation involves *synthesizing* what the various biblical passages teach, so that each item taught finds its proper place in the *organism* of revelation as a whole." Packer said that "progressive revelation" "is not an evolutionary process of growing spiritual discernment through which cruder notions come to be left behind," but instead it is one in which "earlier revelation became the foundation for later revelation" (p. 155–56).
4. "*The response for which the text calls* must be made explicit. It is ... possible to find in every ... [book of the Bible] universal and abiding principles of loyalty and devotion to the holy, gracious Creator; and then to detach these from the particular situations to which, and the cultural frames within which, the books apply them, and to reapply them to ourselves in the places, circumstances, and conditions of our own lives today" (p. 157).

In the past, liberalism was able to peel off those doctrines or ethical teachings of the Bible, which some from a liberal perspective found out-of-date or bothersome, as one would peel an onion to get to the center. Over against this cavalier way of approaching the text, Packer's approach (as is mine) was to look for what was being taught in the text first of all, detach it from the particularity of the local cultural situation in the Scriptures, and identify the principle that transcended that cultural difference as he applied it to our day.

Admittedly, this quest for applying the Scriptures has not always produced results that have been salutary in the long term. For example, in

---

17. James I. Packer, "Understanding the Bible: Evangelical Hermeneutics," in *Honouring the Written Word of God: The Collected Shorter Writings of J. I. Packer*, vol. 3 (repr., Carlisle, UK: Paternoster, 1999), 147–60.

the nineteenth century, the North and the South in the United States were deeply divided over the issue of slavery, with both sides claiming the support of biblical principles. Reformed theologians likewise handled the issue of apartheid in South Africa from different perspectives even though both sides appealed to the same Bible. Similar interpretation problems continue today on other issues, such as the use of the gifts of the Holy Spirit and the role of women in ministry. Add to these dilemmas new issues that have arisen, such as reproductive technologies, genetic engineering, euthanasia, environmental concerns, and other moral issues. Scripture must have a part in these discussions, but on what bases and by what procedures?

In order to obtain contemporary relevancy for questions that seem to "go over the edge" of the Bible, must we go beyond the "surface teaching" of the individual texts of Scripture? And if we do go beyond that literal reading, what are the criteria and how do we set the trajectory? Will that trajectory have the same authoritative meaning as the surface meaning? What will that claim to be moving off the sacred page say about the doctrine of the "sufficiency of Scripture"?

"Going Beyond" the Text of Scripture

The most recent statement of this problem and a new approach to it came in I. Howard Marshall's 2004 book, *Beyond the Bible*.[18] In it he called for some new principled criteria that would guide us in the interchange between the Scriptures and many of today's ethical issues. He proposed that the early Christians not only built on their biblical sources, but actually went beyond those sources so that a pattern of diversity emerged between the earlier and later biblical materials.

Marshall pointed out three areas that exhibited this phenomenon of going beyond the Bible: (1) the way the early Christians used the Old Testament in their citations of it in the New, (2) the way Jesus' teaching took the early church beyond both the Old Testament and the gospel writers, and (3) the way Paul's teaching went beyond the "apostolic deposit" with further revelations and teachings as the early Christians reacted against the errors of the Judaizers and others.

---

18. I. Howard Marshall, *Beyond the Bible: Moving from Scripture to Theology* (Grand Rapids: Baker, 2004).

While aspects of some of these so-called advances were seen previously in the discussions of progressive revelation, there seems to be one huge difference. In earlier discussions, the so-called going beyond–ness always had an organic connection and a seminal attachment with what preceded it. The perfection (or so-called transcendency of the latter question) that came later always was a seminal perfection of the seed form that was embedded in the older form, rather than a departure or a setting on a new trajectory that had little if any relationship to the literal or surface meaning. For example, Geerhardus Vos taught: "The organic nature of the progression of revelation ... [includes] the absolute perfection of all stages.... The organic progress is from seed-form to the attainment of full growth."[19]

However, Marshall's illustrations of where the New Testament writers went beyond the Old Testament merely illustrate what has been traditionally known as the progress of revelation. The same could be said for his illustrations of the teachings of Jesus and Paul. Basically, Marshall's method could still be explained in these traditional terms.

More difficult to assess are the views of William J. Webb's "redemptive-movement trajectories."[20] Webb defines this "going beyond" as a need to progress beyond "the frozen in time aspects of the ethical portrait found in the Bible" or the "time-restricted elements of the Bible."[21] Even though Webb agrees that there is an embedded element of meaning at the abstract level in the text, he wants us to go beyond the concrete specifics of the instructions in the Bible. But he has forgotten to show any organic or seminal connection between what the text said and the end of the trajectory. It is as if the "redemptive movement trajectory" laid down a path of its own that was apart from the concrete realities of the Scriptures in all their "time-restricted elements."

A preferred way of accomplishing the desired results of this approach without getting away from Scripture is principlization (see pages 163–67 in chapter 12). As I explained well over twenty-five years ago, in my book *Toward an Exegetical Theology*, "Principlization seeks to bridge the 'then' of the text's narrative [or any other biblical genre] with the 'now' needs

---

19. Geerhardus Vos, *Biblical Theology: Old and New Testaments* (Grand Rapids: Eerdmans, 1954), 15.

20. William J. Webb, *Slaves, Women and Homosexuals: Exploring the Hermeneutics of Cultural Analysis* (Downers Grove, Ill.: InterVarsity, 2001), or his *Brutal, Bloody and Barbaric: War Texts That Trouble the Soul* (Downers Grove, Ill.: InterVarsity, 2009).

21. These comments are taken from Webb's chapter, "A Redemptive-Movement Model," in Gary T. Meadors, gen. ed., *Counterpoints: Four Views on Moving beyond the Bible to Theology* (Grand Rapids: Zondervan, 2009).

of our day, yet it refuses to settle for cheap and quick solutions which confuse our own personal point of view [good or bad] with that of the inspired writer."[22]

Principalizing, of course, is unlike allegorizing or spiritualizing. Instead of importing a new meaning into the text and imposing that meaning over the ancient word, this method seeks to see what the natural development of the seed or seminal idea was in the surface meaning of the text and then to carry that germ of the "plant" out to its full growth in the developed form or in similar situations.

All that is good and preferable in those types of trajectories that would otherwise purport to take us beyond the Bible have been operative as part of the best practices of Protestant hermeneutics for centuries now. The case for principlizing a text will help us reach the contemporary applications or significances of each text of Scripture.

The Search for Deeper Meanings in the Text

Nevertheless, there still remained a search for something deeper and more spiritual than what could be found on the surface of most biblical texts. As we saw in chapter 6, one answer came from Father Raymond E. Brown, who presented the now-standard definition of the *sensus plenior* interpretation of scriptural texts. Nevertheless, as we also saw earlier, Bruce Vawter effectively argued that the real meanings of Scripture were not somehow divinely hidden from the human writers as the text was "exhaled" into them in "words taught by the Holy Spirit" (1 Cor. 2:13).

Up to this point in time, it has been held that the writers of Scripture were conscious of what they were writing, for no creedal statement argued for any dictation theory of inspiration in which the writers were mere automatons who wrote as the words were whispered to them. No creed ever held that view, nor do I. Moreover, what they did write, they attributed not to themselves, but to the Holy Spirit who guided them all the way up to the writing process. But the unique style and vocabulary of each writer were preserved and are obvious to all who read the texts in their original tongue. The apostle John's vocabulary and style are simple with profound concepts, while the styles of the books of Job and Hebrews are complex

The unique style and vocabulary of each writer were preserved and are obvious to all who read the texts in their original tongue.

22. Walter C. Kaiser Jr. *Toward an Exegetical Theology: Biblical Exegesis for Preaching and Teaching* (Grand Rapids: Baker, 1981), 198.

because of the wide-ranging Hebrew vocabulary in Job and the complicated Greek syntax in Hebrews.

Do the Scripture Writers Deny They Understood Their Own Words? (2 Peter 1:19–21)

The apostle Peter declared in 2 Peter 1:19–21 that what he and other Scripture writers had as a result of the word from the prophets was a "more certain" word from God. In fact, "prophecy never had its origin in the will of man, but [these] men spoke as they were carried along by the Holy Spirit." Despite the clarity of this text, some still claim that the prophets did not always understand or demonstrate their ability to interpret their own words! Peter refuted this claim by asserting that he and the others were "eyewitnesses" of Jesus' glory on the Mount of Transfiguration (vv. 16–18).

The Scripture writers claim that they did not originate any sort of free creations in their messages, as if these concepts came by their own overt wills; nor did any of their words come about through their own "loosing" or "freeing" (Gk., *epiluseos*). To render this word "interpretation," as the NIV does (v. 20), would mean that *all* prophetic writings were closed to their writers. But then, how could anyone, much less the writers themselves, have given more careful attention to these same prophetic teachings? The "light" that was in these words would, in that scenario, have been little more than darkness itself.

Anchoring the Interpretation of the Bible in Space and Time

More than any other religious book, the Bible needs to be anchored in space and time; otherwise it lacks reality and verifiability. It is for this reason that the Bible has such a high number of geographical, cultural, and historical references. Given the fact that the message of the Bible is for persons in our world and in our space and time, we are marked by divine revelation as the invaded planet: God sent his Son, not to some other planet, but to the earth.

It is therefore of no small consequence that the revealed word began with a couple in the Garden of Eden and then went on to the divine election of Abraham and his family as God formed "a people" and a "holy nation" through which he would humbly make his arrival the first time, and to

Given the fact that the message of the Bible is for persons in our world and in our space and time, we are marked by divine revelation as the invaded planet: God sent his Son, not to some other planet, but to the earth.

which he will triumphantly introduce his eternal reign in his second arrival at the conclusion of historic times.

This ongoing narrative and the preparation for the arrival of God's Son in the Abrahamic-Davidic line is totally unlike any of the other religious myths, fables, or legends. Both the facts that the text records and the trustworthiness of the texts themselves are replete with an overwhelming number of artifacts and manuscripts that bear out both the genuineness and the antiquity of the Bible's claims and authenticity.[23]

How, then, does all of this affect the work of the interpreter? In this way: for more than two centuries now the method for interpreting the Bible has been known as the grammatical-historical interpretation of the Bible.[24] The word *grammatico*, or as it is rendered today, *grammatical*, does not refer to the grammar and syntax of a passage; rather, it approximates what we mean by the term *literal*. The first users of the term *grammatico-historical* intended to point to the simple, plain, ordinary, or natural meaning of a text. Likewise, the word *historical* referred to the setting of the text—the times, persons, and events. Therefore, the role of history was an essential one if the interpreter was to locate the context for the author's statements.

Nevertheless, it is possible to so overplay the historical role as one tries to find out what went on behind the text that little space and time are left for hearing and describing the theological and ethical injunctions of that text. When this distortion takes place, as so frequently occurs in modern Bible commentaries, suddenly what had been an assistance in the interpretive process is transformed into either a cold academic exercise or a straightforward apologetic presentation, with an emphasis on searching for how the text came to be or on demonstrating that the events described really happened. Certainly there is a place for each of these concerns, but they must not preempt the primacy that must rest on the message, teaching, theology, or guidance that the text wishes to give to us from God himself.

Conclusion

When the Bible is rightly interpreted, it reads as one story from the beginning of Genesis to the end of Revelation. Attempts to get to the spiritual message of the Bible prematurely can lead to rabbit trails that promise to

---

23. For more specific details, see Kaiser and Silva, *Introduction to Biblical Hermeneutics*, 117–18; and Walter C. Kaiser Jr., *The Old Testament Documents: Are They Reliable and Relevant?* (Downers Grove, Ill.: InterVarsity, 2001).
24. This name was first used by Karl A. G. Keil in 1788.

deliver a quick insight into assorted mysteries, deeper meanings, or divine intentions that allegedly superseded the disclosures given to the human penmen who first wrote these words. But in the end, the best method for interpreting texts is the tried and true method of grammatical-historical interpretation.

In those cases in which we do ask questions that go beyond the text of Scripture, we can depend on the method of principlization of the text. In this method, we move from the specificity of the text to a general principle, which is then related to the specifics of the case.[25]

---

25. For more detail here, see my discussion and diagram of the "Ladder of Abstraction" in Walter C. Kaiser Jr., *Toward Rediscovering the Old Testament* (Grand Rapids: Zondervan, 1987), 164–66.

The Unity *of the* Bible *and* Expository Preaching *and* Teaching

The expository method ... [of preaching and teaching should] be restored to that equal place which it held in the primitive and Reformed Churches; for, first, this is obviously the only natural and efficient way to do that which is the sole legitimate end of preaching, convey the whole message of God to the people.

—Robert L. Dabney[1]

Perhaps because of the extremely heavy emphasis on discontinuity and diversity in the Scriptures in the past decades, there has been a gentle disaffection in the believing body away from solid exposition of the Scriptures. Rather than teachers and pastors expounding paragraphs in sequence in the context of a whole book of the Bible and their aiming at covering the entire corpus of the sixty-six books as a well-balanced ministry over the life of their stay in that role, they have tended to replace solid exposition of the Word with a number of alternative teaching and preaching strategies. In fact, already by 1981 the contemporary situation appeared to me to be as follows:

> It is no secret that Christ's Church is not at all in good health in many parts of the world. She has been languishing because she has been fed ... "junk food." ... The Biblical text is often [used as] no more than a slogan or refrain in the message.... Biblical exposition has become a lost art in contemporary preaching. The most neglected of all biblical sections is the Old Testament—[extending]

1. Robert L. Dabney, *Sacred Rhetoric* (repr., Edinburgh: Banner of Truth, 1979), 78–79.

over three-fourths of divine revelation!... Motto preaching may please the masses in that it is filled with a lot of epigrammatic or proverbial slogans and interesting anecdotes, but it will always be a powerless word lacking the authority and validation of Scripture.... American parishioners ... are often rewarded with more or less the same treatment: repetitious arrangements of the most elementary truths of the faith, constant harangues, which are popular with local audiences, or witty and clever messages on the widest-ranging topics interspersed with catchy and humorous anecdotes geared to cater to the interests of those who are spiritually lazy and do not wish to be stirred beyond the pleasantries of hearing another good joke or story.[2]

It would appear that in the finer moments of teaching and preaching in the history of the church, those who turned to the Bible for the substance and authority of their ministries have been more inclined to practice what is now widely known as the expository method of preaching. It was more common then, than now, for congregations to be treated to preaching or teaching through whole books of the Bible in a series of messages over weeks or months.

Some describe the first six decades or so of the twentieth century as years in which the dearth of good preaching seemed to especially hit churches in the West. Among those who mourned this state of affairs was Dallas Seminary professor Merrill F. Unger. In 1955 he wrote, "To an alarming extent the glory is departing from the pulpit of the twentieth century."[3] Whether the precise dating is accurate or not, one cannot say; however, even now into the twenty-first century a famine of hearing solid proclamation of the Word of God (Amos 8:11) still exists in many Western countries with some wonderful exceptions to the contrary.

In the finer moments of teaching and preaching in the history of the church, those who turned to the Bible for the substance and authority of their ministries have been more inclined to practice ... the expository method of preaching.

Basic Definitions

To better understand what an expository sermon or lesson is, a brief discussion of several other alternative types may be helpful. First, there is the *topical sermon*. It is generally built around some selected subject or idea that remains primary in the presentation. The idea for the sermon may be borrowed from the Bible, or it may come from outside the Scriptures. Sometimes doctrinal sermons lend themselves to this type of presentation,

2. Walter C. Kaiser Jr., *Toward an Exegetical Theology: Biblical Exegesis for Preaching and Teaching* (Grand Rapids: Baker, 1981), 7, 19, 37, 191, 20.
3. Merrill F. Unger, *Principles of Expository Preaching* (Grand Rapids: Zondervan, 1955), 11.

especially if the doctrine is enforced by a number of scattered scriptural texts from the whole range of the Bible rather than from a chair or teaching passage (*sedes doctrinae*) where that doctrine received its fullest disclosure in the sacred text. In my opinion, however, taking a topic and then appealing to a wide range of scattered biblical texts is one of the poorest ways to teach or preach. I have repeatedly told students during my past half century of teaching, "Preach a topical sermon once every five years—and then repent and go back to expository preaching of the Bible after receiving forgiveness." Of course, I do this with my tongue in cheek, for some can use this method with such care that they avoid most, if not all, of the problems usually associated with it.

A second form of proclamation is the *textual sermon*. This form of preaching is based on a verse or two from the Bible with typically no, or very little, reference to the biblical context or its historical and cultural settings. The gifted orator Charles H. Spurgeon more often than not built his sermons around a single verse or two from the Bible, though he often, but not always, had to resort to more of what we would today call allegorical exegesis. The danger in this method is that the preacher may practice imposition on a text rather than exposition from a text. In this case the text is a springboard from which to start the sermon, but the Scripture often ends up being merely a peg on which to hang something the speaker wanted to say. The problem is whether that peg was divinely intended to hold the weight that it is now being called upon to bear.

Likewise, ethical and biographical treatments of Scripture often end up with the speaker falling into the trap of saying what he or she wanted to commend and to apply to the audience, but the message may be lacking in the authority and sufficiency of the powerful Word of God. All too often the proclaimer fails to distinguish between what the Bible *reports* and what the Bible *teaches*. Thus approval of one aspect of a biblical character's life does not automatically mean an endorsement of all that person did. The same is true when certain ethical descriptions are noted in the text without any divine editorial comment, as often occurs in biblical narratives. For example, to preach that lying is approved in certain situations, since the midwives lied to Pharaoh that they had delivered no baby boys from the Israelite women, or since Rahab lied about harboring the Israelite spies, is to rely on the description in the passage without taking the full unity of the Bible into account. Certainly the midwives were blessed by God, but not because they lied. They were blessed because they feared God more than they feared Pharaoh. The same goes for Rahab: she was blessed not because she lied, but because she feared God and not the king of Jericho. That is why she is listed in the hall of faith in Hebrews 11.

What then is expository preaching? Expository preaching is that method of presenting the Word of God that takes a minimum of a paragraph (in a narrative genre it would be a scene; in poetry, a strophe, and so forth) of the biblical text and from that derives both the *content* and the *shape* of the message. However, in most instances it will be more than a paragraph, for it must include the whole pericope, or teaching block, which may often stretch for an entire chapter.

Some have misjudged this method to mean that it is a repetition of all that the commentaries have to say on a particular passage. But that is hardly a worthy exemplar of the method, for it substitutes talking *about* the text (a form of teaching) for talking *to* God's people about what God is saying in the text. Sometimes some get so bogged down in the details of archaeology, history, customs, and culture that they never do come back to what it is that God is saying to us in the text. For example, a passage that begins with "To the church at Corinth" seems to open up for some preachers so much about the archaeological excavations at that site that most parishioners are bored to death, with their only hope for mercy and deliverance coming in the form of the elapsing of the appointed hour for the meeting. Others see Jesus as the Good Shepherd (briefly alluded to) as an opportunity to describe all they have recently learned about Middle Eastern shepherds, sheepfolds, and the like, to the abandonment of the text of Scripture.

Good expository preaching, however, begins by dividing a book of the Bible into its natural sections, which successively unlock the themes of the stated or implied purpose of that book. And the purpose of that individual book forms a part of the overarching purpose and theme of the entire Bible in its unified cohesiveness. The divine plan of the whole Scripture is worked out in each book, for there is a unity to the whole corpus of Scripture. The whole and the parts work together in the interpretation of both.

The identified sections of the biblical book are then divided into paragraphs in the prose portions of the Bible (scenes in narrative, strophes in poetry). These paragraphs (and their parallel forms in other genre) are then grouped according to their blocks of subjects (pericopes) to form the bases for the messages to be offered weekly in sequence, as one pericope after another unfolds in the biblical book. It is the consecutive interpretation and practical enforcement of each passage in the biblical book that constitutes expository preaching.

Expository preaching is that method of presenting the Word of God that takes a minimum of a paragraph ... of the biblical text and from that derives both the content and the shape of the message.

The Biblical Roots of Expository Preaching and Teaching

Ecclesiastes 1:1 used the word *Qohelet*, which is usually rendered "preacher" or "caller." The root of that word is *qahal*, meaning "to call out." From this we gain the idea that the preacher or teacher is the one who speaks out in front of the assembled people of God. This is similar to the word *qara* found in Isaiah 61:1, where the proclaimer also calls to the people. But best of all is the word *basar*, which means "to announce glad tidings," found, for example, in Isaiah 61:1 and Isaiah 40:9.

But the classic Old Testament picture of preaching has to be Nehemiah 8, where several key terms are used to describe how the word of God was disseminated on that day. Especially important is verse 8: "They read from the Book of the Law of God, making it clear and giving the meaning so that the people could understand what was being read."

The word translated "making it clear" is the Hebrew word *parash*. It can be rendered "distinctly," or "distinguishing or specifying clearly." Clarity has always been a key objective for all proclamation of the Word of God. A second key term is the Hebrew word *sekel*, meaning "to give the sense," or "giving the meaning." Finally, the word the interpreting Levites use in this passage is the Hebrew word *bin*, meaning they "caused [the people] to understand." Here is a great picture of what expository preaching is all about. It is helping God's people to understand what is written in God's Word.

Some additional aspects of expository preaching can be found in the New Testament terminology. Not to be left out of the hall of great preachers is none other than our Lord Jesus himself. Luke 24:27 reads: "And beginning with Moses and all the Prophets, [Jesus] *explained* to them what was said in all the Scriptures concerning *himself*" (emphasis added). The word translated "explained," or "expounded" is the Greek word *diermeneuo*. The idea here is once again that of "explaining through" or "expounding" a passage.

This Lukan text is an important description of what is involved in expository preaching. Exposition emphasizes the systematic presentation of Scripture. Jesus "explained through" the Old Testament systematically as he began with Moses and then went on to the Prophets, telling what Scripture said about himself as the predicted Messiah.

Some take a second principle from this passage. They argue that every exposition of the Scripture must be a Christ-centered presentation. Many at this point appeal to Charles Spurgeon, who said that when he took a text of Scripture, he quickly beat a straight path to Jesus. However, said he, if there was no path to Jesus in the text, he made one! That is quite an admission—one I would not recommend for interpreters today.

Beating a path that is not in the text poses a serious problem. To impose even a christological meaning on a text, even if it is done with a good heart and for a great cause, is still eisegesis and an imposition of meaning over a text that in many cases has nothing to do with the Messiah or the second person of the Trinity. The texts that our Lord used, you can be sure, were those he had originally inspired to carry just such a meaning as could be determined by following the author's asserted meanings.

Another New Testament contribution to the terminology of expository preaching is found in Acts 17:2–3. "As his custom was, Paul went into the synagogue, and on three Sabbath days he *reasoned with* them from the Scriptures, *explaining* and proving that the Christ had to suffer and rise from the dead. 'This Jesus I am proclaiming to you is the Christ,' he said" (emphasis mine). The Greek word Paul used was *dialegomai*, "to speak through," or "to reason with." Biblical exposition is a logical presentation of what the Scriptures have to say. Another Greek word Paul used in this situation was *dianoigo*, meaning "to open thoroughly," or "explaining." This same word was used in Luke 24:32, "They asked each other, "Were not our hearts burning within us while he talked with us on the road and *opened* the Scriptures to us?" (emphasis mine). This form of Bible teaching is committed to drawing from the Scripture itself the substance of what is opened up before the listening audience.

The Advantages of Expository Preaching

The most important advantage of using expository messages is that it makes it possible for the preacher or teacher to grow continually in his or her understanding of the Word of God. Dipping here and there in the Scriptures for lessons or sermons, without any systematic plan, will stunt one's spiritual growth. Some are content to take what they know of the grace of God and pour it into different Scripture readings. But their sermons almost always have the same content and provide little impact, for the text serves as little more than a springboard or a jumping-off point in the sermon.

A second advantage of using expository messages is that the expositor has to work hard to plow new ground in his or her spiritual development.

The tendency toward laziness is avoided as the researcher is pushed to more in-depth exploration.

Third, expository preaching saves hours of fussing over what topic to preach on next time. Going through whole books of the Bible relieves this anxiety and conserves precious hours of research for the real work of studying the next passage in one's sequence of teaching blocks.

A fourth advantage to expository preaching is that it forces the expositor to face passages that he or she might otherwise have overlooked or deliberately avoided. A preacher may have a good reason for avoiding a certain passage, such as not wanting to create the impression that someone in the congregation is being "singled out" or "picked on" for a particular sin or habit. If, for example, a preacher decides out of the blue to preach on the topic of homosexuality, parishioners are likely to play a guessing game as to who the pastor might have in mind. But when a text that may possibly be offensive to some occurs in the natural flow of the passages being treated in sequence, there is little basis for asserting that someone is being singled out as the object of a message.

A fifth advantage is that expository preaching yields unusual confidence in the one who stands before God's people to deliver a message. Armed with the *authority* of the Word of God and confident in the *sufficiency* of the inspired Scripture to meet the needs of the audience, attention is taken away from the speaker's own sense of worth or acceptance and focused instead on the Lord who has given the Word. The Word is from God and not of the preacher's own making.

An Issue of Unity: Must Every Old Testament Sermon Make Reference to the New Testament?

Elizabeth Achtemeier took the position that the Old Testament was not a word to the believing church today. She wrote: "The fact is ... that apart from the New Testament, the Old Testament does not belong to the Christian church and is not its book. The Old Testament is the word of God to Israel."[4] Elsewhere she added: "The ... basic presupposition that we must hold as we preach from the Old Testament is that the Old Testament is directed to Israel.... Unless we therefore have some connection with Israel, the Old Testament is not our book, and it is not a revelation spoken to

---

4. Elizabeth Achtemeier, *Preaching from the Old Testament* (Louisville: Westminster John Knox, 1989), 56.

us.[5] Furthermore, she added: "It must be emphasized that no sermon can become the Word of God for the Christian church if it only deals with the Old Testament apart from the New. In every sermon rising out of an Old Testament text, there must be reference to the New Testament outcome of the Old Testament's word."[6]

But contrary to what Elizabeth Achtemeier claimed, the two testaments are not two books, but one unified whole in which the story begun in the Old is completed in the New. The testaments are fused in their writings, in that the Old anticipates the New, and the later sees itself as the continuation of the older. It is the person of Jesus the Messiah who unites the two testaments.

Does this mean that the Old Testament must be interpreted from the perspective of the New? Some attempt to support this stand by appealing to 2 Corinthians 3:15–16, which reads: "Even to this day when Moses is read, a veil covers their hearts. But whenever anyone turns to the Lord, the veil is taken away." It does not, however, read that "whenever anyone turns to the New Testament" the veil is taken away; the turning is in faith to the Lord. It is exceeding the boundaries of what is said to make this text demand that every Old Testament exegesis must have a christological focal point not just in context but in substance.

My argument is against eisegesis—reading material *into* the text back from the New Testament—but it is not an argument for truncating the revelation of God so that the light of the New Testament must never be brought to bear on any Old Testament passage. I contend only for the fact that the New Testament must not be used as an "open sesame" for explaining what the Old Testament meant in the first place.

Where, then, does the problem lie? If the case for the unity of the Scriptures is as strong as I have claimed it to be in this group of chapters, why would anyone object to using the New Testament christocentrically?

The tension can be illustrated in two separate quotes. First, Chris Wright maintained:

> We may legitimately see in the event, or in the record of it, additional levels
> of significance in light of the end of the story—i.e., in the light of Christ. [He
> went on to say:] Looking back on the event [of the exodus] ... in the light of the
> fullness of God's redemptive achievement in Jesus Christ, we can see that even

5. Elizabeth Achtemeier, "From Exegesis to Proclamation," in *Studies in Old Testament Theology*, ed. Robert L. Hubbard Jr. et al. (Dallas: Word, 1982), 50.
6. Elizabeth Achtemeier, *The Old Testament and the Proclamation of the Gospel* (Philadelphia: Westminster, 1973), 142.

the original exodus was not merely concerned with the political, economic, and social aspects of Israel's predicament. There was also a level of spiritual oppression in Israel's subjection to the gods of Egypt.[7]

Notice that Wright carefully used the words "additional levels of *significance*" that could come from the "end of the story." This is a whole world apart from what Sidney Greidanus argued after he surveyed the fact that some scholars prefer to use "*sensus plenior,* or the *analogia fidei* ("rule of faith"):

> I continue to favor the name that refers to the broadest possible context and gives due recognition to God's acts in history, "redemptive-historical interpretation." Whatever name we use, the important point is that a passage understood in the contexts of the whole Bible and redemptive history may reveal more meaning than its author intended originally. For example, it is not likely that the author of Numbers 21 realized that in relating the story of the bronze serpent he was sketching a type of Christ. The type in this passage is discovered only from the New Testament perspective when Jesus makes use [John 3:14] of this event to proclaim his own saving work.[8]

Everything in this quote was going well until Greidanus used the words "may reveal *more meaning* than its [human] author intended originally." Had Greidanus used "may reveal more *significance* than its [human] author intended originally," I would have no quarrel. But there lurks in evangelical thought the occultic idea that a hidden meaning lay just outside the purview of the human authors of the Old Testament that can be unlocked now that we have the New Testament. This is damaging to the case for inspiration and for unity of Scripture. It posits that there exists somewhere in cyberspace a meaning that cannot be reached by the grammatico-historical interpretation of the text. But since it is not in the words, grammar, or syntax of the sentences or paragraphs, it must be located between the lines. If that is so, then it is not *graphe*—that is, what is "written"—that is said to be inspired by God (2 Tim. 3:16–17), but rather what is not written.

Nevertheless, Greidanus's concept of "redemptive history" is a good one. Moreover, exegetes of the Old Testament cannot pretend that the New Testament has not come as yet. As David Larsen so wisely said, "God's saving work is everywhere in the Old Testament. In this holistic sense, all the Old Testament prepares for is fulfilled in Christ. We can't preach the Old

---

7. Christopher J. H. Wright, *Knowing Jesus through the Old Testament: Rediscovering the Roots of Our Faith* (Downers Grove, Ill.: InterVarsity, 1992), 28–29.
8. Sidney Greidanus, *Preaching Christ from the Old Testament: A Contemporary Hermeneutical Method* (Grand Rapids: Eerdmans, 1999), 233.

Testament as if the fulfillment had not come."[9] It is proper that the end of the story accompany the beginning and the middle of the story after the Old Testament passage has been fairly exegeted.

It is this important observation that makes the case for the unity of the Bible so very significant. As Bryan Chapell clearly stated: "Context is part of text.... No text exists in isolation from other texts or from the overarching biblical message. Just as historico-grammatical exegesis requires a preacher to consider a text's terms in context, correct theological interpretation requires an expositor to discern how a text's ideas function in the wider biblical message."[10]

How, then, can expositors of the Word of God include the end of the story in their exegesis of parts of the beginning and the middle of the story? Must they superimpose ideas that are foreign to the text or include as a postscript to their messages something like this: "Now a word in closing about Christ's substitutionary penal death and bodily resurrection, the present work of the Holy Spirit, and the second coming of our triumphant Lord"? No all of that would be, as included in the question, a "superimposition" and an odd "attachment" to a passage not referring to any of these topics.

From the work of biblical theology, we are taught that the Bible has an overall plan, purpose, and unifying story. I have argued that it is the "promise-plan of God."[11] The parts of God's revelation can best be seen in terms of the overarching cohesive whole. It can also be seen best in its progressiveness, which is organic in nature. This means that the truth of God may be spoken in earlier texts in seed form, but that seed will continue to build as God's revelation progresses to become a full plant in full bloom by the time it comes to its full maturation.[12] Thus Moses may not have had in his authorial intentions what Jesus had in mind when he spoke the words of John 3:14 ("Just as Moses lifted up the snake in the desert, so the Son of Man must be lifted up"), but the seed and germ of the truth shared in both the Old Testament and the New Testament contexts is the same: If one does not look to and believe in God's provision, he or she will die!

The truth of God may be spoken in earlier texts in seed form, but that seed will continue to build as God's revelation progresses to become a full plant in full bloom by the time it comes to its full maturation.

---

9. David L. Larsen, *The Anatomy of Preaching: Identifying the Issues in Preaching Today* (Grand Rapids: Baker, 1989), 167.
10. Bryan Chapell, *Christ-Centered Preaching: Redeeming the Expository Sermon* (Grand Rapids: Baker, 2005), 275.
11. Walter C. Kaiser Jr., *The Promise-Plan of God: A Biblical Theology of the Old and New Testaments* (Grand Rapids: Zondervan, 2008).
12. This concept was stated beautifully by Geerhardus Vos in *Biblical Theology* (Grand Rapids: Eerdmans, 1975), 5–7.

Conclusion

Preaching Christ, especially from the Old Testament, does not mean that every verse in the Old Testament directly reveals the Messiah. Instead, it argues from a concept of the unity and cohesiveness of the whole Bible that the same overarching story begins, continues, and ends where it had always been intended to end in the plan of God.

If this is central, it in no way undermines a host of other topics relating to ethics, morality, and other doctrines that radiate out from this center. To appeal to Paul's tactical decision when he was in Corinth ("I resolved to know nothing while I was with you except Jesus Christ and him crucified," 1 Cor. 2:1–2), is to make one special case normative for his total ministry. But in his writings to that same city, Paul treated a number of other issues that admittedly were tangential to Christ and his death and resurrection. For example, he took up the problems connected with taking fellow believers to court to sue them, the issue of divisions in the church, and the challenges of remaining single. His claim to know "nothing but Jesus Christ and him crucified" is a hyperbole used here to emphasize what is central, but not to exclude other areas given to him by revelation of God.

Epilogue

The case for the unity of the two testaments enjoyed a much easier route in the beginning of "the Way," as the church was called at first in the book of Acts (9:2; 19:9, 23; 22:4; 24:14, 22). In the days of the apostles, believers in Yeshua (= Jesus) were regarded as a sect within the synagogues of Judaism.

But what really blew things apart was the heavy tax imposed by Emperor Vespasian after the Jewish War and the fall of Jerusalem in AD 70.[1] All Jewish households, including those who worshiped in a Jewish way—which would include the Christians who were called people of "the Way"—had to pay the *Fiscus Judaicus* tax. This became an incentive for Gentile believers to start distancing themselves from Judaism.

It was about this time, after the destruction of Jerusalem, that the synagogues began introducing a curse on believers in Yeshua as a new benediction in their daily liturgies. Those worshipers who would not pray this curse against Yeshua and his believers were expelled from the synagogue. Thus began an animosity between Jewish leaders and Gentile or Jewish believers

---

1. For what follows, I have been aided by reviewing many of the events in the tragic history of relations between the Jews and Christians found depicted in the fine work by D. Thomas Lancaster, *Restoration: Returning the Torah of God to the Disciples of Jesus* (Marshfield, Mo.: First Fruits of Zion, 2005), 13–28.

in Yeshua. This excommunication from the synagogue created deep animosity and offense between persons who once had worshiped together.

Vespasian's son, Emperor Domitian, anticipating another Jewish revolt, unleashed a new series of persecutions against Jewish people and Christians associated with them. In one of those waves of persecution, the apostle John was exiled to the island of Patmos. But by now the anti-Jewish sentiment was at such a high pitch in the second Christian century that non-Jews who worshiped together in the synagogues wanted to break all contacts with their Jewish brethren.

The Second Jewish Revolt against Rome came in the third decade of the second century in the days of Emperor Hadrian. The Jewish population was led in this revolt by Shimon Bar Kokba, "Shimon, son of [the] Star," whom Rabbi Akiva had declared to be the Messiah. Bar Kokba's followers had to swear allegiance to him as the Messiah, a declaration that followers of Yeshua could not do. This became the final break between the believers in Judaism and believers in the Way.

But the break was not all that sudden even as late as AD 135, for the Ante-Nicean church fathers, such as Ignatius and Justin Martyr, and the pseudo-epistle allegedly composed by Barnabas, Paul's missionary companion, continued to war against Gentile believers who kept the Sabbath and against those who found delight in dancing and clapping in their services. Justin Martyr, in his dialogue with a Hellenistic Jew named Trypho, claimed that the Torah of God was given to the Jews as a punishment for their wickedness and hardness of heart. The early church, however, did excommunicate the great heretic Marcion in AD 144 for his denunciation of the Old Testament and for his reduction of the New Testament to portions of Luke and ten of Paul's epistles.

Another controversy that widened the gap between the Jewish and Christian communities and became the final straw was the Easter controversy. Resurrection Sunday had been celebrated every year on the Sunday that followed Passover, though that day had been given an older name for a pagan springtime festival called Easter. The Roman Church, however, wanted its members to stop reckoning Easter by the Passover, thus elevating Easter above all other festivals, which had the accompanying result of eliminating the Jewish elements and festivals from Christian practice. In the end, the Roman Church prevailed and Easter was moved from the Sunday following Passover.

When Emperor Constantine converted to Christianity and made it a legal religion in the empire, he made the divorce between Judaism and Christianity final with the Council of Nicea (AD 325). His estimate of the Torah was "let us have nothing in common with the detestable Jewish rabble."[2] The Council of Antioch (AD 341) followed suit by forbidding Christians from celebrating Passover with the Jews, and the Council of Laodicea (AD 363) forbade Christians from celebrating the seventh-day Sabbath. But it is clear that all the way up to the fourth century of the Christian era some believers were still keeping parts of the Torah.

Late in the fourth century the gifted preacher John Chrysostom gave a series of eight sermons at Antioch against Jews and Judaizers. His rhetoric at times was intemperate and filled with anti-Jewish expressions. He saw the response to the Torah as a disease:

> What is this disease? The festivals of the pitiful and miserable Jews are soon to march upon us one after the other and in quick succession: the Feast of Trumpets, the Feast of Tabernacles, the fasts [i.e., the Day of Atonement]. There are many in our ranks who say they think as we do. Yet some of these are going to watch the festivals and others will join the Jews in keeping their feasts and observing their fasts. I wish to drive this perverse custom from the church right now.... But now that the Jewish festivals are close by and at the very door, if I should fail to cure those who are sick with the Judaizing disease ... [they] may partake in the Jews' transgressions.[3]

Despite all of Chrysostom's oratorical gifts, these eight sermons showed he wanted a clear cleavage between the law of Moses and Christianity. He, along with many of the church fathers, and many of their modern descendants, have gotten their wish by and large in the contemporary church of today.

Fast forward the historical chart to AD 1517 as the Augustinian monk, Martin Luther nailed his Ninety-five Theses on the Wittenberg Church door. His protest was not against the papacy or against images of the saints or against Mary as the mother of God; it was strictly against the sale of indulgences—charging people for the forgiveness of their sins in order to build St Peter's cathedral. By now the Mass was in Latin, a language known only by a few of the intelligentsia. The Bible was written in Latin, and the laity were forbidden to own a copy.

Luther, at first enthusiastic about the prospect of the Jewish people coming to own Yeshua as their Messiah, finally lashed out against the Jewish people when he saw they were adamant in not accepting Christ as their

---

2. Eusebius, *Life of Constantine* 3:18–19.
3. John Chrysostom, *Against the Jews: Homily* 1.5.

Savior. He wrote two encyclicals titled *Against the Sabbath Keepers* and *Against the Judaizers*. Protestant believers were warned to keep their distance from the Jewish people and their Torah. Even more damaging was his 1543 paper *On the Jews and Their Lies*. In it he urged synagogues to be burned down in every town and Jews to be forced to convert.

However, it was the events of World War II that tended to sober up many Christians as anti-Semitism came to its full fruition under the leader of the Third Reich, Adolph Hitler. Hitler justified his attempted genocide of the Jewish people by freely quoting Christian writers, especially Luther. The Holocaust will go down in history as one of the most unbelievable atrocities against humanity in the history of all mortals.

It may be more than a trivial fact, but on November 29, 1947, the same day that the United Nations voted to partition Palestine and grant to Israel statehood, Professor Eleazar Sukenik of the Hebrew University went in disguise on a secret trip to Kahil Iskander Shahin, a shoemaker in Bethlehem, to purchase the rest of the scrolls (later to be known as part of the Dead Sea Scrolls) from this shoemaker who had bought them from three Bedouin boys (Muhammed edh-Dhib and his two cousins). These events each have had a revolutionary effect on the Christian supersessionism and the distant treatment of the Old Testament by Christian scholars.

Conclusion

With so much history lying behind the Christian use and integration of the Old Testament with the New Testament, it is little wonder that the case for the unity of the Bible has suffered in recent years, but it has lagged behind in most of the Christian era. Nevertheless, this history cannot take priority over the claims found in the text that what is exhibited throughout both testaments is that both are the work of one divine mind, plan, and purpose for the whole.

Even allowing for the obvious amounts of diversity, the Scriptures stand before us unparalleled by any other form of writing. To repeat a few of the facts once again: here are sixty-six books written in three different languages by forty human authors living in three different areas of the world—Africa, the Near East and Europe—over a period of 1,500 to 1,600 years. The heart of the book takes place right where east meets west so that it is neither exclusively an Oriental or an Occidental book.

The coherence, unity, and progressiveness of the story of the promise-plan of God; the centrality of God's call to Israel; and the focus on the death, resurrection, and second coming of Jesus Christ, with the supporting doctrines, make the Hebrew and Greek Scriptures of the Old and New Testaments one great unified message.

Bibliography

Alexander, Neil. "The United Character of the New Testament Witness to the Christ-Event." In *The New Testament in Historical and Contemporary Perspective*, edited by Hugh Anderson and William Barclay, 1–33. Oxford: Basil Blackwell, 1965.

Allis, O. T. "Modern Dispensationalism and the Doctrine of the Unity of Scripture." *Evangelical Quarterly* 8 (1936): 22–35.

———. "Modern Dispensationalism and the Law of God." *Evangelical Quarterly* 8 (1936): 272–90.

Allrik, H. L. "The Lists of Zerubbabel (Nehemiah 7 and Ezra 2) and the Hebrew Numeral Notation." *Bulletin of the American Schools of Oriental Research* 136 (1954): 21–27.

Archer, Gleason L. *An Examination of the Alleged Discrepancies of the Bible*. Grand Rapids: Zondervan, 1982.

Armstrong, Ryan Melvin. "Canonical Approaches to New Testament Theology: An Evangelical Evaluation of Childs and Trobisch." Th.M. diss.: Southeastern Baptist Theological Seminary, 2007.

Baker, D. L. *Two Testaments, One Bible: A Study of Some Modern Solutions to the Theological Problem of the Relationship between the Old and New Testaments*. Downers Grove, Ill.: InterVarsity, 1977.

Barr, James. "Typology and Allegory." *Old and New In Interpretation: A Study of Two Testaments*, 103–48. London: SCM, 1966.

Barton, John. "Unity and Diversity in the Biblical Canon." In *Die Einheit der Schrift und die Vielfalt des Kanons*, edited by John Barton and Michael Wolter, 11–26. Berlin: De Gruyter, 2003.

Barton, John, and Michael Wolter, eds. *Die Einheit der Schrift und die Vielfalt des Kanons (The Unity of Scripture and the Diversity of the Canon)*. Beihefte zur Zeitschrift für die neutestamentliche Wissenschaft 118, v–307. Berlin: De Gruyter, 2003.

Blomberg, Craig L. *The Historical Reliability of the Gospels*. Downers Grove, Ill.: InterVarsity, 1987.

———. "The Legitimacy and Limits of Harmonization." In *Hermeneutics, Authority, and Canon*, edited by D. A. Carson and John D. Woodbridge, 135–74. Reprint, Grand Rapids: Zondervan, 1995.

———. "The Unity and Diversity of Scripture." In *New Dictionary of Biblical Theology*, edited by T. Desmond Alexander et al., 64–72. Downers Grove, Ill.: InterVarsity, 2000.

———. "When Is a Parallel Really a Parallel?" *Westminster Theological Journal* 46 (1984): 78–103.

Boice, James Montgomery. "A Response to Unity of the Bible." In *Hermeneutics, Inerrancy and the Bible*, edited by Earl D. Radmacher and Robert D. Preus, 663–68. Grand Rapids: Zondervan, 1984.

Bruce, F. F. "All Things to All Men: Diversity in Unity and Other Pauline Tensions." In *Unity and Diversity in New Testament Theology*, edited by Robert Guelich. Grand Rapids: Eerdmans, 1978.

———. "Is Paul of Acts the Real Paul?" *Bulletin of the John Rylands Library* 58 (1976): 282–305.

Carson, Donald A. "Unity of Diversity in the New Testament: The Possibility of Systematic Theology." In *Scripture and Truth*, edited by D. A. Carson and John D. Woodbridge, 65–95; 368–75. Grand Rapids: Zondervan, 1983.

Cazelles, H. "The Unity of the Bible and the People of God." *Scripture* 18 (1966): 1–10.

Childs, Brevard. "The Nature of the Christian Bible: One Book, Two Testaments." In *The Rule of Faith*, edited by Ephraim Radner and George Sumner. Harrisburg, Pa.: Morehouse, 1998.

Christiansen, Duane L. *The Unity of the Bible: Exploring the Beauty and Structure of the Bible*, 1–314. New York and Mahwah, N.J.: Paulist Press, 2003.

Davis, John J. "The Unity of the Bible." In *Hermeneutics, Inerrancy and the Bible*, edited by Earl D. Radmacher and Robert D. Preus, 641–59. Grand Rapids: Zondervan, 1984.

Dentan, R. C. "The Unity of the Old Testament." *Interpretation* 5 (1951): 153–73.

Dillard, R. B. "Harmonization: A Help and a Hindrance?" In *Inerrancy and Hermeneutic: A Tradition, a Challenge, a Debate*, edited by Harvey Conn, 151–64. Grand Rapids: Baker, 1988.

Duda, Daniel. "The Development of a Course Based on a Book-by-Book Approach to the Bible." D.Min. diss.: Andrews University, 1992.

Dunn, J. D. G. *Unity and Diversity in the New Testament*. London: SCM, 1977; 2nd ed., 1990.

Erlandson, Seth. "Faith in the Old and New Testaments: Harmony or Disagreements?" *Concordia Theological Quarterly* 47, no. 1 (1983): 1–14.

Filson, F. V. "The Unity of the Old and New Testaments: A Bibliographical Survey," *Interpretation* 5 (1951): 134–52.

———. "The Unity between the Testaments." *The Interpreter's One-Volume Commentary on the Bible*. Edited by C. M. Laymon, 989–93. Nashville: Abingdon, 1971.

Freedman, David Noel. *The Unity of the Hebrew Bible*. Ann Arbor: University of Michigan Press, 1991.

———. "The Unity of the Bible." *Western Watch* 7, no. 14 (December 15, 1956): 7–14.

———. "The Unity of the Bible." In *The Messiahship of Jesus: What Jews and Jewish Christians Say*. Compiled by Arthur W. Kac, 178–84. Chicago: Moody, 1980.

Fuller, Daniel P. *The Unity of the Bible: Unfolding God's Plan for Humanity*. Grand Rapids: Zondervan, 1992.

———. "The Importance of a Unity of the Bible." In *Studies in Old Testament Theology*, edited by Robert L. Hubbard, Robert K. Johnston, and Robert P. Meye, 63–75. Dallas: Word, 1992.

Gaebelein, Frank E. "The Unity of the Bible." In *Revelation and the Bible: Contemporary Evangelical Thought*, edited by C. F. H. Henry, 389–401. Grand Rapids: Eerdmans, 1957.

Glen, J. Stanley. "Jesus Christ and the Unity of the Bible." *Interpretation* 5, no. 3 (1950): 259–67.

Goldingay, John. "Diversity and Unity in Old Testament Theology." *Vetus Testamentum* 34 (1984): 153–68.

Haley, John W. *An Examination of the Alleged Discrepancies of the Bible*. Boston: Estes and Lauriat, 1874. Reprint, Grand Rapids: Baker, 1951.

Harrison, Carol, "'Not Words but Things': Harmonious Diversity in the Four Gospels." In *Augustine*: *Biblical Exegete*, edited by Frederick Van Fleteren and Joseph C. Schnaubelt, 157–73. New York: Peter Lang, 2001.

Hasel, Gerhard F. "Proposals for a Canonical Biblical Theology." *Andrews University Seminary Studies* 34, no. 1 (1996): 23–33.

Hicks, R. Lansing. *Forms of Christ in the Old Testament*: *The Problem of the Christological Unity of the Bible*, 1–45. Evanston, Ill.: Seabury-Western Theological Seminary, 1968.

Honeycut, R. L. "The Unity and Witness of Scripture." *Foundations* 8, no. 4 (1965): 292–98.

Hunter, A. M. *The Unity of the Bible*. Philadelphia: Westminster, 1943.

Janowski, Bernard. "The One God of the Two Testaments." *Theology Today* 57, no. 3 (2000): 297–324.

Johnson, Luke Timothy. "Fragments of an Untidy Conversation: Theology and the Literary Diversity of the New Testament." In *Biblical Theology*: *Problems and Perspectives*: *Essays in Honor of J. Christiaan Beker*, edited by Steven J. Kraftchick, Charles D. Myers, Jr., and Ben C. Ollenburger, 276–89. Nashville: Abingdon, 1995.

Kaiser, Walter C., Jr. *The Promise-Plan of God: A Biblical Theology of the Old and New Testaments*. Grand Rapids: Zondervan, 2008.

———. *Toward Old Testament Ethics*. Grand Rapids: Zondervan, 1983.

Kloch, Klaus. "Two Testaments, One Bible." *Bangalore Theological Forum* 28, nos. 1–2 (1996): 38–58.

Köstenberger, Andreas J. "Diversity and Unity in the New Testament." In *Biblical Theology*: *Retrospective and Prospect*, edited by Scott J. Hafemann, 144–58. Downers Grove, Ill.: InterVarsity, 2002.

———. "Early Doubts of the Apostolic Authorship of the Fourth Gospel in the History of Modern Biblical Criticism." In *Studies on John and Gender*: *A Decade of Scholarship*, 17–47. New York: Peter Lang, 2001.

———. "Review of David Wenham's *Paul: Founder ... or Follower.*" *Trinity Journal* 16, n.s. (1995): 259–62.

Lalleman, Hetty. *Celebrating the Law? Rethinking Old Testament Ethics.* London: Paternoster, 2004.

Lemcio, E. E. "The Unifying Kerygma of the New Testament," *Journal for the Study of the New Testament* 33 (1998): 3–17; 38 (1990): 3–11.

Lohse, Eduard. "Changes of Thought in Pauline Theology? Some Reflections on Paul's Ethical Teaching in the Context of His Thought." In *Theology and Ethics in Paul and His Interpreters: Essays in Honor of Victor Paul Furnish*, edited by Eugene H. Lovering Jr. and Jerry L. Sumney, 146–60. Nashville: Abingdon, 1996.

Longenecker, Richard N. "On the Concept of Development in Pauline Theology." In *Perspectives on Evangelical Thought*, edited by Kenneth S. Kantzer and Stanley N. Gundry, 195–207. Grand Rapids: Zondervan, 1979.

Longman, Tremper III. *Making Sense of the Old Testament: Three Crucial Questions.* Grand Rapids: Baker, 1995.

Ludlow, Morwenna. "Theology, Allegory: Origen and Gregory of Nyssa on the Unity and Diversity of Scripture." *International Journal of Systematic Theology* 4 (2002): 45–66.

Lyman, Mary Ely. "The Unity of the Bible." *Journal of Bible and Religion* 14, no. 1 (1946): 5–12.

Maier, Gerhard. "The Unity of Scripture." In *Biblical Hermeneutics*, translated by Robert W. Yarbrough, 187–208. Wheaton: Crossway, 1994.

McConville, J. G. "Using Scripture for Theology: Unity and Diversity in Old Testament Theology: The Old Testament as a Hermeneutical Problem." *Scottish Bulletin of Evangelical Theology* 5 (1987): 39–57.

Minear, Paul S. "Diversity and Unity: A Johannine Case-Study." In *Die Mitte des Neuen Testaments*, 162–75. Göttingen: Vandenhoeck und Ruprecht, 1983.

Morgan, Robert. "Unity and Diversity in New Testament Talk of the Spirit." In *Holy Spirit and Christian Origins*, 1–13. Grand Rapids: Eerdmans, 2004.

Morrison, John D. "Review of Daniel P. Fuller's *The Unity of the Bible: Unfolding God's Plan for Humanity.*" *JETS* 39, no. 3 (2006): 516–18.

Motyer, Steve. "Two Testaments, One Biblical Theology." In *Between Two Horizons*, edited by Joel B. Green and Max Turner. Grand Rapids: Eerdmans, 2000.

Neil, William. "The Unity of the Bible." In *The New Testament in Historical and Contemporary Perspective*: *Essays in Memory of G. H. C. MacGregor*, edited by Hugh Anderson and William Barclay, 237–59. Oxford: Blackwell, 1965.

Nieuwenhove, Rik van. "Diversity and Unity in the Scripture: The Patristic Perspective." In *The Many Voices of the Bible*: *Concilium*, edited by Sean Freyne and Ellen van Wolde, 92–101. London: SCM, 2002.

Outler, Albert C. "Toward a Postliberal Hermeneutics." *Theology Today* 42, no. 3 (2006): 281–91.

Packer, James I. "Upholding the Unity of Scripture Today," *Journal of the Evangelical Theological Society* 25 (1982): 409–14.

Paul, S. M. *Studies in the Book of the Covenant in Light of Cuneiform and Biblical Law*. Supplements to Vetus Testamentum 18. Leiden: Brill, 1970.

Payne, J. Barton. "The Validity of Numbers in Chronicles." *Bibliotheca Sacra* 136 (1979): 109–28, 206–20.

Perrin, Nicholas. "Dialogic Conceptions of Language and the Problem of Biblical Unity." In *Biblical Theology*: *Retrospect and Prospect*, edited by Scott J. Hafemann, 212–24. Downers Grove, Ill.: InterVarsity, 2002.

Pierson, Arthur T., ed. *The Inspired Word: A Series of Papers and Addresses Delivered at the Bible-Inspiration Conference, Philadelphia, 1887*. New York: Anson D. F. Randolph & Co., 1888.

Preus, R. D. "A Response to the Unity of the Bible." In *Hermeneutics, Inerrancy and the Bible*. Edited by Earl D. Radmacher and Robert D. Preus, 671–90. Grand Rapids: Zondervan, 1984.

———. "The Unity of Scripture." *Concordia Theological Quarterly* 54 (1990): 1–23.

Reicke, Bo. "Unity and Diversity in New Testament Theology." In *Good News in History: Essays in Honor of Bo Reicke*, edited and translated by L. Miller, 173–92. Atlanta: Scholars, 1993.

Reumann, J. *Variety and Unity in New Testament Thought*. Oxford: Oxford University Press, 1991.

Rhodes, David. "Diversity in the Bible," *Dialog* 26, no. 1 (1986): 14–19.

Roop, Eugene F. "The Problem of Two Testaments: We Can't Have the New without the Old." *Brethren Life and Thought* 19, no. 3 (1947): 157–65.

Roth, John D. "Harmonizing the Scriptures: Swiss Brethren Understandings of the Relationship between the Old and New Testament during the Last Half of the Sixteenth Century." In *Radical Reformation Studies*, edited by Werner O. Packull and Geoffrey L. Dipple. Brookfield, Vt.: Ashgate, 1999.

Rowley, H. H. *The Unity of the Bible*. London: Carey Kingsgate, 1953.

———. "The Unity of the Bible." In Rowley, H. H., *The Relevance of the Bible*. New York: Macmillan, 1944.

———. "The Unity of the Old Testament." *Bulletin of the John Rylands Library* 29 (1945–46): 326–58.

Sabourin, Leopold. "The Bible and Christ: The Unity of the Two Testaments." *Biblical Theology Bulletin* 8 (1978): 77–85.

Saphir, A. *The Divine Unity of Scripture*. Reprint. Grand Rapids: Kregel, 1984.

Scholer, David M. "Issues in Biblical Interpretation." *Evangelical Quarterly* 88, no. 1 (1988): 5–22.

Schultz, Richard L. "Unity or Diversity in Wisdom Theology? A Canonical and Covenantal Perspective." *Tyndale Bulletin* 48 (1997): 271–306.

Scobie, H. H. "Structure of Biblical Theology." *Tyndale Bulletin* 42 (1991): 178–79.

Scroggie, W. Graham. *Ruling Lines of Progressive Revelation: Studies in the Unity and Harmony of the Scriptures*. London: Marshall, Morgan & Scott, 1918.

Seitz, Christopher R. "Two Testaments and the Failure of One Tradition History." In *Biblical Theology: Retrospect and Prospect*, edited by Scott J. Hafemann, 195–211. Downers Grove, Ill.: InterVarsity, 2002.

Sloan, Robert B. "Unity in Diversity: A Clue to the Emergence of the New Testament as Sacred Literature." In *New Testament Criticism and Interpretation*, edited by David Alan Black and David S. Dockery, 437–68. Grand Rapids: Zondervan, 1991.

Stenschke, Christoph W. "Die Einheit der Scrift und die Vielfalt des Kanons: The Unity and Diversity of the Canon." *Religion and Theology* 12, no. 1 (2005): 88–91.

Thirion, Willem Gabriel. "A Practical Model for the Relationship of the Old Testament/New Testament." D.D. diss.: University of Pretoria (South Africa), 2002.

Thomas, Robert L., and Stanley N. Gundry. "Problems and Principles of Harmonization." In *A Harmony of the Gospels*. Chicago: Moody, 1978.

Thomas, T. Glyn. "The Unity of the Bible and the Uniqueness of Christ." *London Quarterly & Holborn Review* 191 (July 1966): 219–27.

Tiessen, Terrance. "Toward a Hermeneutic for Discerning Universal Moral Absolutes." *Journal of the Evangelical Theological Society* 36, no. 2 (1993): 189–207.

Topping, Richard R. "Revelation, Holy Scripture and Church in the Hermeneutic of James Barr, Paul Ricoeur and Hans Frei." Ph.D. diss.: University of St. Michael's College (Canada), 2005.

Van Ruler, A. A. *The Christian Church and the Old Testament*. Translated by G. W. Bromiley. Grand Rapids: Eerdmans, 1971.

Wall, Robert W. "The Canon and Christian Preaching." *Christian Ministry* 17, no. 5 (1986): 13–17.

Ward, Timothy. "The Diversity and Sufficiency of Scripture." In *The Trustworthiness of God: Perspectives on the Nature of Scripture*, edited by Paul Helm and Carl R. Trueman, 192–218. Grand Rapids: Eerdmans, 2002.

Ware, James H., Jr. "Rethinking the Possibility of a Biblical Theology." *Perspectives in Religious Studies* 10 (1983): 5–13.

Wenham, David. "Appendix: Unity and Diversity in the New Testament." In G. E. Ladd, *A Theology of the New Testament*, 2nd ed., 684–719. Grand Rapids: Eerdmans, 1993.

———. *Paul: Founder of Christianity or Follower of Jesus?* Grand Rapids: Eerdmans, 1996.

Wenham, John W. *The Goodness of God*. London: Inter-Varsity, 1974.

———. "Large Numbers in the Old Testament." *Tyndale Bulletin* 18 (1967): 19–53.

Williams, Rowan. "The Unity of the Church and the Unity of the Bible: An Analogy." *International Kirchliche Zeitschrift* 91, no. 1 (2001): 5–21.

Wright, Christopher J. H. *Walking in the Ways of the Lord: The Ethical Authority of the Old Testament*. Leicester: Apollos, 1995.

Wright, G. Ernest. "The Unity of the Bible." *Interpretation* 5, no 2 (1950): 131–33.

———. "The Unity of the Bible: A Summary." *Interpretation* 5, no. 3 (1950): 304–17.

————. "The Unity of Scripture." *Scottish Journal of Theology* 8, no. 4 (1955): 337–52.

————. "Wherein Lies the Unity of the Bible?" *The Journal of Bible and Religion* 20, no. 3 (1952): 194–98, followed by four "Responses" by Virginia Corwin, John A. Hutchison, S. Vernon McCausland, and Robert H. Pfeiffer; and G. Ernest Wright's "Brief Rejoinder," 199–201.

Youngblood, Ronald. "From Tatian to Swanson, from Calvin to Ben David: The Harmonization of Biblical History." *Journal of the Evangelical Theological Society* 25 (1982): 415–23.

Scripture Index

Genesis

1–11 . . . . 83, 184
1 19
1:26–27. 129
2 19
3 19
3:15. . . . . 73, 129, 144
4:19. 106
5:24. 180
6:2. 106
6:3. 184
6:4. 130
6:9. 184
9 51
9:27. 73
11 48
11:4. 130
11:7–8 185
12 . . . . 51, 148, 177
12:1. 101
12:2. 130
12:2–3. 144

12:3. 73, 116, 119, 131, 139,
   143–44, 184–86, 192
12:10–20. 100
12:13. 100
13 177
13:16. 144
14 . . . . 177, 199
14:1, 4. 199
15 . . . . 51, 144, 176
15:1–6. 144
15:1–5. 177
15:2–5. 176–77
15:2. 187
15:5–6. 101
15:5. 144
15:6. . . . . 176–77, 179
15:8. 187
15:14. 94
15:16. 95
16 144
17 . . . . 51, 114
17:1–22. 114

17:2. 114
17:5–6. 114–15
17:6. . . . . 130, 144
17:7–8 . . . . 114, 145
17:7. 111–12
17:16. . . . . 114, 130
17:19. 114
17:21. 114
18:18. . . . . 144, 185
19:14. 106
19:14. 106
19:30–38. 107
20:1–18. 100
22 . . . . 92, 101, 148
22:1. 92
22:5. 181
22:17. 144
22:18. . . . . . . 139, 144, 185
26:4. . . . . 139, 144, 185
26:6–11. 101
28:3–4 144
28:14. . . . . 144, 185

28:21 145
35:11–12 144
35:11 . . . . 130, 144
36:7 87
46:3 144
48:3–4 144
49:10 . . . . 73, 130
49:11–12 73

Exodus

1:17–21 101
1:18–19 90
2:6 105
2:24 145
3:13 145
3:15 145
3:18–20 94
3:20–21 94
3:21–22 93
3:21 94
3:22 93
4:21 88
4:22–23 . . . . 113, 145
5:1–3 94
6:3 . . . . 112, 180
6:6–7 112
6:7 145
7:3 88
7:5 88
7:13, 14 88
7:17 88
7:22 88
8:10 [6] 88
8:15 [11] 88
8:19 [15] 88
8:22 [18] 88
8:25–26 94
8:32 [28] 88
9:7, 12, 14 86
9:29 88
9:34, 35 88
10:1 . . . . 88, 107
10:2 88

10:7 94
10:9–10 94
10:20, 27 88
11:2–3 93
11:10 . . . . 88, 107
12 177
12:7, 12 178
12:35–36 93
12:36 93
12:38 88
13:15 88
14:4 . . . . 88, 107
14:8 88
14:17, 18 88
15–16 145
15:18 128
15:22–26 92
16:4 92
19:5–6 . . 113, 115, 145, 192
19:5 113
19:6 . . . . 113, 186
20 . . . . 50, 52
20:3 52–53
20:4 52–53
20:7 52–53
20:8 52–53
20:12 . . . . 52, 54
20:13–17 52
20:18–20 92
21–23 . . . . 109, 162
21:10 106
22:14[18] 93
23:7 179
25–40 162
25:9 . . . . 150, 162, 178
25:40 . . . . 150, 178
26:30 162
27:8 162
29:45 162
32 52
32:4 53
32:29 186

32:34 132
34:6 . . . . 157, 172
34:16 106
38:25–26 44

Leviticus

11:45 145
16 177–78
16:17 178
18–20 162
18:5 161
18:21 . . . . 92, 97
18:23, 24 97
18:28 95
19 180
19:1–18 163
19:2 180
19:12–18 150
20:2 92
20:3 . . . . 97, 191
22:33 145
23:29 139
24:10–16 52–53
24:15–16 53
25:23 53
26:9–13 114
26:11–12 114
26:12 145
26:44–45 145
26:45 145

Numbers

1–10 162
1:16 44
1:46 44
6:24–26 192
15:17–21 123
15:32–36 52–53
15:35 54
15:41 145
21 217
26:51 44
28:22 178

Deuteronomy

1:31 145
3:20 246
4:27 115
4:30–31 146
4:31 145
4:40 145
5 50, 52
5:7, 8 52
5:11, 12 52
5:16–21 52
7:1–2 96
7:7 171
8:2 92
8:16 92
9:5 97
9:10 115
10:4 115
12:9–10 146
12:14 146
12:21 146
12:28 145
17:14–15 131
18:15 139
20:10–18 96
21:15–17 87
21:18–21 . . . . 52, 54
21:20, 21 54
24:14–15 166
25:4 166
25:19 146
26:17 145
29:4 122
29:12–13 145
30:10–14 161
32:6 145
32:21 121
33 50

Joshua

1:13 146
2:1–14 101
2:2–7 90

6:25 101
7 52, 54
9:1 40
10:40 40
23–24 50

Judges

2:21–2 92
3:1–4 92
3:15–26 102
3:15 103
4:17–21 102
5:24 103
6:15 44
8:22–23 131
8:23 108
8:24 93
9–10 108
9 131
17:6 108
18 108
18:1 108
19–30 54
19–21 . . . . 52, 54
19 108
19:1 108
21 108
21:25 108

1 Samuel

1:28 93
2:10 . . . . 71, 147
2:35 . . . . 71, 104, 147
7 45
8:1–3 130
8:5, 7 131
10:19–21 44
11–12 54
12:12 128
13:1 43
13:14 . . . . 104, 131
14:41 43
15:11, 29, 35 31

15:33 108
16 102
16:2 101
16:13 131
16:13–14 174
17:4 45
25:43 106
30:11–13 39
30:11–12 40
30:13 40

2 Samuel

2:4 131
5:3 131
7 118, 131, 138, 146
7:5 146
7:10–11 146
7:12 146
7:12–13 131
7:13 146
7:14–15 146
7:16 . . . . 131, 146, 187
7:18–19 187
7:19 . . . . 119, 146, 191
7:20–29 187
7:25, 26 146
7:29 146
10:18 45
11–12 52
11 104
12:16 105
12:25 100
12:28 119
18:5 105
21:1–9 108
21:19 45–46
24 104
24:24 44
50 45

1 Kings

2:5–8 102–3
4:26 45

8:41–43 188
8:43 . . . . 115, 119
11:36 147
17:1 149
18 32
19:18 165
21 . . . . 52, 53, 55
22:2–33 90

2 Kings
2:23–25 104
4:3 93
6:5 93
6:8–23 102
10:9 179
17:24 190
24:8 45
25 48

1 Chronicles
16:23–33 187–88
19:18 45
20:5 46
21:25 44
28:7 146
29:11 128
29:23 140

2 Chronicles
6:32–33 142
7:14 119
9:8 140
9:25 45
20:25 93
21:7 147
26:10 40
32:31 92
36:9 45
36:16 105

Ezra
2 45
4:8–6:18 26
7:12–26 26

Nehemiah
7 45
8 213
8:8 213

Job
13:18 179
14:14 181
19:25–27 181

Psalms
2 189
2:2 . . . . 71, 132, 147
2:6 132
2:7 132
2:9 140
16 . . . . 74, 138, 181
16:5 139
16:10 74
18:26 94
18:48–49 189
20:6 147
22:28 128
24:1 113
26:2 92
28:8 147
32 104
33 189
44:23 29
45:6 131
49 181
50:4–11 189
51 104
51:10 174
51:11–12 174
52:13–53:12 189
65:16 147
67 189
67:1 . . . . 123, 189
67:2, 3 189
67:7 . . . . 189, 192
69:5 189
69:22–23 122

72:8 131
72:11 131
72:17 . . . . 131, 147
73:17 181
77:9 89
80:1 116
80:8–19 116
84:9 147
89:26–37 147
89:27 140
89:36 131
89:51 71
95:7 116
95:11 146
96 . . . . 187, 189
96:1, 2, 3 187
96:4–6 188
96:6, 7, 9, 10 187
96:11–12 188
98 187
110 140
100:3 116
103:12 178
103:19 . . . . 128, 133
117 189
121:4 29
132:10 71
132:11 138
132:12 146
132:17 71
145 . . . . 42, 189
145:11–13 128
145:14, 15 42
146:10 128

Ecclesiastes
1:1 213
2:14–16 181
9:1–3 181
12:13–14 32

Isaiah

1:9 116
1:14 87
2:2 132
4:1 119
5:1–7 116
5:23 179
6:5 128
6:9–12 106
8:14 . . . . 121, 161
9:2, 3 39
9:7 132
10:5 91
10:22–23 116
12:6 132
13:2 40
15:16–19 89
19:14 91
19:24–25 115
22:22 140
26 180
26:19 181
26:20 89
28:16 161
29:10 122
32:15 132
40:3 22
40:7 191
40:9 213
41:8, 9 147
42 191
42:1–7 189
42:1–4 190
42:5 191
42:6 190–92
44:1, 2, 21 147
45:4 147
45:6 189
45:22 190
48:20 147

49 191
49:1–7 189
49:3 147
49:5–7 147
49:6 190–92
49:8 191
53:10 91
54:5–8 115
54:7–8 89
56:2–6 54
56:6–8 . . . . 115, 137
58–66 31
58:13 54
59:20–21 147
61:1 213
61:11 62
62:5 115
66:18–21 137

Jeremiah

2:2 115
4:1–2 147
4:10 90–91
5:4 190
7 54
7:8–11 51–52
7:9 52
7:10 119
8:7 190
14:9 119
15:19 139
16:15 139
17:21 54
20:7 91
23:8 139
24:6 139
25:29 119
28 32
31:3 89
31:8 40

31:31–34 . . . . 124, 160
31:33 132
32 55
38:15–16 102
38:27 102

Ezekiel

11:19–20 160
14:9–10 91
14:9 90
14:12–16 91
16:55 139
17:23 139
21:27 130
30:3 132
34:15 116
36:17 191
36:25–32 174
36:26–27 160
37 55
38:8 132
38:16 132

Daniel

2:4–7:28 26
2:34 132
2:44 132
4:3 128
4:34 128
7:13, 14 132
9:18–19 119
9:25 . . . . 71, 147
9:26 . . . . 71, 132
12:2 181
26 147

Hosea

1:2, 3, 4 106
1:6 . . . . 106, 116
1:9 . . . . 106, 116
1:10 116

2:19 89
2:23 116
3 106
3:1 107
4:2 52
11:1 . . . . 115, 200, 139

Joel
1:15 132
2:1 132
2:28–29 132
3:14 132

Amos
3:7 95
5:21 87
8:5 54
8:11 210
9:9–15 119
9:11–15 119
9:11–12 . . . . . 118–19, 191
9:11 132
9:12 . . . . 87, 132

Obadiah
15 132
19–21 87
21 128

Micah
4:1 132
5:2 44

Habakkuk
2:3, 4 179
3:13 . . . . 71, 147

Zephaniah
1:7 132
1:14 132

Zechariah
2:11 115
10:6–12 32
14:16 147

Malachi
1:2–3 87
1:6–7 192
1:10, 11, 12 192
1:13–14 192

Matthew
2:15 . . . . 115, 200
2:22 200
5–7 152
5:1 40
5:17–20 150
6:24 87
6:33 133
7:11 42
7:21 133
8:1–11:1 152
8:11–12 136
10:5–6 61
10:10 62
10:37 87
11:2–13:53 152
11:9 149
11:11 149
11:25–27 134
12:40 39
12:49–50 116
13:11 133
13:54–19:2 152
15:24 61
16:17 134
16:18 61
18:3–6 133
18:17 61
19:3–26 152
19:14 133
19:16–26 172
19:17 41
21:43 136
23:23 163
23:38–39 136
24:23 62

Mark
1:14–15 . . . . 127, 132
2:18–20 115
3:5 87
4:11–12 107
4:11 . . . . 133, 152
7:19 61
8:34 62
10:14 . . . . 87, 133
10:17, 18 41
10:45 152
10:38, 39 62
12:1–12 116
15:42 64

Luke
1:3 152
1:32–33 137
1:46–55 138
1:51–55 137
1:69–75 137
1:70–73 138
1:78–79 137
3:7 90
5:32 153
6:17 40
8:10 133
10:7 62
10:9 137
10:25–37 173
11:13 42
11:20 137
14:26 87
16:13 87
18:19 41
18:20 52
19:10 153
19:12 138
19:14 138
20:37–38 180
21:24 . . . . 124, 136

22:1 64
23:54 64
24:27 213
24:32 214

John

1:17 . . . . 157, 172
1:29 . . . . 149, 154
1:36 154
1:41 71
2:17 87
3 173
3:1, 3, 5, 8 173
3:14 217–18
3:18 90
4:25 71
6:29 172
7:38–39 175
10:1–30 116
11:33 87
11:38 87
13–17 154
14:16–17 175
14:17 42
14:26 174
15:1–8 116
15:26–27 174
16:12–15 174
19:14 64
19:31 64
20:31 154
21:22–23 134

Acts

1:3–8 138
1:5 175
1:6 . . . . 134, 139
1:11 138
2–3 138
2 175
2:23 91
2:25–33 74
2:31–35 138

2:30–31 74
2:30 . . . . 74, 138
3:19 139
3:25 186
4:12 176
7:2–3 148
7:17 148
7:48 65
8 175
8:3 151
8:12 128
9:2 221
9:15 61
10 175
10:36 68
13:32–37 74
13:32–33 143
15 . . . . 65, 117
15:8 118
15:14–18 118
15:17 119
16:3 65
17:2–3 214
19:8 128
19:9 221
19:23 221
20:24–27 . . . . 128, 132
20:28 116
21 65–66
21:20–26 65
22:4 221
24:14, 22 221
26:6–8 142
28:16 121
28:23, 31 129

Romans

1:4 123
1:16–17 62
1:16 120
2:9, 10 120
2:17 120

2:27–29 159
2:28 120
2:29 . . . . 120, 159
3:1 120
3:9 120
3:21–28 66
3:21 158–59
3:28 159
3:29 120
3:31 158
4:13–17 142
4:13 185
4:17 137
4:20 142
6:14 158
7:6 158
7:6 158–60
7:8–9 101
7:9 158
7:12 159
7:14 159–60
8:3–4 158
8:3 160
9–11 120
9:2 121
9:4–5 136
9:4 . . . . 121, 143
9:6–8 . . . . 122, 147
9:6–7 121
9:6 121
9:8–9 121
9:9 121
9:13 87
9:22–24 116
9:24–29 116
9:27–29 116
9:30–10:13 160
9:30–10:4 122
9:30–33 . . . . . . 120–21, 160
9:32–33 122
10:2 161
10:3 161

10:4 . . . . 158, 162
10:5 161
10:10 161
10:14–21 122
10:18 121
11:1–10 122
11:1 151
11:2–4 122
11:5, 7, 8 122
11:9–10 122
11:11–15 122
11:11 121
11:12 . . . . 124, 136
11:14 . . . . 121, 123
11:15–16 161
11:15 123
11:16–24 123
11:23–26 124
11:25–26 136
11:25 124–25
11:25 148
11:26–27 124
11:28 122
11:29 . . . . . . 121, 148, 132
12:7 14
13:9 52
14:14 63
15. 65
15:8–9 143
15:8 120
15:15–21 136
15:27 120
16:26 61

1 Corinthians

2:1–2 219
2:13 204
6:9, 10 61
7:10 62
9:11–12 166
9:14 62
9:20–21 66

11:23–26 61
15:12–13 123
12:12–13 175
15:21 123
15:42 123
16. 65

2 Corinthians

3:6 159
3:8 188
3:11 158
3:14–15 158
3:15 134
3:15–16 216
8–9. . . . . 61, 65
10:1 66
10:16 66

Galatians

1–2. 63
1:12 63
2:11 66
2:16 151
2:21 173
3:6–8 149
3:8 . . 143, 151, 184–86, 200
3:11 151
3:14 137
3:18 137
3:19–25 158
3:19 144
3:21 . . . . 137, 158, 162
3:24 151
4:1–5 158
5:21 61

Ephesians

1:13 137
2:14 117
2:15 158
3:1–13 136
3:1–6 123

3:5, 6 117
3:11–16 123
4:32 165

Philippians

2:8 178
3:9 66
4:2 165

Colossians

1:15 113
2:14 158

1 Thessalonians

1:3 66
2:16 90
4:15 62
5:4 62
5:9 90

2 Thessalonians

1:11 66

1 Timothy

5:1–2 116
5:18 166

2 Timothy

1:6–7 153
1:13 14
3:16–17 217

Hebrews

1:1 24
3:17 143
4:2 143
4:12 20
6:13–15 142
6:13 148
6:17–18 148
6:17 142
10:1–4 178
10:37 179
11:9 147

13:20 116
39–40 140

James

2:11 52
2:17, 18, 24, 26 66

1 Peter

1:10–11 75
1:23, 25 20
2:5 . . . . 145, 186
2:9–10 113
2:9 . . . . 113, 145
2:10 116
3:18–20 184
5:2–4 116

2 Peter

1:16–18 205
1:19–21 205
1:20 . . . . 22, 205
1:21 22
2:5 184

Revelation

1:1–3 154
1:5–6 139
1:5 113
1:6 . . . . 113, 145, 186
1:9 140
2:26–27 140
3:7 140
3:21 140

5:10 . . . . 113, 145
11 154
11:15 154
12:9 154
13:1 154
14:10 90
15:1 90
16:13 154
18:2 154
19:10 154
20, 21 19
21:2 115
21:4 111
21:9 115
22 19
22:17 115

Author Index

Achtemeier, Elizabeth, 215–16
Alexander, Neil, 225
Allis, O. T., 225
Allrik, H. L., 45, 225
Althamer, Andreas, 37
Archer, Gleason L., 38–39, 225
Aristotle, 18, 89
Armstrong, Ryan Melvin, 225
Augustine, 13–14, 36
Baker, D. L., 225
Baron, David, 70
Barr, James, 226
Barton, John J., 47–51
Barton, John, 25, 28, 226
Bauer, Walter, 59
Beardsley, Monroe C., 197
Becker, Joachim, 71–72
Beecher, Willis J., 82–83, 129, 135, 141–42, 149
Berkhof, Louis, 76
Bietenhard, H., 115

Blass, F., 75
Blaw, Johannes, 183
Blomberg, Craig L., 40–42, 63, 226
Bock, Darrell, 137–38, 152
Boice, James Montgomery, 226
Brauch, Manfred, 38
Bretschneider, Karl Gottlieb, 63
Briggs, Charles, 188
Bright, John, 127
Brown, Raymond E., 76, 204
Bruce, F. F., 37–38, 226
Buber, Martin, 131
Bullinger, E. W., 39
Bultmann, Rudolf, 23, 59
Bush, George, 103
Buswell, J. Oliver, 161
Calvin, John, 106
Campenhausen, H. Freiherr, 11, 13–15
Carson, Donald A., 67, 226

Cazelles, H., 226
Chafer, Louis Sperry, 172
Chapell, Bryan, 218
Charlesworth, James H., 71
Childs, Brevard, 226
Christiansen, Duane L., 227
Chrysostom, 36
Clements, Roy, 166
Clendenen, E. R., 196
Coleridge, Samuel Taylor, 35
Collins, Anthony, 80
Cooper, Oliver St. John, 37
Cranfield, C. E. B., 159
Cuvier, Georges, 18–20
Dabney, Robert L., 209
Davids, Peter H., 38
Davidson, Samuel, 37
Davis, John J., 227
de Vaux, Roland, 17, 92
De Young, James, 198–200
Debelius, M., 16

DeBrunner, A., 75
DeHaan, M. R., 37
Delitzsch, Franz, 70, 72, 81–82
Dentan, R. C., 227
DeWette, W. M. L., 81
Dillard, Raymond B., 36, 44, 227
Dodd, C. H., 23, 67–68
Downing, David C., 38
Duda, Daniel, 227
Dumbrell, William, 146
Dunn, James D. G., 23, 59, 64, 159, 227
Edersheim, Alfred, 70, 72
Egan, Hope, 61
Eichhorn, J. G., 81
Eichrodt, Walther, 58
Ellison, H. L., 85
Erlandson, Seth, 227
Eusebius, 36
Ezra, Eben, 106
Farris, T. V., 176
Fausset, A. R., 103
Fernandez, F. André, 75
Filson, F. V., 227
Fisher, Milton, 105
Fohrer, Georg, 16
France, R. T., 128
Freedman, David Noel, 47–57, 227
Fuller, Daniel, P., 117, 227
Gaebelein, Frank E., 227
Gardiner, Frederic, 77
Gelston, A., 190
Glen, J. Stanley, 70, 228
Goldingay, John, 25, 29–32, 114, 228
Goldsworthy, Graeme, 78
Goodwin, Thomas, 176
Greene, William B., Jr., 90–91, 95
Greidanus, Sidney, 217

Gressman, Hugo, 106
Grogen, Geoffrey W., 173
Gundry, Robert H., 151
Gundry, Stanley N., 232
Haley, John W., 37, 228
Hanson, Paul D., 33
Harrison, Carol, 228
Hasel, Gerhard, 17, 228
Heavenor, E. S. P., 106
Hengstenberg, E. W., 70, 106
Henry, Carl F. H., 36
Herder, J. G., 81
Herschel, Abraham, 89
Hesse, F., 15
Hicks, R. Lansing, 228
Hirsch, E. D., 79–80, 196–97
Honeycut, R. L., 228
Hopkins, Ezekiel, 102
Hunter, A. M., 228
Hurty, Sarah, 198–200
Ingersoll, Robert, 104–5
Irenaeus, 14–15
Janowski, Bernard, 228
Janzen, J. Gerald, 164
Jenni, E., 73
Johnson, Luke Timothy, 150, 228
Johnston, G., 62
Josephus, 13
Juel, Daniel, 71
Justin Martyr, 13
Kaiser, Walter C., Jr., 71, 228
Käsemann, Ernst, 59
Keil, C. F., 106
Kelley, Page H., 17
Kimchi, David, 106
Klein, Gunter, 16
Klein, W. W., 196
Kloch, Klaus, 228
Köstenberger, Andreas J., 59, 63–64, 66–68, 228
Kraft, Charles H., 170

Lalleman, Hetty, 157, 229
Larsen, David L., 218
Lawlor, John I., 92
Lehrer, Steve, 116
Lemcio, Eugene E., 23–24, 229
Lindsell, Harold, 46
Lohse, Eduard, 229
Longenecker, Richard N., 229
Longman, Tremper III, 229
Ludlow, Morwenna, 229
Luther, Martin, 106
Lyman, Mary Ely, 229
Maier, Gerhard, 15–16, 229
Maimonites, 106
Mann, Thomas, 37
Marshall, I. Howard, 167, 201, 203
Matera, Frank J., 59
McCaul, Alexander, 78–79
McConville, J. G., 57–58, 229
Mendenhall, G. E., 44
Minear, Paul S., 229
Morgan, Robert, 229
Morrison, John D., 229
Motyer, Steve, 229
Mounce, Robert H., 37
Mowinckel, Sigmund, 71
Neil, William, 230
Neusner, Jacob, 71
Nieuwenhove, Rik van, 230
O'Donovan, Oliver M. T., 13
Origen, 14
Orr, James, 15
Osiander, Andreas, 106
Outler, Albert C., 230
Packer, James I., 201, 230
Paul, S. M., 230
Payne, J. Barton, 43–45, 71–72, 75, 83, 230
Peck, John R., 192
Pentecost, J. Dwight, 133
Perrin, Nicholas, 230

Peters, George W., 188
Pinnock, Clark H., 170, 196
Poythress, Vern, 196
Preus, Robert D., 14, 230
Provence, Thomas, 159
Redlich, E. B., 15
Reicke, Bo, 230
Reumann, J., 230
Rhodes, David, 230
Riehm, Edward, 70
Robertson, O. Palmer, 119
Rodd, Cyril, 164
Roop, Eugene F., 230
Ross, Allen P., 177
Roth, John D., 231
Rowley, H. H., 231
Rushdoony, R. J., 90
Ryrie, Charles, 169
Sabourin, Leopold, 231
Sanders, E. P., 151
Saphir, Adolph, 70, 231
Sauer, Erich, 133
Scholer, David M., 231
Schultz, Richard L., 75, 231
Schuter, Michael, 166
Scobie, H. H., 23
Scroggie, W. Graham, 18–19, 28, 231

Seitz, Christopher R., 231
Sherlock, Thomas, 81
Simpson, A. B., 174
Sloan, Robert B., 231
Smeaton, George, 176
Smend, Rudolf, 16
Smith, James, 71–72
Smith, R. Payne, 70
Snaith, N. H., 190
Speiser, Ephraim, 100
Spurgeon, Charles H., 211, 213
Stein, Robert H., 38
Stenschke, Christopher W., 231
Strauss, D. F., 63
Stuhlmacher, Peter, 59
Swaim, J. Carter, 37
Terry, Milton S., 195
Tertullian, 14–15
Thaddaeus, Johannes, 37
Theodoret, 36
Thielman, Frank, 151
Thirion, Willem Gabriel, 231
Thomas, Robert L., 232
Thomas, T. Glyn, 232
Tiessen, Terrance, 232
Topping, Richard R., 232
Unger, Merrill F., 210
Van Gorder, Paul R., 37

van Groningen, Gerald, 71
van Hoonacker, Albin, 106
Van Ruler, A. A., 232
Vawter, Bruce, 76–77, 204
von Hengstenberg, E. W., 81
von Rad, Gerhard, 29–30, 58
Vos, Geerhardus, 93, 203, 218
Waite, J. C. J., 173
Wall, Robert W., 232
Waltke, Bruce, 134, 146
Walvoord, John, 137
Ward, Timothy, 232
Ware, James H., Jr., 232
Webb, William J., 167, 203
Weinfeld, M., 114
Wenham, David, 60–61, 65, 232
Wesley, John, 159
Williams, Rowan, 232
Wimsatt, William K., 197
Wright, Christopher J. H., 71, 164, 216–17, 232
Wright, G. Ernest, 11–12, 56, 232
Yancey, Philip, 69
Youngblood, Ronald, 36, 233

Subject Index

Abarbanel, 94

Abimelech, 100, 108, 131

Abraham, 99–101; appeared to, 112; believed, 179; called out, 142; a covenant with, 114; example of, 65; faith of, 170–71, 177; God orders, 92–93; line of, 130; received the gospel, 149; relationship with, 114; and the seed, 73, 144;

Abram. See, Abraham

adulterers, examples of, 104

advent, 75

Ahab, 90–91

amillennialism, 135

Ammonites, 95

Amorites, 96

analogia fidei, 217

Ancient of Days, 132

anger, way we define, 89; of God, 86, 88–89

Anointed One, 132

application: in our day, 167; of Scripture, 201

atonement, 93, 168, 178

Augustine, 94

authority: of their ministries, 210; of the Word of God, 215

authors: beyond the human, 196; intention of, 78–79, 196–97; were consciously expressing, 201. See also, authorship, writers

authorship: diversity in, 26, unitary, 56. See also, authors, writers

Baal, 96, 122

baptism, of the Holy Spirit, 175

Bathsheba, 104

Benjamin, 108

beyond the Bible, 167–68

Beyond the Bible, 202

Bible, the: beyond, 167–68; diversity of the, 12; ethics of, 163; going beyond, 202; interconnectedness of, 155; needs to be, 205; process of interpreting, 195; structural unity of, 20; study of, 37. See also, Scripture, Word of God

biblical studies, ways of approaching, 16

biblical theology: as to what, 12; central concept of, 16–17

blessing, 148

born again, 173

bride, 115

bridegroom, 115

Buddhist Scriptures, 15

Canaanite culture, 95–97

canon, the: not closed, 199;

to establish doctrine, 60; conclusion of, 72; removed from, 19; unity of, 85

Catharists, 87

ceremonial laws, 163. See also, law

characters, of the Old Testament, 99

children: they cursed, 104–5; of harlotry, 106; names of, 116

Christ: fulfilled in, 158, 217; is the telos, 162. See also, Jesus Christ, Messiah

Christianity: Judaism and, 222; was made up of, 64; type of, 65

Christians, Jews and, 221–22

chronous, 139

Chrysostom, John, 223

church, the: doctrine of 61; family called, 117; formation of, 136; mission of, 151; as people of God, 111–12; "the Way" as, 221. See also, church fathers, church history, people of God

church fathers, early, 165

church history, unity of the Bible in, 13–17

circumcision, 117

civil laws, 163. See also, law

clarity, a key objective, 213

community, law is for the, 168

Constantine, 222

context, terms in, 218

contradictions: abound in, 15; famous historical, 45; troubling, 28; types of, 30–32; usually means, 30

covenant: with Abraham, 144; is called a, 114; that God gave, 50–51; of Moses, 153; is new covenant, 124; with the

patriarchs, 121; for the people, 191

covenantal nomism, 151

covenant theologians, 139

crucifixion, timing of the, 64

culture: bogged down in, 212; of the Bible, 165; Canaanite, 95–97

Dan, tribe of, 108

Daniel, 73

David, 92, 99, 101; decapitated the giant, 45–46; delivering seven, 108; house of, 73, 118; a Man of Promise, 130; the prophet, 74; time of, 146

Day of Atonement, 178

death, life after, 180–81. See also, resurrection

Decalogue, the, 50–54, 56, 163–64

deception, 90–92

development, idea of, 82

dialegomai, 214

discipleship, 153

discrepancies: famous alleged, 36–37; sources for, 38–39. See also, contradictions

diversity: case for, 15; concept of, 12–13; degrees of, 30; legitimate kinds of, 56–58; in the New Testament, 60; presence of, 25; theological, 29–30; types of, 26–27

divorce, Jesus' teaching on, 62

doctrinal unity, of the Bible, 22

doctrine: of the Messiah, 71; Paul developed, 61

dwell, the verb, 73

Ecclesiastes, 32

Egypt, out of, 200

Egyptians, 93–94, 112

eisegesis, 214, 216; example of, 78

election, of God, 186

Elijah, 102

Elisha, 102; cursing the forty-two children, 104–5

El Shaddai, 112

Emites, 95

Enlightenment, 14, 16

Enneateuch, 48–49, 55

Enoch, was taken, 180

Epistles, the, complement each other, 19

errors, of transmission, 39

eschatology, 135

eternal punishment, 97

ethics, of the Bible, 163

evangelicals, 196

Eve, line of, 184

evil, hatred of, 88–89

exegesis: aims at understanding, 78; extreme form of, 70; historical-grammatical, 218; must have a christological, 216; with a concept of unity, 58

Exodus, book of, 112

exodus, time of the, 145

expository preaching, 209–19; advantages of, 214; biblical roots of, 213; can not be reached by, 217

Ezekiel, 73

faith: justified by, 151, 171; in the Messiah, 161; object of, 170; and righteousness, 122; what is, 179; by their works, 66

family of God, 115–16

firstborn, in this context, 113

fulfillment, times of, 148

fullness, 76; the term, 124

genres, diversity of, 27
Gentiles: eating with the, 66; by faith, 161; fullness of the, 124; grafted in, 123; heirs together with Israel, 136–37; include both, 116; Jews and, 118–25; people from the, 117; plan to include the, 119–20
Gideon, 108
gifts, of the Holy Spirit, 202
Girgashites, 96
Gnosticism, 14, 64, 88
God: changing his actions, 31; character of, 92, 97; concept of, 29; of the Old Testament, 90; of wrath, 86, 88–90. See also, Christ, El Shaddai, Yahweh, Yeshua
gospel, the: Abraham received the, 149; announce, 61; essence of, 73; to the Gentiles, 121; are important to each other, 19; to the law, 150; law's relationship to, 157–58; living from, 62; motif was, 67–68; in the Synoptic Gospels, 172
gospel of John, 60, 63–64, 154
grace: gospel of, 158; means of, 171–72
grammatical-historical interpretation, of the Bible, 206–7, 218

halakhah, 28
Handel, George, 80
haram, 96
harlots, they married, 105–7
harmonization: overworked, 46; practice of, 36–37; the term, 35
harmony, points of, 13
hasid, the word, 75

Hebrew, the language, 26
Hebrew Bible, unity of the, 47–51, 55. See also, Old Testament
hell, 168
hermeneutics, and unity of the Bible, 195–206. See also, interpretation
historical-grammatical exegesis, 206–7, 218
historic unity, of the Bible, 21
history: concentration on, 56; end of, 64; fulfilling, 142; interpretation of, 17; lying behind, 224; of preaching, 210; of the promise doctrine, 143–55; role of, 206; symmetry of, 20
Hittites, 96
Hivites, 96
holiness, life of, 180
Holy Spirit, the: baptism of, 175; coming of, 174; gifts of, 202; guided them, 204; indwelt believers, 42; meaning of, 76; moved by the, 22; power of, 118; promise of the, 152; poured out, 132; regenerated by, 160; work of, 171
homoeoteleuton, 42
Hosea, 105–7; gave to his children, 116
house of David, 73, 118
human authors. See authors
human sacrifice, 92

idiom, for getting married, 106
incest, they committed, 107
inclusivists, 170
insertions, type of, 41
inspiration, case for, 217
interpretation: antiauthorial intention, 196; must replicate, 198; grammatical-historical, 205; in space and time, 205; is a dialectic, 57; of messianic prophecy, 74–80; of the Old Testament, 81; primary goals of, 164; principles to govern, 201; rabbinical methods of, 78; slipperiness in, 77. See also, hermeneutics
interpretive keys, 134
ippissima vox Jesu, 41
Isaac, 101, up as a sacrifice, 92–93
Israel: election of, 114; future for, 120; heirs together with, 117; history of, 142; Jesus and, 61; offered through, 119; as people of God, 111–12; the people of, 21; as the people of promise, 147; rejection of, 122–23; restoration of, 116, 123, 135, 191; had been warned, 95. See also Jews

Jacob and Esau, 87
Jael, 103
James: differences between Paul and, 66; spoke up, 118
Jebusites, 96
Jeremiah, 101
Jericho, 101
Jerusalem Council, 117
Jesus Christ: as the Messiah, 64, 139; and Paul, 60–63; supremacy of, 153. See also, Christ, Messiah
Jews: and Christians, 221–22; and Gentiles, 118–25. See also Israel
Job, 32
Jonah, 191
Joseph and Mary, 200

Judah, tribe of, 73
Judaism, and Christianity, 222
Judaizers, 151; against the, 224
Judges, period of the, 108
justice, interpreted politically, 190
justification: emphasis on, 61; by faith, 171–72, 179; Paul's use of, 62, 66
Justin Martyr, 222

kairoi, 149
kerygmatic core, 56
kerygmatic unity, of the Bible, 23
Ketubim, 48––49
king: as God's "Anointed One", 132; Israel demanded a, 131; origin of the, 130–31
kingdom of God, the: aspects of, 133–35; concept of, 129–30; and David's throne, 137–38; to establish, 127; future fulfillment of, 135; "now-already" aspect to, 139; in the Old Testament, 128; and the promise-plan, 152; stress on, 61
knowledge, is relative, 197
Koine Greek, 26
Koran, the, 15

Lactantius, 88–89
Ladder of Abstractions, 166–67
language, diversity in, 26
Last Supper, account of the, 62
law, the: is a gift, 168; and the gospel, 150, 157–58; and the Spirit, 159; and the unity of the Bible, 157–68;
lawless, they were, 108
Law of the Tooth, 109
Levite, 108

lex talionis, 109
liars, 100
liberalism, 201
light, metaphorically, 190–92
literal meaning: the term, 206; versus a deeper meaning, 198;
literary convention, of square brackets, 107
literary form, diversity in, 26
Lot, 107
love: expressions of God's, 171; royal law of, 150
Luther, Martin, 223
lying, 101–2

Manichaeism, 87
Man of Promise, 180, 184
Marcion, 86–88, 97, 222
Mary, 150
meaning: distinction between, 79; search for deeper, 204; and significance, 197; texts do have, 198
Melchizedek, a good type for, 200
men and women, of the Old Testament, 99
Messiah, the: claims of the coming, 69; comings of the, 22; concept of a, 72; doctrine of the, 71; Jesus as the, 64; promise of, 82–83; proofs that Jesus was, 80; resurrection of the, 138; term for, 75, 147
Messianic Hope, origin of the, 72
messianic prophecy, 74–81
Midianites, 131
midrash exegesis, 77
mishpahah, 185
mishpat, 190
mission, of the church, 151

missions: in the Old Testament, 183–92; in the Psalms, 188
Mitte, 16
Moab, 95
Moabite Stone, 96
modern interpretive movement, origins of the 197
Molech, 92
monarchial era, 130
moral issues, 202
moral laws, 163. See also law
Moses, 99; begged, 145; covenant of, 153; and Pharaoh, 94–95; speeches of, 50
Mount Sinai, 115
murderers, examples of, 102–3
mystery, 124, aspects of, 136; taught Paul, 117

nacham, 31
nations: Israel to serve the, 191; will be blessed, 149
Nebi'im, 48
new covenant, 124, 153
New Testament, the: diversity in, 60; and the Old, 85; reinterprets the Old, 134; unity of, 59–68
Nicodemus, 173–74
nissah, 93
Noah, 97, 184–85
numbers, transcription of large, 43–45

oath, 148
obedience: conditioned on, 145; to the law, 151; was the expression, 121
Old Testament, the: coherence in, 33; deeper meanings of, 199; diversity in, 56–58; God of, 86, 90; Holy Spirit in, 175; kingdom

of God in, 128; men and women, 99; and the Messiah, 69–70; mission in the, 183–92; multiplex nature of, 29; and the New, 85; New Testament reinterprets, 134; organization of, 47, 56; salvation in, 169–71. See also Hebrew Bible

olive tree, theology of the, 123–25

omission, of words, 42–43

original text, 41

pagans, extermination of, 95

parables: Jesus' use of, 107; on wealth, 61; on the wise, 62

paradigm, concept of, 163–64

paradox, the theme of, 58

Passover, the, 64

patriarchs, time of the, 130, 144

Paul: of the Book of Acts, 64–66; and James, 66; Jesus and, 60–63; interlaced Jew and Gentile, 120

Pentecost, 118, 176

people of God: metaphors for, 115–16; unity of the Bible and the, 111–19. See also, church

Perizzites, 96

Peter, rebuke, 66

Pharaoh: the case of, 87–88; hardening of, 107; stubbornness of, 94–95

plagues, purpose in sending the, 88

pledge, 148

pleroma, 124

posterity, emphasis fell on, 114

preaching, 209–19; advantages of, 214; biblical roots of, 213. See also, teaching, sermon

premillennialism, 135

priesthood, of believers, 113, 145

principlization, seeds to bridge, 203

prison epistles, 152

proclamation, of the Word, 213

program of God, concept of the, 140

progressive revelation, 201, 203

promise: arrival of the, 149; definition of, 141–42; the term, 148

promise-plan of God, 82–83, 141–55; kingdom in the, 129

prophecy: centers of all, 22; language of, 69; had only a single, 81

prophetic unity, of the Bible, 22

prophets, 48–49, 55; exilic, 73; missions in the earlier, 186; Old Testament, 74; preaching of the, 147

Psalms, missions in the, 188

Rahab, 90, 101, 211

redaction criticism, 40

redemptive-historical interpretation, 217

redemptive movement trajectory, 203

Reformation, the, 14, 16, 37, 179

remnant, 116, 121–22

repent, 31

repentance, 153

resurrection, the, 123; from the dead, 180–81; hope of, 171; of the Messiah, 138; spoke of, 74

revelation, progress of, 63, 134, 203

Revelation, the book of, 154

revenge, they sought, 108–9

righteousness: Paul's use of, 62;

ways of obtaining, 161

rule of faith, 217

Sabbath, 54

sacrifices: in "every place", 192; in the Old Testament, 178

salvation: applied to, 18; doctrine of, 169–81; by means of grace, 171

Samuel, 101, 108

sanctification, 171, 180

Sarah, 100–101

Saul, 101; broke the oath, 108; as their first king, 131

Scripture: application of, 201; authority in, 165; beyond the text of, 202; center or Mitte to, 16; claim of, 33; exposition of the, 209; role of, 153; simply was not, 77; writers of, 79, 204–5. See also, Bible, Word of God

second coming, of Jesus, 75, 90

seed, the: of Abraham, 73, 200; of all the nations, 146; a posterity, 144; promise of, 176–77; prophecy of, 129–30

segullah, 113

sensus literalis, 78

sensus plenior, 204, 217; defined, 76, 77–78

sermon: textual, 211; topical, 210. See also, teaching, preaching

significance, 79; levels of, 217; meaning and, 197–98

Simeon, 150

sin: cleansing from, 171; forgiven, 178; presence of, 88

slavery, issue of, 202

Sodom and Gomorrah, 97, 116

Solomon, 99; prayer of, 188

Son of Man, 75, 132

soteriology, tractate on, 120

Spirit. See, Holy Spirit

spiritual unity, of the Bible, 23

Stephen, 65; before the Sanhedrin, 148

sufficiency, of Scripture, 164, 215

symmetry, 20

synagogues, 221

Synoptic Gospels, and the gospel of John, 60, 63–64

systematic theology, 12, 58, 142

teaching, 209–19; advantages of, 214; biblical roots of, 213. See also, preaching, sermon

temple, for Yahweh, 146–47

Ten Commandments, 50–54, 56, 163–64

textual criticism, 39, 41–43

The Messiah, 80

theological diversity, as a special problem, 29–30. See also, diversity

theology, 58

thrones, the two, 140

times, of restoration, 139

tooth, for tooth, 109

topical sermon, 210

Torah, the: 48–49, 223; missions in, 184; written on the hearts, 132

Tower of Babel, 185

trajectories, 64, 167

transcription, of large numbers, 43–45

translation, 39

transmission, errors of, 39

trinity, the term, 162, 168

typology, 78

Ugarit, 96

unity: between the two testaments, 85–97; in church history, 13–17; doctrinal, 22; and expository preaching, 209; of the Hebrew Bible, 47–51; historic, 21; kerygmatic, 23; of the law and gospel, 158; nature of, 20; of the New Testament, 59–68; problem of, 11–12; prophetic, 22; spiritual, 23; types of, 18–20

universalists, 170

war, conduct of, 103

Way, the, 221–22

wickedness: presence of, 88–89; of these nations, 97

women, role of, 202

Word of God, authority of the, 215. See also, Bible, Scripture

works: faith by their, 66; pursued it by, 161

worship, 154

wrath, God of, 86, 88–90

writers, of Scripture, 204–5. See also, authors, authorship

Writings, the, of the Hebrew bible, 48–49, 55

Yahweh, 115; was presented, 87; references to, 128–29; is called the "Tester", 92. See also, God, El Shaddai, Yeshua

Yeshua, 221. See also, God, El Shaddai, Yahweh

Zamzummites, 95

Zechariah, 73, 150

Zedekiah, 101

zeugma, used to modify, 106

Zoroastrian Scriptures, 15

Printed in the USA
CPSIA information can be obtained
at www.ICGtesting.com
JSHW062055030124
54652JS00003B/5

9 780310 529934